Indian and
Northern Affairs

Affaires indiennes
et du Nord

Issued under the authority of the Honourable Judd Buchanan, PC, MP, Minister of Indian and Northern Affairs

Produced by the Conservation Group, Office of the Public Information Adviser Design: Gottschalk+Ash Ltd.

Canadian Historic Sites: Occasional Papers in Archaeology and History will be published as papers become available. Manuscripts may be submitted to Chief, Research Division, National Historic Parks and Sites Branch, Indian and Northern Affairs, Ottawa, Ontario K1A 0H4, Canada.

Canadian Historic Sites:
Occasional Papers in Archaeology
and History — No. 9

National Historic Parks and
Sites Branch
Parks Canada
Indian and Northern Affairs
Ottawa, 1974

Cover: Lighthouse at Peggy's Cove,
Nova Scotia (*Photo by Malak.
Infocan Phototheque.*)

The Canadian Lighthouse

by Edward F. Bush

Canadian Historic Sites
No. 9

Illustrations

Abstract
This study traces the evolution of the Canadian lighthouse from the first structure at Louisbourg to the latest developments in lighthouse design and technology within the past decade. The treatment is regional, with emphasis on the older extant structures. An appendix lists data on individual lighthouses within regional agencies.

Submitted for publication 1973
by Edward F. Bush,
National Historic Parks and Sites
Branch, Ottawa

The murmur rose soft as I silently gazed
On the shadowy waves playful motion
From the dim distant land, till the
lighthouse fire blazed
Like a star in the midst of the ocean.

Thomas Moore
(*composed on leaving Halifax aboard*
a British frigate, October 1804)

Introduction
The purpose of this study is to trace the evolution of the Canadian lighthouse from its inception in the 18th century to the present time, and to provide, it is hoped, a sound historical reference work on Canadian lighthouses. In no sense, however, should it be considered an architectural treatment, for which the writer is hardly qualified. Architectural reports on specific lighthouses, where available, have been quoted.

Trinity House
Warnings to mariners in the form of towers or other structures bearing lights have been in use for centuries. The lighthouse system in Canada, however, was based on the British "Trinity House," formed in the early 1500s.

Lights in the form of beacon fires and pole lights were frequently maintained by various monastic orders in England throughout the Middle Ages. With the suppression of the monasteries in the reign of Henry VIII, it became apparent to mariners and shipowners alike that some authority should be established to carry on the good offices of the monks along Britain's storm-swept coasts. In 1514 the king granted a charter in the name of the Holy Trinity as the Shipmen of Mariners of England. Its present charter, granted by James II in 1685, describes it under the impressively mediaeval title of "The Guild, Fraternity, or Brotherhood of the Most Glorious and Undivided Trinity and of St. Clement in the Parish of Deptford Stronde in the County of Kent." Its first function, however, was merely the direction of the naval dockyard at Deptford : only in 1573 did it undertake the erection of beacons and sea marks.

In 1604 a board of directors composed of two naval officers, eleven officers from the merchant service and several prominent figures from civil life to be known as the Elder Brethren of Trinity House was selected from the members of this association. In 1609, the Elder Brethren assumed complete executive control, with the otherwise designated Younger Brethren holding the franchise or the election of members to the senior body. The Trinity House charter was suspended during the republican interlude, but was renewed at the Restoration. This internationally celebrated authority has functioned continually from that day to this. Its contribution to lighthouse design and technology can scarcely be overestimated.

In later years, the Scottish coast became the charge of the Northern Lighthouse Board, and similarly the Irish coast of the Irish Lighthouse Board, both of which were fully autonomous.[1] Our own Quebec Trinity House, established in 1804, owed both its inspiration and its title (though not its authority) to the English parent body.

Lighthouse Structure
Basic Principles of Lighthouse Design and Location
Lighthouses may be broadly defined under two heads : wave-swept and land structures. Although the latter may frequently be found in exposed locations, in general the wave-swept tower offers the greatest challenge to designer and builder alike. There are four kinds of construction used in wave-swept towers at present : (1) masonry and concrete, (2) cast-iron plated, (3) caisson foundation and (4) openwork steel. Masonry and concrete construction is preferred at sites where stone or brick is costly to transport. The openwork steel tower is resorted to on shoals, coral reefs or sandbanks in which a secure foundation is to be had only by means of steel piles driven deep where excavation is impractical. Likewise, the caisson foundation often is recommended at such locations.[1] Figure 2 illustrates basic types of construction currently in use.

Lighthouses may also be functionally categorized under four general heads : (1) landfall lights, (2) major coastal lights, (3) secondary coastal lights and (4) harbour lights. Landfall lighthouses are located on shipping approaches generally well offshore to serve as the first landfall for inbound shipping and to provide a first bearing for outbound shipping. As one would suppose, landfall lighthouses are equipped with the most powerful lights available. Examples of several well-known landfall lighthouses are Bishop's Rock off the Scilly Isles (the first sight of the approaching English coast on a course for the Channel), and nearer home, Cape Race and Belle Isle,

from which eastbound shipping out of the St. Lawrence takes its departure. Next in importance are the major coastal lights on the approaches to major ports or at the mouths of principal rivers. The Sambro Island lighthouse on the outer approaches to the port of Halifax and the oldest surviving lighthouse in Canada is an example in this category, as is Prince Shoal at the confluence of the Saguenay and St. Lawrence rivers. These two are fitted with powerful lights, although generally not to the same extent as the landfall lights. Secondary coastal and harbour installations exhibit lights of decreasing power and intensity ; the latter, many of which may aptly be described as shaped like a pepper-shaker 10 or 15 feet in height, are often to be found at the head of piers or jetties.

Wave-swept lighthouse towers are usually of tapering circular design and are frequently set upon square foundations. Land-based lighthouses, by contrast, come in all shapes and sizes. Briefly they may be broken down into three broad types : (1) towers solely, (2) towers with attached dwellings and (3) houses with short towers, cupolas on the roof, or simply exhibiting the light from a window. Simple mast and pole lights are frequently seen on inland waterways other than those of such expanse as the Great Lakes. Towers are in a variety of shapes, circular, hexagonal and octagonal being the most common.

The range of a light ; that is, the distance at which it can be seen in clear weather, is computed in nautical miles and is dependent on two factors : the height of the light above the water,

1 Harbour light, Western Gap, Toronto Harbour.
(*Canada. Department of Transport.*)

1

governing what is termed its "geographic range," and the intensity of the light computed in candela (an internationally recognized unit of luminous intensity equivalent to a British standard candle), called its "luminous range." In the case of major lights of high intensity the range is limited only by the curvature of the earth—hence range varies directly with the elevation of the light. Atmospheric conditions

such as fog, rain, snow or haze greatly reduce the range of all lights.[2] Landfall lights are installed in towers up to 200 feet in height (often, though not invariably, the distance between high water and the focal plane of the light) with ranges of from 20 to as high as 25 nautical miles. Major coastal lights rarely exceed 150 feet.

The height of a lighthouse tower is determined by its location. In general, tall towers are called for on low-lying shores or offshore rocks in order to gain the maximum range. On the other hand, lighthouses built on lofty promontories often call for squat towers, for if at a high elevation the light might too frequently be obscured by fog.

In choosing a lighthouse site an area subject to rapid coastal erosion should be avoided. Many a sturdily built lighthouse has been undermined by this process, necessitating removal to a safer location. Sable Island, with the unenviable title "the graveyard of the Atlantic," is a notorious example of the effect of coastal erosion, and another is Long Point on Lake Erie. The opposite phenomenon is coastal accretion, brought about by offshore currents or river estuaries dumping deposits in such amounts that the shoreline advances, thereby reducing a lighthouse's effectiveness.

Another basic factor fundamental to the very purpose of a lighthouse was under debate in the early 19th century: Should a light serve to warn the mariner to keep well clear or encourage him to approach the location? A case in point again is Sable Island, on which many a ship had foundered. As early as 1801, two lighthouses were recommended for this location, one at either end of the treacherous crescent-shaped isle, to be located as near the hazardous sandbars as possible.[3] Nothing was done, however, other

than the establishment of a rescue station. More than 30 years later, Francis (later Sir Francis) Beaufort, a celebrated naval hydrographer, condemned the project in his "Report on the several documents relating to the Lighthouses of the British Colonies in North America."
Nothing however could be more mischievous than placing there a light, though more than once recommended, it could scarcely be seen further than the shoals extend and could therefore always act as an enticement into danger.[4]

Another 38 years were to pass before the Department of Marine took the long-deferred project in hand and put the first pair of lighthouses in service in 1873. By that time, lights of such sufficient power were available that Francis Beaufort's objections were no longer tenable. Today lights serve both functions, depending on the location and hazards involved.

British Structural Design
The 18th century is noteworthy for the remarkable progress made in lighthouse construction and the beginnings of greatly improved lighting apparatus. Nowhere was this more apparent than in the British Isles, France and Sweden.

English architects pioneered the challenging design and construction of the first wave-swept towers, structures exposed, generally on rocks offshore, to the full onslaught of the sea. The first of these was the Eddystone light, 14 miles off Plymouth and open to the broad Atlantic. Henry Winstanley built the first Eddystone lighthouse, an elaborate tower in the

Baroque tradition featuring galleries and projections. Completed in 1697, it was swept away by an unprecedentedly fierce storm on 26 November 1703. John Rudyerd, a silk mercer of London, assisted by two expert shipwrights completed the second lighthouse on the Eddystone Rocks in 1709. Although sturdily built of bolted and clamped oak timbers, this second structure fell victim to fire in 1775. The third lighthouse, built by John Smeaton between 1756 and 1759, subsequently was condemned due to subsidence of its foundation. The fourth and present Eddystone lighthouse, 133 feet in height, was completed by J. N. Douglass in 1882.

The most difficult project of all fell to a Scottish engineer, R. Stevenson, grandfather of the talented novelist and poet Robert Louis Stevenson. The construction site chosen for the Bell Rock lighthouse consisted of rocks 12 miles off the east coast of Scotland. The site was a peculiarly hazardous one because the foundation work was below high water. This well-known offshore light was completed in 1811. Yet another notable achievement was the building of the Skerryvore lighthouse off the Isle of Tiree, on the mountainous and irregular west coast of Scotland. The Skerryvore light, 158 feet in height, was completed in 1844. These exposed towers required a high measure of skilled design on the part of the engineer or architect, implemented by rugged masonry.[5]

As steam replaced sail on the high seas during the rapidly industrializing 19th century, many waveswept light-

houses were built at exposed sites in various parts of the world. Horsburgh, Singapore in 1851; Minot Ledge, Massachusetts in 1860; Alguada Reef, Andaman Sea in 1865, and Great Basses, Ceylon in 1873 are but a few.[6]

Canadian Tower Construction
Although the two earliest Canadian lighthouses, Louisbourg and Sambro Island, were very solidly built masonry structures, this was not to be the invariable pattern for the future. The British North American colonies were bound by the limitations of a more stringent purse than either the United States or Great Britain. In the case, for instance, of the two St. Paul Island lighthouses built in 1831 and 1839, the Elder Brethren of Trinity House in London strongly recommended stone construction and dioptric apparatus; the Nova Scotia lighthouse commissioners on the other hand, opted for wooden towers fitted with catoptric apparatus. This decision was not solely based on economy: the governor made known in a despatch to the colonial secretary on 23 March 1838 that to proceed otherwise would have resulted in considerable delay.[7]

Wood, although less durable than masonry, was frequently preferred in Canada due to its abundance. The New Brunswick lighthouse commissioners, for example, showed a preference for wood or frame construction for this reason. Normally one would not expect a frame tower to be as durable as a masonry structure, although a number of timber and frame lighthouses have in fact stood the test of time. One of these is the Gannet Rock lighthouse, a rock station 7 miles off the southern tip of Grand Manan Island. This lighthouse, built in 1831 and, apart from the lantern, still in its original state today, was the object of critical remarks on the part of the master of HM sloop *Persian* in 1851. A New Brunswick lighthouse commissioner's defence of the structure has been borne out surely by the test of time.

The building is of wood, as are all the Light Houses of the Province, but this one is of the very best construction, a frame of heavy timber, boarded and shingled in a good state of preservation and repair. The lower flat or first storey is studded off from the frame lath'd and plastered.[8]

Many circular cast-iron lighthouse towers were built along the shores of Newfoundland and were the subject of much dispute. The imperial authorities (Board of Trade and the Admiralty) who built the majority of the more important lighthouses in Newfoundland favoured this type of construction.[9] A typical structure of this type is shown in Figure 31. Local authorities frequently took issue with this imperial predilection for iron towers. Robert Oke, a celebrated Newfoundland lighthouse authority, in his report for 1856 inveighed against the unsuitability of iron towers in so damp a climate. A case in point was Cape Race tower; condensation and hoarfrost on the interior walls had made the living quarters uninhabitable. A marginal notation within the report

indicates that the Board of Trade had been warned of this possibility beforehand.[10] A visiting Canadian engineer, G. F. Baillarge, supported this contention on a visit to Newfoundland nearly 10 years later.[11] Sir Alexander Bannerman, the lieutenant governor, made the same point in a despatch of 22 December 1857, contending that brick was the most suitable material for use in Newfoundland.[12]

Iron towers found favour because of the very little maintenance required compared with brick and masonry. In 1878, the Newfoundland inspector of lighthouses and public buildings strongly recommended an iron tower for the projected Cabot Island lighthouse. Brick and stone required annual maintenance, even in the case of the best materials, whereas iron required but a little paint to counteract corrosion.[13] The subject remained a debatable one in Newfoundland.

John Page, Canadian chief engineer, in his report for 1859, favoured stone work to brick for exterior surfaces. Brick did not lend itself so well to circular construction. Wood, brick and stone had all been used in lighthouse construction throughout British North America, wood being the most prevalent, particularly on inland waters. The wooden St. Paul Island lighthouses had withstood the ravages of wind and weather in that stormy location for the previous 20 years. Page completed his observations with the conclusion that the objection to iron towers was the danger of instability, and that mode of construction should only be resorted to at sites where stone and brick were not available and costly to transport from a distance. The soundest tower design

was to be found in France, in which an insulating air space was left between the inner and outer walls to counteract the deleterious effect of dampness. Only stone of uniform grain should be used; generally speaking in Canada granite and limestone were most satisfactory.[14] Reinforced concrete and steel, available in the early years of the 20th century, were to add a new dimension to lighthouse design.

The Canadian engineer previously cited, G. F. Baillarge, found that American pressed brick lined inside and out with Portland cement was a frequently used alternative to the cast-iron tower in Newfoundland. This combination proved moisture-resistant to a high degree, a prime requisite in a climate as damp as that of Newfoundland. Based on a stone foundation, this type of construction frequently was combined with three or four courses of freestone at the topmost levels, ostensibly the better to withstand the effects of weathering in windswept locations. The freestone was brought in from Wallace, Nova Scotia, priced at 30 to 60 cents per cubic foot. The Boston region supplied the American pressed brick at $7 per thousand.[15]

The Department of Public Works records offer considerable construction detail on the Cape Jourimain lighthouse (Cape Tormentine) completed in 1870. This is worth citing, not because there was anything unusual about this tower but rather because it was representative of the period. It was a timber and frame eight-sided tower 51 feet in height, the sloping sides tapered from a 20-foot

3

length at base to 9 feet at the top. There were four storeys including the lantern room. The joists at ground level and the first storey were 13 inches deep and 4 inches thick. The sides, floor and hatchway of the lantern were sheathed in galvanized iron as a fire preventive. From ground level to the lantern platform the tower was covered with high-quality shingling, and above this level with galvanized iron.

The cost of construction, including a dwelling, was $2,974. The light was ready for service by 5 January 1870.[16]

A perusal of the Admiralty light lists compiled in 1864 covering the coasts and inland waters of British North America indicates that lighthouse towers generally followed a circular, square or octagonal design.[17] The tabular statement of lighthouses for the (pre-Confederation) Province of Canada on the eve of the federal union lists square frame and stone towers as recurrent types in what were shortly to become the provinces of Quebec and Ontario. Brick was not in common use in this region. Hexagonal and octagonal towers were not uncommon with one light at Coteau-du-Lac described as "on top of a house."[18]

The new century, which has so featured accelerating technological change, gave early confirmation of this trend both in lighthouse construction and apparatus. Reinforced concrete and steel skeleton towers made their appearance in the early years of the 20th century. The tower installed at the north end of Belle Isle in 1906, which went into service the following spring, was a cast-iron structure built in sections by the Montreal firm of H. R. Ives. A coat of reinforced concrete was applied a few years later, the whole supported by buttresses resting on rock.[19]

An early forerunner of the now familiar skeleton steel tower was ordered by the Department of Public Works for the north pier at Kincardine, Ontario, in the spring of 1903.[20] Point-au-Baril lighthouse on Georgian Bay (Lake Huron) was of similar design, and was installed the same season. As with most towers of this type, these were square with sloping sides imparting a tapering shape to the whole. The Varennes light in Quebec was a third early installation. Both reinforced concrete and skeleton steel towers had won general acceptance and were to be found at a number of locations by 1917.[21]

Sable Island posed a challenging site for lighthouse construction. In an utterly exposed location far out in the Atlantic, the desolate and notorious island, by reason of its continually eroding and shifting sands, never allowed for permanence of installation. The first pair of lighthouses, wooden structures at either end of the crescent-shaped island, date from 1873. A lighthouse of skeleton steel design was installed in 1917. Built by the Dominion Bridge Company in Lachine, the tower was shipped in sections to Dartmouth at a total cost (fob) of $3,836. An individual foundation for each of the four legs of the tower was provided to a depth of seven to eight feet, in order to cope with the ceaseless undercutting of the sand by the wind. Re-assembled on the site, the work was completed and the light in operation by 18 December 1917.[22] Only nine years later, the corrosive action of the salt air had had its effect on parts of the tower. In 1935 a concrete tower was recommended for Sable Island on the grounds of steel's rapid corrosion at such a location. Nonetheless, a decision in May of the same year again favoured open-work steel construction, still in use today at the site.

A cast-iron cylindrical tower was designed and built at the Prescott depot, complete with lantern and optical apparatus, for assembly at Cape Norman in the Strait of Belle Isle in 1906. Cape Bauld, in the same region on the northern coast of Newfoundland, was being provided for in similar manner the same year.[23] These two installations featured the long familiar circular cast-iron construction but were of Canadian manufacture.

Post-1945 tower construction felt the rapid winds of change. In 1952 an offshore lighthouse, the foundation for which was a cellular crib of reinforced concrete built in the Sault Ste. Marie drydock and towed to the site, replaced the lightship on Gros Cap Reef, Lake Superior. On the cribwork filled with concrete, whose prow-shaped foundation was especially designed to withstand ice pressure, rested a lighthouse, fog alarm and radio. This offshore installation resembles the forepeak and bridge of a lake freighter.[24]

The White Island Shoal lighthouse, replacing a lightship in Lake Superior in 1955, and the Prince Shoal lighthouse on the lower St. Lawrence are of similar design. The foundation consists of a steel pier in the form of a cone on which rests an inverted cone of similar dimensions, its top thus providing a circular flight deck for the reception of helicopters as well as a base for the light and radio installations.[25]

Apparatus: Lights and Optics
The Whale-oil Lamp
The principal handicap of the oil-fed lamp has always been the smoking of the wick, depositing a film of soot on the lantern glazing and so decreasing rapidly the effectiveness of the light. This centuries-old problem was overcome in 1782 by an invention by the Swiss, Ami Argand, of a virtually smokeless oil lamp utilizing a circular, sleeve-like wick through and around which was a free circulation of air, much improving combustion. The lamp, soon to be known by the name of its inventor, was enclosed within a glass chimney reminiscent of the coal-oil lamps used by our grand-

parents before the age of hydro. The Argand burner produced a clear, relatively smoke-free flame. By 1820 some 50 lighthouses along the shores of England and Ireland were fitted with Argand lamps: indeed 60 years later there were still numerous lighthouses in the British Isles so equipped.[1] A further refinement and improvement of the simple Argand burner was the multiple-wick lamp devised by Count Rumford (Sir Benjamin Thompson), American-born scientist and founder of the Royal Institution in 1800.

Parabolic Reflectors: Catoptric Principle

The whale-oil lamp on the Argand principle was still inferior in illuminating properties to a well-tended blazing coal or wood fire. To remedy this deficiency, the Swedes hit upon the use of the parabolic reflector of polished steel as early as 1738, in order to focus the light on the required plane. At Orskär, five parabolic mirrors were fitted with ten burners, but these initial experiments were disappointing mainly because the lamps were not set at the exact focal point of the mirrors.[2] By 1763 a crude type of parabolic reflector was introduced to certain lights along the Mersey in England, but again results were not encouraging.[3] It fell to J. A. Bordier-Marcet of France to perfect what came to be known as the "catoptric system" (from the Greek *katoptron*, a mirror). His *fanal à double effet* employing two reflectors and two Argand lamps won general favour in the French lighthouse service by 1819. Bordier-Marcet's next optic, the *fanal sidéral* or star-lantern, utilized two circular reflecting metal plates, one above and one below the flame, projecting the light in a parabolic curve horizontally. In essence, this device reflected the vertically emitted light to the horizontal plane. Mariners at Honfleur, where the star-lantern was first introduced, enthusiastically dubbed it *notre salut*. This device increased the candlepower of an ordinary Argand lamp from 10 to 70 candlepower, a sevenfold improvement.[4] Catoptric apparatus was used in the Canadian lighthouse service until late in the century because of its relative economy, but in Europe and the United States a light upon an improved principle had largely displaced the simple reflector type by the 1830s and 1840s.

The following passage quoted from the minutes of the New Brunswick Executive Council in 1846, describing the apparatus at Machias Seal Island at the entrance to the Bay of Fundy, illustrates the limitation of the older style catoptric installations with multiple lamps and reflectors.

The Lighthouse lanterns have eight parabolic reflectors of 23 inches diameter, set in a circle of 16 feet circumference, with one large Argand lamp to each, each lamp having a pipe of communication with a common reservoir in the centre, in which oil is kept fluid in winter by an Argand lamp burning under the reservoir—the lantern is only seven feet in diameter, so that the lighthouse keeper really has no room for the necessary operations of feeding and cleaning, and the glass of the outer frame is so near the lamps as to be constantly misted.[5]

By contrast, the largest dioptric light of much greater power than the above installation, 6 feet in diameter with but one lamp, was many times more convenient to service.

Lenses: Dioptric Principle

In 1823 another Frenchman, Augustin Fresnel, perhaps the most celebrated of all the pioneers in lighthouse optics, introduced the first lenticular, or dioptric, lighting apparatus in the Corduouan lighthouse located at the mouth of the Gironde River. The principle of the dioptric (Greek *dioptrikos*, to see through) system was the refraction, by means of lenses and prisms, of light on the desired focal plane. Unlike the catoptric, the dioptric apparatus used only one lamp or light source. At the time of the installation of the first lenticular light in the Corduouan lighthouse in 1823, the facility was considered second to none in the world. The cutting and grinding of lenses called for craftsmanship of a very high order, and so lenticular apparatus was costly, but once installed it required no adjustment. By mid-century both refracting and reflecting elements were combined in the one optic, known as the catadioptric system, but in practice the shorter term continued to be used. By this time, lenticular or refracting lens apparatus had supplanted the simpler reflector type in most of the world's principal lighthouses.

It will be readily appreciated that France was the leading country in the field of lighthouse optics in the early 19th century; particularly was this the case in the fine craftsmanship required for the production of lenticular or dioptric apparatus. In England as early as 1831, the South Shields firm of Isaac Cookson and Company endeavoured quite unsuccessfully to match French quality. The turmoil in France in 1848 drove a number of refugees to seek asylum in England, among whom were Georges Bontemps and an engineer, Tabouret, who had gained an invaluable apprenticeship under the great Fresnel. These two fugitive craftsmen from the continent were engaged by the Birmingham firm of Chance Brothers, a concern which had been commissioned by the government to manufacture dioptric lighthouse apparatus for use on the English and Irish coasts in 1845. As a result, by 1851 Chance Brothers could boast a product on a par with that of their French forerunners and future competitors.[6] The English firm enjoyed a monopoly in its field for many years in Britain and its products were exported to all parts of the world. Throughout the 19th century, until the debut and gathering experience of the Dominion Lighthouse Depot in the early years of this century, Chance Brothers supplied a large portion of Canada's requirements.

As early as 1845, the imperial Trinity House had expressed a decided preference for the dioptric type of light. This also was the trend along the American seaboard, where their numbers increased from three in 1851 to no fewer than 310 five years later. Indeed the American authorities announced a programme of total replacement of the old reflector-type lights,

whereas as late as the year 1860 there were but 10 dioptric lights in service in the old Province of Canada.[7] By this date there was no doubt concerning the superiority of the dioptric or refracting light. Expressed in terms of the percentage of light produced reaching the bridge of a ship, the following figures are significant:

open light (without reflectors)	3½%
catoptric (the best)	17%
dioptric	83%

Assuming equivalent oil consumption, the dioptric apparatus emitted a light five times the strength of the catoptric.[8] Furthermore, as previously indicated, one light source sufficed with the dioptric system whereas the catoptric required multiple lamps. One cannot do better than to quote a report compiled by a British engineering firm, D. and T. Stevenson, for the Commissioners of Northern Lighthouses, about the year 1850.

It has been determined that in revolving lights, the effect of one of the eight annular lenses, in a First Order Light, is equal to that of eight of the largest reflectors in use; and that to produce by reflectors to the most perfect kind the effect of Lenticular apparatus of the best description, a lantern must be provided capable of accommodating from fifty-six to seventy-two reflectors; an arrangement all but impracticable.[9]

Dioptric lights were classified according to the internal diameter of the optical apparatus; the largest, lights of the 1st Order, designed for installation in landfall lighthouses, were 72½ inches in diameter. The smallest, lights of the 6th Order used as harbour lights,

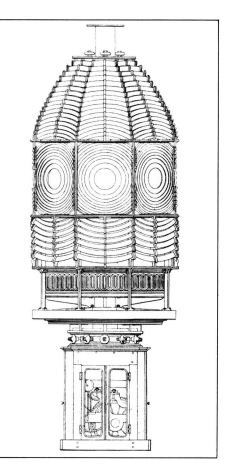

4

were less than a foot in diameter. Lights of the 2nd Order were used in coastal lighthouses, to be found frequently at the mouths of large rivers or in the vicinity of dangerous shoals.[10]

This elaborate construction of precisely ground lenses and prisms has survived to the present, although invariably the light source is now electric. Current electric lamps, because their light source is so concentrated, do not require such complex refracting optical apparatus as their predecessors. None-

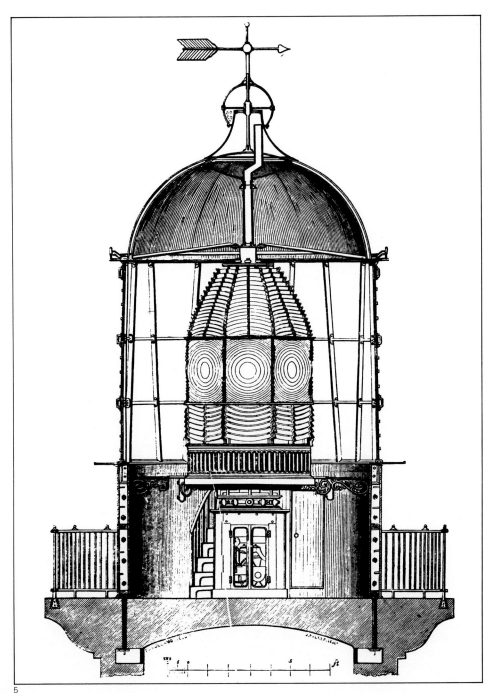

theless, dioptric apparatus of the type depicted in Figure 4 has continued to be used with an electric light source at major lighthouses. As this apparatus is replaced over the course of time, much simpler and less costly optical apparatus will be used with comparable effectiveness.

The Coal-oil Lamp
Until the 1850s in British North America, lighting apparatus was based on the Argand burner with its reservoir of sperm oil, with variants of porpoise or fish oils in maritime regions. At going rates in 1861 of $1.69 to $1.85 per gallon, the traditional sperm oil was expensive and likely to become more so due to the diminishing supply. Already by the early sixties far-ranging whaling fleets operating in the southern seas had depleted the whales. The British and French lighthouse services had in large measure turned to the use of vegetable oils such as colza and rape seed, which was at once cheaper and more readily available. In 1860 John Page, in his report to the Commissioner of Public Works, observed that Canadian experience confirmed the superiority of colza to sperm oil. Although a larger quantity of the vegetable oil was required to produce an equivalent effect, the cost was little more than half that of the traditional material. Despite the fact that lighthouses in the British and French service had converted with few exceptions to the use of colza oil (the source for which was France and Holland), at the time lighthouses both in the Prov-

ince of Canada and in the United States were still largely dependent on sperm oil.[11]

A highly significant Canadian contribution to both the lighthouse service and to domestic lighting in general was the distillation in 1846 of kerosene from coal devised by Dr. Abraham Gesner, a physician from Cornwallis, Nova Scotia. Although having taken a medical degree in London in 1827, Gesner later forsook medicine for geology, in which field he made a major contribution to the development of lighthouse illuminants.[12] Popularly known as "coal oil," kerosene was first tried in the early sixties in lighthouses on the upper St. Lawrence between Beauharnois and Kingston. According to Superintendent D. C. Smith, coal oil "afforded much better and more brilliant light than the sperm oil."[13] At a cost of a mere 65 cents per gallon, coal oil offered the strong inducement of economy. In 1864, Smith recommended the total conversion of all lights in his agency to coal oil, and received the chief engineer's sanction the following year. Mariners plying the upper St. Lawrence reported enthusiastically on the effectiveness of the new kerosene lights.[14] Although there was no doubt but that coal oil produced both a brighter and steadier flame with catoptric apparatus, John Page cautioned against its use with dioptric apparatus which was gaining favour for the more powerful lights. Coal oil used in the concentric ring burners required to produce "the large, uniform shape and density of flame required for lights of this class" would have insufficient combustion to be effective.[15] But for reflector or catoptric lights coal oil provided at once a much cheaper and more effective illuminant. Until late in the century, this older-style apparatus was still favoured in Canada. In 1861 coal oil was introduced with excellent results at the Father Point lighthouse on the lower St. Lawrence.

Until the advent of petroleum vapour and acetylene lamps early in the 20th century, the circular-wick burner using colza oil and the flat-wick lamp using kerosene held sway in the Canadian lighthouse service. Figure 7 illustrates flatwick coal-oil lamps, so favoured for use with the more numerous catoptric lights until the end of the century. The mammoth burners were fitted with 18- and 24-inch reflectors : their kerosene consumption ran at about double the rate of the smaller models. These kerosene lighthouse lamps, some of which were still in service until post-war years, remind one of the domestic coal-oil lamps which were so much a part of rural households in our grandparents' generation. In the main, these two basic lamp types, fitted with more elaborate refracting and reflecting elements, saw the Canadian lighthouse service through into the early years of the present century.

The Gas Mantle
Around the turn of the century an ingenious device utilizing a familiar illuminant was introduced to lighting technology and survived at some locations well into the post-war period. The incandescent oil vapour light was first installed at L'Ile Penfret lighthouse in France in 1898. The novel principle, trebling the power of all former wick lamps, consisted of the burning of vaporized coal oil within an incandescent mantle. In England Arthur Kitson perfected a lamp on this principle which became well-known as the "Kitson burner," and by 1902 this equipment was widely adopted in the British lighthouse service. In 1921 David Hood introduced an improved mantle of viscous silk doubling the brilliance of mantles up to that time.[16] By 1904 petroleum vapour lights had captured the attention of the Canadian authorities, not surprisingly, inasmuch as a 345 per cent increase in candlepower was claimed for the oil vapour lights compared with the flat-wick lamp. The new lights came in four sizes ranging from 25 to 85 millimeters.[17] Although the well-established English firm of Chance Brothers was credited with producing the best quality petroleum vapour lights at the time, an early Canadian competitor in the field was the Diamond Heating and Lighting Company of Montreal.[18] As early as 1909 a 1st Order dioptric apparatus at the Heath Point lighthouse, Anticosti Island, produced a brilliant light of one-half million candlepower.[19]

A concurrent development of the early 20th century and one to find increasing favour with unwatched lights was that of the acetylene light. First tried in Canada in the Father Point lighthouse in 1902, the acetylene light was reported on favourably by mariners. It was claimed that the range of this reflector-type light was increased

6 Types of oil lamps used in lighthouses in the 19th century. (*Canada. Department of Transport.*)

7 Flat-wick lamps utilizing coal oil, generally in conjunction with catoptric or reflector-type apparatus. (*Canada. Department of Transport.*)

8 Oil vapour lights with incandescent mantles. Introduced in the 20th century, this apparatus gave a much brighter light. (*Canada. Department of Transport.*)

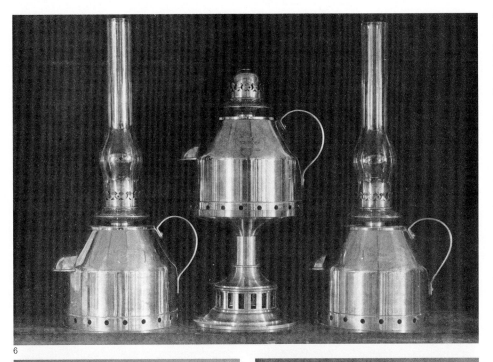

6

7

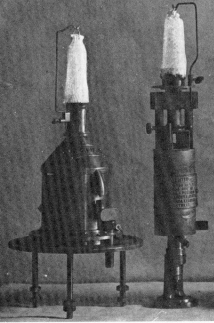

8

from 14 to 28 miles as a result of the conversion.[20] In 1903 the department decided to convert all the kerosene lights on the upper St. Lawrence to acetylene and tests conducted that same year demonstrated a five-fold increase in candlepower over the former kerosene flat-wick lamps.[21] On the whole, the acetylene light was more applicable to use in buoys than in lighthouses. The advantage of acetylene was that it could be left untended for a period of time, a factor which became significant in the lighthouse service at a much later date. An untended kerosene device, the Wigham lamp, which could be left to its own devices for up to a month at a time, was manufactured in Dublin. The principle of this lamp, which found favour on the Pacific coast, was that of a horizontally burning wick fed slowly over a roller, the burner surrounded by a combustion cone and fitted with lenticular optical apparatus.[22] Although both petroleum vapour and acetylene were to be eventually supplanted by electricity, both were in service at scattered locations in very recent years.

Revolving Lights and Colour Characteristics

Until late in the 18th century, all lighthouses exhibited fixed white lights. The first revolving light to sweep the horizon with its beam was tested at Carlston, Sweden, in 1781. By 1790 revolving lights had been widely adopted in the French and British services. Weight-driven clockwork, on the same principle as that used in grandfather clocks, provided rotary power until the advent of the electric motor. The early revolving lights were restricted in size because of frictional losses produced by the light's rollers in the raceway; friction was overcome by 1890, with the introduction of the mercury float mechanism, removing at one stroke the principal restriction on the size and weight of the intricately designed apparatus. The first such light in Canada was installed at Southwest Point, Anticosti Island in 1831. Its beam completed a revolution 100 feet above high water every minute.[23]

Figure 9 illustrates the two systems of rotary gearing in common use about the middle of the last century. The French system employed offset gearing, and the Scottish, central. Greater stability and smoother operation was claimed for the latter, conditions which were very important with apparatus of great weight.[24]

Although it was early known that white light was visible at a greater range than coloured, the desirability of colour characteristics in the interests of readier identification was admitted. To an English customs agent, Benjamin Milne, goes the credit for devising the first colour characteristics in lighthouse optics. Produced by 21 parabolic reflectors mounted on a three-sided frame, the whole rotated by means of a vertically mounted axle. The reflectors on one of the three sides were covered with red glass, pro-

ducing a red beam periodically followed by white. This apparatus was installed in the Flamborough Head lighthouse on the Yorkshire coast in 1806. Light colours now used internationally are white, red and green. White is preferred because of its range, which exceeds that of red or green.

Light Characteristics
The trend in the early years of the 20th century was the replacement of catoptric by dioptric apparatus, increased power in lights generally, and the replacement of fixed with flashing and occulting lights in the interests of easier identification. The flashing light displays its beam for a briefer span than the subsequent period of darkness, or eclipse; the reverse is the case with the occulting light. In order to render identification yet more certain, combinations of flashing and occulting sequences, sometimes with the additional feature of a colour phase, were devised for different locations. Below are shown the characteristics of lights that are exhibited internationally.
fixed – continuous or steady light; little used today.
flashing – single flash at regular intervals; duration of light less than darkness.
group flashing – a group of two or more flashes at regular intervals.
occulting – steady light with a sudden and total eclipse at regular intervals, duration of darkness being always less than or equal to that of light.
group occulting – steady light with a group of two or more sudden eclipses at regular intervals.
fixed flashing – a fixed light varied by a single flash of relatively greater brilliance at regular intervals.

fixed and group flashing – a fixed light varied by a group of two or more brilliant flashes at regular intervals.
quick flashing – a light that flashes continuously more than 60 times a minute.
interrupted quick flashing – same as preceding but with total eclipse at regular intervals.
group interrupted quick flashing – same as above, but with relatively longer periods of eclipse.
alternating – any of foregoing but which alter in colour.[25]

Electrification
Electricity for lighthouse purposes was tried first at South Foreland, England, as early as 1858. The first electric light in regular service was at the Dungeness lighthouse on the coast of Kent in 1862. The results cannot have been encouraging, for both prototypes were subsequently replaced with the reliable mineral oil lights. The practical adaptation of electricity to lighthouse use was contingent upon two developments; inexpensive transmission of electrical power (or self-contained generating equipment) and the tungsten filament lamp or bulb, the forerunners of which were too short-lived to be practical. In Canada, hydroelectric power became readily available for domestic and industrial use during the first decade of the 20th century and tungsten filament lamps were on the market by 1907. Reed Point, New Brunswick, was the first lighthouse in Canada exhibiting an electric light (1895), but the first electrically operated light and fog alarm was established at Cape Croker,

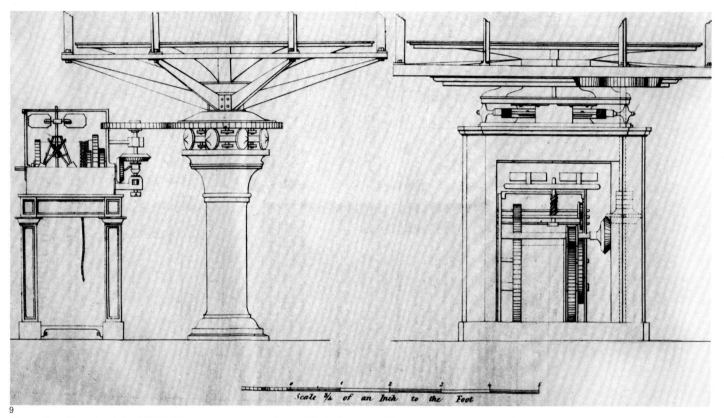

9

Georgian Bay, in July 1902. The Ottawa firm of A. Trudeau furnished the generating plant.[26]

Electrification continued apace in the inter-war years, and was completed following World War II. The Commissioner of Lights for the season 1914-15 listed a total of 23 electrically equipped lighthouses of which 8 were in Nova Scotia, 6 in British Columbia and 5 in Ontario.[27]

By 1931, electricity supplied both light and rotary power in an increasing number of lighthouses. Known as "multi-flashing apparatus" this equipment was first given a trial in 1930 at Musquash, New Brunswick, and at Cranberry Island and Guion Island, Nova Scotia.[28] And so compact electric motors came to replace the clockwork and weight mechanisms of yesteryear. Experimental work at the Prescott depot delved into the use of cellophane to impart colour characteristics, safety devices for the protection of optics and, most significant for the future, the now widely used mercury vapour lamp. The advantage of the latter, which is now recently replacing the filament lamp, is greatly extended life, running to many thousands of hours. Electrification of Canadian lights was completed following the Second World War, although the acetylene or oil light has survived in some locations.

Of equal significance in the evolution of the modern lighthouse service at home and abroad was the introduc-

10 Occulting apparatus used at Machias Seal Island
  lighthouse, Bay of Fundy. (*Canada. Department of
  Transport.*)

11 Mercury vapour electric light fitted with bulldog
  plastic lenses. This is the apparatus most favoured
  in the modern lighthouse service. (*Canada. Department of Transport.*)

12 A 300-mm. lantern fitted with mercury vapour light.
  On right is the circular screen to produce flashes.
  (*Canada. Department of Transport.*)

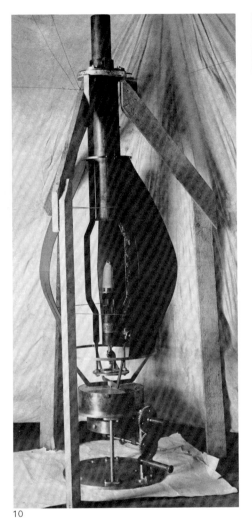

10

11

12

tion of the automatic, or untended light. Gustaf Dalen (1869-1937) of Sweden, a brilliant engineer tragically blinded in an accident early in his career, invented the first automatic beacon lighting using acetylene, an innovation which won him a Nobel Prize in 1912. He is also credited with the invention of the first sun valve, a photometric device activated by light, switching the light off once dawn had broken and on with gathering dusk. With the passing of the years more and more lights could be left untended. The advantage of automation, particularly with the introduction of the automatic lamp changer, was particularly obvious for lights in remote locations in the north. Today in Canada the function of the traditional lighthouse keeper is being rapidly phased out; in his stead is the itinerant technician making his rounds at periodic intervals by motor, supply ship or helicopter.

The principal post-war developments in the more than two-century evolution of the Canadian lighthouse were the completion of the electrification programme, introduction of radar aids to the lighthouse service (for example radar reflectors), and the conversion of a great many lighthouses to automatic and untended operation.

The completion of electrification in the post-war years was made possible by the extension of hydro-electric power to regions hitherto without it, and of yet greater significance, by the widespread introduction of diesel generating units. By this means the convenience and efficiency of electricity was introduced to the high Arctic. As early as 1948, 481 of 2,469

lighthouses and navigational lights had been electrified. At time of writing (1970) virtually all lighthouses throughout the country have been converted to electricity, as well as a good many buoys.[29]

Hand in hand with the electrification of lighthouses previously equipped with acetylene or oil vapour apparatus went the development of new high-intensity electric lights. Many of these were installed in the original dioptric lens and prism apparatus; but with the much greater concentration of electric light, very much simpler optics of moulded glass and plastic served equally well at a fraction of the cost. In its report for 1951, the department observed that "major high intensity electric units established for trial service have been favourably reported."[30] The superiority of the new mercury vapour bulb over the incandescent lamp was obvious by 1961, the advantage being a light of higher intensity and much longer life; these much smaller bulbs lasted for two or three years, an important consideration with the trend toward unwatched lights.[31]

A new, lightweight, anti-corrosive aluminum alloy lantern was introduced in 1955. These gradually will replace the heavy cast-iron types with anticipated lower maintenance costs.[32] The xenon light developed in Britain and Germany, one of which was installed at Prince Shoal in 1964, produced a light of such unprecedented intensity (32 million candlepower) that it is used only in thick fog.

Electronically operated remote control systems, developed jointly by the National Research Council and the Department of Transport, were designed to operate both lights and fog

alarms. The offshore Pelee Passage lighthouse in Lake Erie was the first light station so equipped. The significance of automatic remote control for light stations in remote locations in the far north was obvious. A microwave control system was introduced at the Holland Rock fog alarm near Prince Rupert in 1961.[33]

Conversion to electricity was more than two-thirds completed by 1961; of the 3,054 lights in service (including buoys), 2,518 were in automatic operation.[34]

Fog Alarms
From earliest times various devices had been used at light stations to sound fog warnings in thick weather. Bells, gongs and cannon were all tried at various times and places with varying effectiveness. It was well known that sound transmission over water was subject to peculiar and capricious vagaries, a signal sometimes becoming inaudible close inshore while easily heard farther out to sea. Fog signals due to deflection or echo often gave false bearings. Such difficulties have yet to be resolved completely.

The first steam fog whistle in British North America was installed in 1860 at the Partridge Island lighthouse in Saint John Harbour. Mariners were enthusiastic over the installation, consisting of an 8-horsepower engine producing a pressure of 100 pounds per square inch and costing £350 local currency. Its range in calm weather was established at 10 miles. The whistle was controlled by clockwork, sounding 10 seconds in each minute.[35]

In 1899, a fog siren was introduced at Belle Isle half way between the upper and lower lights at a cost of $20,112.64. Power to drive the air compressor was derived from a water-wheel. The signal was produced by a double siren driven by compressed air; the siren was located 250 feet above high water, and the air compressor in a power house at the landing stage. The equipment was English-made[36] and, along with a somewhat similar device known as a "Scotch siren" also of British make and in use at Louisbourg and Father Point, gave the best results before the appearance of the diaphone, the product of a Canadian inventor.

Diaphone Apparatus

In 1902, J. P. Northey, a Toronto manufacturer, developed the diaphone, a major improvement in fog alarm equipment and one still in widespread use today. Basically a modification of the Scotch siren and operating on the principle of a high-velocity pulsating piston rather than a rotating drum, Northey's diaphone produced a blast of more constant pitch for about one-eighth the power expended by the Scotch siren.[37] By 1904, diaphones had replaced the older fog alarm equipment at most of the important light stations.

The new diaphone equipment required skilled attendants known as "fog alarm engineers" at major light stations. This attendant shared the keeper's meagre salary. Some light-keepers, more versatile than their fellows, qualified as fog alarm engineers and so could dispense with assistance. The larger diaphones were fitted with steam-driven air compressors, but the smaller installations were petrol-operated.[38]

The diaphone continued in use throughout the country, notwithstanding the introduction of electronic aids. In 1952, engineers developed a new resonator which greatly increased the audible range. In the mid-sixties Canada once again contributed to fog alarm development with the "Airchine." The Airchine was not designed to replace the diaphone, the largest of which were unsurpassed in range. The Airchine did, however, offer the signal advantage of economy with a signal of almost comparable range. Its air compressors were driven by small electric motors, the whole plant being about one-fifth the dimensions of the standard diaphone. The first Airchine went into service in 1965.[39]

The electronic fog alarm, a curiously shaped structure (see Fig. 14) of English manufacture, must be considered a major departure in the more than a century's progress in this field. This Stone Chance apparatus has been reported highly satisfactory in the Canadian service.

Submarine Signaling Apparatus

Submarine signaling apparatus, an invention of A. J. Mundy of Boston and Professor Elisha Gray, was another fog alarm system introduced at major light stations early in the century. It was based on an underwater bell connected by cable with the lighthouse; when sounded in foggy weather, the resultant underwater signal was picked up by a direction-finding receiver installed in a vessel's bow. The range of submarine signals varied between 5 and 12 miles.[40] The equipment had its limitations, among which was that very few ships were fitted with direction-finders — the *Tunisian* and *Ionian* of the Allan Line, and the *Mount Temple* and *Lake Manitoba*, early transatlantic CPR vessels. Nonetheless, this equipment was installed at 21 lighthouses under contract to the Submarine Signal Company of Boston.[41] Submarine signaling was quickly displaced by radio in the early twenties.

Radio

Twentieth-century progress in communications was nowhere more apparent than in the fields of radio and aviation, the first of which had an early contribution to make to the lighthouse service in Canada and throughout the world. The first wireless coast station designed for ship-to-shore communications was established at Spezia, Italy, in the summer of 1897. The *Lake Champlain*, launched in 1900 and initially operated by the Beaver Line, was the first passenger liner equipped with radio. Although Department of Marine wireless coast stations were often separate establishments, some lighthouses, particularly in the early days, combined the functions of light station and radio coast station. In 1904, for example, wireless facilities were installed at the Fame Point, Belle

13 Drawing of the first steam fog alarm installed at Partridge Island lighthouse at the entrance to Saint John Harbour, New Brunswick. (*Public Archives of Canada.*)

13

Isle, Cape Ray, Cape Race, Heath Point and Point Amour lighthouses. By 1915, no fewer than 21 lighthouses below Quebec were radio equipped. In the same region, Crane Island, Money Point, Point Lepreau and Partridge Island had telephone facilities.[42] By these means, a closer check was kept on ship movements.

Note has already been made of the eccentricities, under certain geographic or climatic conditions, of the familiar bellow and grunt of the fog alarm. The radio beacon installed at a number of radio coast stations and some lighthouses used in conjunction with loop direction-finding apparatus aboard ship was to prove a surer guide to the navigator than the audio signal from diaphone or siren. Cross bearings, however, were themselves subject, under certain conditions, to coastal refraction and hence dangerously misleading. In any case, radio bearings were considered less reliable than visual bearings on a light.

In 1923, the Lighthouse Board recommended the installation of radio transmitter beacons at either the Cape Bauld or Belle Isle light stations, and at Heath Point, Anticosti Island. These experimental radio beacons had a range of about 50 miles. Initially this equipment was to be the responsibility of the lightkeeper.[43] The first radio beacon on the Great Lakes was installed at the Southeast Shoal lighthouse in 1927, transmitting a signal every 2½ minutes on a wave-length of 1,000 meters.[44]

By 1929, radio direction-finding equipment had definitely supplanted submarine signaling apparatus. It should not be overlooked that at this date there were 153 diaphone fog alarms in service, some of which had been operating since 1906. Indeed the fog alarm, as a glance at the latest list will confirm, has been far from displaced; despite the proliferation of electronic aids, mariners still appreciate the discordant blast of the foghorn.[45] In 1929 more powerful radio beacons of 200-watt output became available; this equipment was installed at, or near, the Cape Whittle, West Point Anticosti, and the Pointe-des-

Monts lighthouses in the Gulf of St. Lawrence. On the Great Lakes (never behind-hand) similar equipment was supplied to the Main Duck Island (Lake Ontario), Long Point and the Southeast Shoal (Lake Erie), Cove Island (Lake Huron), and the Michipicoten (Lake Superior) lighthouses.[46] The words of the *Liverpool Journal of Commerce* are as applicable to the Canadian as to the British lighthouse service.

Wireless stands as science's great contribution to safety at sea, and future developments, so far as lighting and lighthouses are concerned, may be of no less remarkable import than those of the last fifty years until the time, perhaps, lighthouses as we know them today, and as they have been known for centuries, may be superseded.[47]

This speculation, dating from 1929, has yet to be fulfilled.

Administration

From 1763 until 1805, boards of commissioners were appointed for specific public works in Lower Canada. In that year, following the British tradition, a corporate body to be known as the Quebec Trinity House was created by statute, with

full power and authority, to make, ordain and constitute such and so many Bye laws, Rules and Orders, not repugnant to the maritime laws of Great Britain or to the laws of this Province. . . . for the more convenient, safe and easy navigation of the River Saint Lawrence, from the fifth rapid, above the city of Montreal, downwards, as well by the laying down, as taking up of Buoys and Anchors, as by the erecting of Light houses, Beacons or Land Marks, the clearing of sands or rocks or otherwise howsoever.[1]

14

In addition to the master and his deputy, two wardens were appointed in Quebec and three in Montreal, a subordinate branch of the parent body. The same bill made provision for divers other officials as a harbour master for Quebec, and at Montreal water bailiffs, superintendent of pilots and a lighthouse keeper at Green Island "with a farm belonging to the Corporation."[2] A little over a quarter-century later, a Montreal Trinity House was instituted, the enabling statute receiving royal assent on 25 February 1832.[3] These two authorities were not unworthy of their namesake in London, co-operating fully with the Admiralty, the imperial boards of trade, and the various boards of lighthouse commissioners in the Atlantic provinces, to be succeeded only at Confederation by the newly created Department of Marine and Fisheries.

By the year 1824, the colony of Nova Scotia was maintaining five lighthouses along its shore solely financed by means of light dues. Apparently the Nova Scotian authorities at this time felt that they were contributing somewhat more than their share in relation to their neighbours, for in the words of a despatch from Government House dated 14 September 1824, "It may not be improper for me to observe here, that from the geographical position of Nova Scotia, the navigation to and from the Provinces of New Brunswick and Prince Edward Island derive very considerable security from its Light Houses."[4] From this date, 1824, more than two decades were to pass before the first lighthouse was built on the shores of Prince Edward Island; but whether the Nova Scotia governor's implication with respect to the efforts of New Brunswick's lighthouse commissioners was well taken is perhaps debatable.

In 1834, there were 11 lighthouses in Nova Scotia, the south coast, fronting on the Atlantic and extending about 250 miles, having five by this date. In addition there was the Halifax Harbour light and one under construction at Cross Island in the vicinity of Lunenburg.[5]

By 1832, the New Brunswick lighthouse commissioners were well content with the lighting of the Bay of Fundy; so much so that in their report they contended that "an increase in lights would rather tend to perplex and embarrass the mariner on his voyage from seaward."[6] An accurate hydrographic survey of the region, so subject to frequent and dense fog and high tides, seemed more to the point than further lighthouse construction. In 1832, New Brunswick was maintaining five lighthouses on the Fundy shore — Gannet Rock, Point Lepreau, Cape Sable (not to be confused with Sable Island), Seal Island and Partridge Island. In their report for 1840, the New Brunswick commissioners contended, on the testimony of American naval and merchant service authorities, that "The New Brunswick Lights are the best kept of any on the American coast."[7]

The hydrographic survey was entrusted to Captain W. F. W. Owen, R.N. He was commissioned in July 1843 to carry out the project in HMS *Columbia*. By 1847 a good part of the Bay of Fundy had been surveyed, greatly adding to the accuracy and detail on navigational charts.[8] Similar work had been carried out on the St. Lawrence and the Great Lakes at an earlier date.

In common with the other colonies, New Brunswick levied a light duty for the upkeep of her lighthouses at the rate of 2-7/10 pennies per ton on all vessels other than coasters and fishing trawlers. The lighthouse return for 1847 listed 10 establishments maintained by the province at annual costs ranging from £99 to as high as £301 (Partridge Island).[9] In addition, New Brunswick contributed to the upkeep of lighthouses at Cape Sable, Seal Island and Brier Island in the neighbouring colony of Nova Scotia.[10] The New Brunswick commissioners,

like their contemporaries in Nova Scotia, maintained that their province had done more than its share toward the provision of lighthouses in the Bay of Fundy. Nova Scotia, for example, contributed nothing toward the establishments at Machias Seal Island, Gannet Rock, Head Harbour, Point Lepreau and Partridge Island, lights contributing as much to the safety of Nova Scotian vessels as to those of New Brunswick.[11]

A peculiarity until 1848 of New Brunswick lighthouse administration was the existence of two boards of lighthouse commissioners, one of which sat at Saint John and the other at St. Andrews. In 1842, on an address from the House of Assembly, the Saint John board was constituted the sole authority in the colony. This decision was resisted for a season by the St. Andrews body, which refused to sit with its associate. The Saint John board resolved on 27 April 1842, since separate appropriations had been provided, to carry on under the old system for another season while recommending the increased efficiency to be derived from a single authority. By 1848 this policy had obviously been implemented, for in the minutes of the executive council, reference is made to one board of lighthouse commissioners.[12] No doubt this resulted in a saving to the colony.

As with the other colonies, in Newfoundland a board of lighthouse commissioners was responsible for those

15

lighthouses which did not fall under the aegis of the Admiralty. By legislation passed in 1855 the lighthouse commissioners' authority was henceforth vested in the newly created Board of Works, made up of the surveyor general as chairman, the attorney general, the colonial secretary, the president of the legislative council, and three members from the House of Assembly.[13]

By the late 1830s it was obvious that Upper Canada's lighthouse service left much to be desired. In the words of Captain Sandom, master of the *Niagara*, whose strictures reached the Colonial Office,

The total neglect of the local government with respect to the Lighthouses, that a very important one (on Long Point) has literally been allowed to fall to ruin, the oil being carefully stored in the contractors' rooms; another (also important) upon Pelée Island, is in spite of frequent remonstrances by my officers with the keeper and contractor, kept in utter darkness. I am given to understand the "Inspector of Lighthouses" is a sinecure office, at present held by . . .in the City of Toronto.[14]

Notwithstanding Sandom's sharp criticism, the inspector general on his 1839 tour of inspection found the Pelee Island establishment, along with those at False Ducks Island and Nine Mile Point on Lake Ontario, in reasonable order. He observed, however, that the reflectors in most of the lights had been damaged by careless cleaning.

The few good stations notwithstanding, it was nonetheless apparent by 1840 that a closer supervision of lightkeepers was required, and that some attention should be given to apparatus designed to improve circulation of air within the lantern. The purchase of supplies by public contract became mandatory only in 1837. The inspector general recommended that lightkeepers' salaries be paid only on certification that the lights in question had been properly maintained either by ship's captains or local customs collectors.[15] Shortly after the Act of Union, lighthouses in Upper Canada, or Canada West as it was to be known until Confederation, passed under the jurisdiction of the Board of Works. A uniform pay scale was introduced for lightkeepers: £65 per annum on shore stations, £85 on island locations, and a special stipend of £100 per annum for False Ducks Island.[16] A stricter and more stringent selection of candidates for lightkeeping duties was instituted in March, 1844; henceforth, mariners with lake experience would be given preference.[17] Clearly the lax ways of the pre-union period were a thing of the past, including the mischievous practice of hiring deputies (sub-contracting the duties to third parties) which so often had contributed to carelessness and neglect.

But not all complaints could be traced to a negligent keeper. Frequently the sperm oil lamps smoked, darkening the lantern glazing and so diminishing the effectiveness of the light. In December 1844, J. S. McIntyre reported to the Board of Works that the trouble lay with poor combustion due to inadequate ventilation. The solution to this problem was a properly designed air vent in the roof of the lantern. He also observed that many of the burners were not set at the exact focal point of the reflectors, and to correct this fault he made all of the reflectors adjustable.[18] He also recommended the standardization of all the lamps and reflectors in use on the lakes, and this was later implemented. Other improvements were made in the lamps to regulate the flow of oil to the wick and reduce oil wastage.[19] Of all the lights on the lower lakes, McIntyre found the worst attended was that at Port Burwell.

It is fortunate that this Light is not of much consequence for it is certainly the worst attended to on the Lakes. . . . The reflectors are of very little use as the lamps are three inches outside of the focus, and there is no way of altering them, without making an entire new stand.[20]

McIntyre's modifications of apparatus and reforms respecting personnel had their effect, for by 1845 he was able to report that all the lights on Lake Erie were of a new and improved design, as were those at False Ducks, Main Ducks and Point Petre on Lake Ontario.[21]

With the creation of the new Department of Marine, not many years were to pass before it assumed responsibility for aids to navigation from its colonial predecessors in the various provinces of British North America. In 1870, the new federal parliament enacted legislation transferring responsibility for all lighthouses and buoys between Quebec and the Strait of Belle

Isle from the Quebec Trinity House to the Department of Marine. The Montreal Trinity House surrendered its jurisdiction in like manner on 1 July 1873.[22]

In 1867 the total number of lighthouses established and in service in the old Province of Canada (Quebec and Ontario) was tallied at 131.[23]

Strait of Belle Isle to Quebec	24
Quebec to Montreal	27
above Montreal	69
above Montreal (privately run)	11

Although this may have seemed at the time an impressive total, with the rapid development of steam navigation the new department early in its career recognized the urgency for both expansion and improvement in quality. The minister, in his fifth annual report (1872) stated,

I was under the necessity of asking for moderate sums, and erecting a cheap description of strong wooden-framed buildings, taking care, however, to use nothing but high-class powerful lighting apparatus ; . . . this Department has succeeded in erecting ninety-three new lighthouses and has established four new lightships, and ten new steam fog alarms on the coasts of Canada, besides having under contract forty-three lighthouses, eight steam fog alarms, and two new lightships, all of which has been done within five or six years. The Canadian petroleum oil used for these lights, being a powerful illuminant, and being procured at a very small cost, has enabled this Department to maintain not only brilliant and powerful lights, but to do so at, probably, a cheaper rate than any other country in the world.[24]

In the summer of 1872, a visiting committee of the imperial Trinity House toured both Canada and the United States in order to observe the quality and efficiency of their respective lighthouse services. The visitors found the Canadian lights superior to the American, although the latter service comprised a greater number of solidly built masonry and brick structures. The Canadian service, they pointed out, had to operate on a much slimmer budget and so was one of simplicity and economy, well-suited to the needs of a new country. Lightkeepers were not highly trained as they were in England, nor were they well paid ; most Canadian keepers considered their lightkeeping wages subsidiary to other sources of income. According to the visiting Brethren,

Their buildings appear to be easily and quickly erected at small cost ; the mineral oil is a powerful illuminant requiring little care in management in catoptric lights, and is inexpensive ; moreover, as our experiments show, a higher ratio of illuminating power is obtained from mineral oil in catoptric lights than in any other arrangement. Such a system seems admirably adapted for a young country.[25]

The Department of Marine handled lighthouse construction estimated at under $10,000 — Bird Rocks, Cape Norman, Ferolle Point and Cape Ray. Projects on a bigger scale fell to the Department of Public Works.[26]

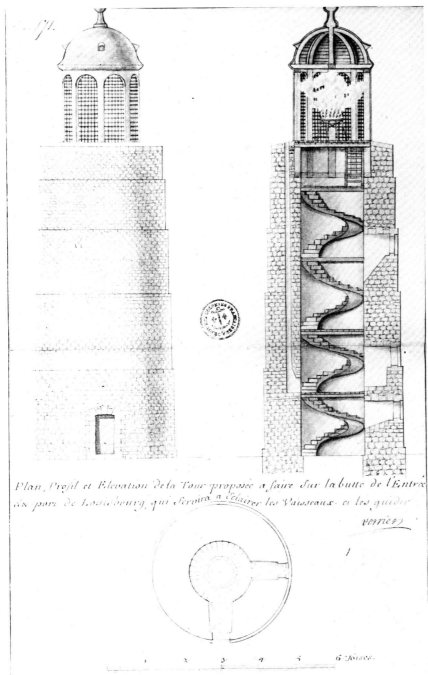

16

The Canadian lighthouse service, in these early post-Confederation years, scarcely compared with that in the British Isles. In Britain, the equivalent of $100,000 was not considered unusual for the construction of an ordinary coastal lighthouse consisting of a stone or masonry tower fitted with dioptric apparatus. A comparable lighthouse in Canada, frequently of frame construction and fitted with catoptric apparatus, could be had for only $8,000. The normal staff for a light station in Britain consisted of three or four uniformed keepers, each of whom had been thoroughly trained; in Canada, by contrast, frequently there was but one keeper per light, assisted by his family. Lightkeeping was not considered a skilled occupation in Canada, hence the preference for simple apparatus in these early years. In the seventies and eighties, the British lighthouse service still used whale oil, costing the equivalent in Canadian currency of 80 or 90 cents per gallon, whereas in Canada coal oil, a superior illuminant for use with catoptric lights, cost but 19 cents per gallon.

In like manner the American system reflected a more costly service, stone towers with several keepers being the rule rather than the exception. Likewise, American lard oil was considerably more expensive than Canadian coal oil. The one disadvantage of coal oil was its inflammable nature. Apart from a score or so of superior lighthouses of masonry construction fitted with lenticular apparatus, the usual Canadian facility was of frame construction with simple reflector apparatus.[27] The very length of the Canadian shore line, both tidewater and inland, particularly with the addition of the Pacific coast on the entry of British Columbia into Confederation in 1871, dictated a measure of economy.

By 1876, the Department of Marine had established six regional agencies responsible for lighthouses, buoys and lightships within their designated limits:

Prince Edward Island Division
Nova Scotia Division
New Brunswick Division
Quebec Division (St. Lawrence below Montreal and Gulf)
Ontario Division (above Montreal)
British Columbia Division[28]

Germane to these enterprising developments in lighting equipment was the institution of the Dominion Lighthouse Depot in a former Prescott starch factory in 1903. Still active in its original premises, the depot by its inventive enterprise has largely rendered Canada independent of overseas suppliers. It has carried out both experimental and manufacturing processes with all types of burners, lanterns, illuminants and lenses tested exhaustively to determine which combinations were best suited to Canadian conditions.

In 1904, a twin development augured well for the future of the Canadian lighthouse service. The Lighthouse Board of Canada, made up of the deputy minister of Marine, the department's chief engineer, the commissioner of lights, the president of the Pilots' Corporation, and a representative of the shipping interests, was instituted by statute with broad terms of reference

to inquire into and report to him [Minister of Marine and Fisheries]

from time to time, upon all questions relating to the selection of lighthouse sites, the construction and maintenance of lighthouses, fog alarms and all other matters assigned to the Minister of Marine and Fisheries by Section 2 of Chapter 70 of the Revised Statutes of Canada.[29]

In 1911, the Lighthouse Board was re-organized on a regional basis: the Atlantic division comprising the east coast, Hudson Strait and as far inland as the head of ocean navigation; the Eastern Inland division embracing the region from Montreal to Port Arthur at the head of the lakes, and the Pacific division, including all inland waterways west of Port Arthur (now Thunder Bay) and the Pacific coast.[30] The Lighthouse Board was active until the creation of the Department of Transport in 1936, and indeed has never been officially disbanded.

In 1908, the Department of Marine introduced an elaborate and detailed classification of lighthouses and aids to navigation under no fewer than 19 categories. Devices in the first six categories were fitted with fog alarms and the first of these included a rescue service. Categories 7 to 11 comprised lighthouses without fog alarms, and the final 8 categories were classed as minor stations "where the exclusive services of the keeper are not expected." Of these the last two (18 and 19) consisted of wharf lights and lights attended under contract.[31] Lights in the first category, complete with fog alarms and a rescue service, were Pelee Passage (western end of Lake Erie), Bird Rocks (Gulf of St. Lawrence northeast of the Magdalens), Belle Isle (northeast and southwest ends) and Cape Race.[32] The second category (main seacoast lights with fog

alarms) comprised another 14 lighthouses, including such well-known establishments as Point Amour (Labrador coast, western end, Strait of Belle Isle), Scatarie Island (eastern tip of Cape Breton Island), and Machias Seal Island and Gannet Rock in the Bay of Fundy.[33]

At the outbreak of war in 1914, the total number of lights, principally lighthouses, along the Canadian seacoast and inland waterways (especially the Great Lakes), stood at 1,461 of which 105 were equipped with fog alarms.[34]

By the spring of 1917, the proliferation of lights along our shores led the department to discontinue a number of minor ones and to improve others by means of superior illuminants and better optics. Based on a 1911 recommendation submitted by the Lighthouse Board, agency boundaries were adjusted to conform more closely to geographical regions. For example, the lighthouses at Belle Isle, Shippegan (northern New Brunswick) and Bird Rocks were placed under the jurisdiction of the Charlottetown agency, whereas Cape Race and Sable Island became the responsibility of Halifax.[35] It should be noted that the principal lighthouses on Newfoundland's shores were a Canadian responsibility, and in earlier times, British. The majority of Newfoundland's lighthouses fell under the jurisdiction, as one would expect, of that colony's Board of Works.

In November 1936, a new federal department fell heir to the Department of Marine dating from Confederation, and to that of Railways and Canals, established in 1879, so combining the function of both. The new Department of Transport assumed responsibility for all marine aids to navigation, embracing the functions of the former commissioner of lights, the chief engineer, and the supervisor of harbour commissions, hitherto within the purlieu of the old Department of Marine. The Navigational Aids Branch terms of reference were broadly defined. *This branch has charge of the construction, repairs, and maintenance of all lighthouses, fog alarms, and other aids to navigation such as lightships, buoys and beacons, and the Sable Island Humane Establishment; the surveying, for registration, and recording of all lands acquired for lighthouse sites; the . . .publications of "List of Lights", three volumes; the issuing of Notices to Mariners; . . .and the administration of all agency shops and the Dominion Lighthouse Depot at Prescott.*[36]

Regional agencies, in general continuing the organization of the old Department of Marine, were established at Halifax, Charlottetown, Saint John, Quebec, Montreal, Prescott, Parry Sound, Victoria and Prince Rupert, with subsidiaries at Port Arthur, Kenora and Amherstburg, each of which operated its own supply depot.[37] In his first annual report, the minister stated that the Canadian Lighthouse Service extended over 52,800 miles of coast line and inland waterways.

With the addition of Canada's tenth province to confederation in 1949, all the lighthouses along the Newfoundland coast came under the jurisdiction of the Department of Transport; hitherto, it will be recalled, only landfall and major coastal lights had been under Canadian operation. Top priority was given to the modernization of the Newfoundland facilities to bring them up to the standard pertaining in the rest of the country. To this end, a comprehensive survey of all Newfoundland's lights and fog alarms was at once conducted by department engineers and technicians. St. John's became the scene of a new regional agency serving the same function as those in the rest of Canada.

Lighthouses Along the Atlantic Coast

Until well into the 18th century the coasts of North America presented a menacing prospect to navigators. The first lighthouse to exhibit a light on this continent on 14 September 1716 was that on Little Brewster Island in Boston Harbor.[1] Beacon fires on headlands at the mouths of rivers or entrances to harbours may have been maintained in earlier times. Presumably vessels under sail and close inshore anchored by night.

The Louisbourg Lighthouse

A cryptic map reference dated 1828 and prepared under the auspices of the lieutenant governor of Placentia implies that this early settlement on the shores of Newfoundland merits the distinction of having been the site of Canada's first lighthouse. "The old castle where ye lighthouse is erected . . .1727." Unfortunately research to date has produced no further evidence to substantiate this claim. Lighthouse literature, including the work of D. Alan Stevenson and a book of recent publication by T. E. Appleton, *Usque ad Mare*, concur that the French fortress of Louisbourg was the site of the first lighthouse to grace our shores and the second on the continent.

The project was first broached in November 1727 and was planned to form a complex along with a hospital and shops on an island in the harbour entrance. The initial plan envisaged the use of a coal fire as illuminant. The following month, December 1727, estimates were called for. A. M. Verrier, the engineer in charge of the project, scotched the suggestion, based no doubt on motives of economy, that a coal fire be exhibited from atop the clock tower in the town on the grounds that the tower was not strong enough for such a purpose. No doubt the fire hazard also figured in his reasoning.[2]

The decision to build on the rocky promontory at the harbour entrance was taken in the spring of 1729. To finance the project, a light duty of five *sols* per ton on ocean-going vessels and six *livres* on coastal craft was levied in the summer of 1732.[3] The substantial stone tower, a circular structure of coursed rubble some 70 feet in height, was begun on 22 August 1731 and completed two years later, but delay in delivery of the lantern glazing imported from France (400 10-inch by 8-inch panes) held up the first lighting of the lantern until 1 April 1734. A retired sergeant was appointed as lightkeeper. This simple sperm-oil light consisted of a circlet of oil-fed wicks set in a copper ring mounted on cork floats, initially without reflectors. The range of the light was said to be six leagues (roughly 18 miles) in clear weather.[4]

17 Lantern and light apparatus, Louisbourg lighthouse.
(*Public Archives of Canada*.)

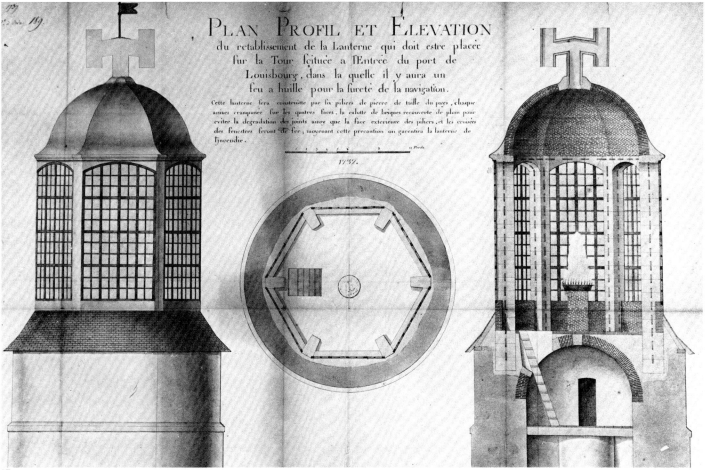

17

Faulty design of the lantern incorporating combustible elements resulted in the gutting of this first structure by fire on the night of 11-12 September 1736. So great was the heat that the cast-iron reservoir was fused by the fire. Thereupon A. M. Verrier, who had charge of the lighthouse's construction, opted for a larger reservoir fully 3½ feet in diameter and 6 inches deep so that, with the lamps spread further apart, heat within the lantern would be less intense.[5] Further safeguards against fire included the elimination of combustibles in the lighting apparatus and the setting of the reservoir containing the cod oil in a water jacket or bath. Perhaps most significant of all, as shown in Figure 17, the lantern itself was designed with six stone pillars surmounted by a vault-shaped brick roof covered with lead. The lantern was fitted with small vents on each face.[6] Cork and solder were ruled out in the lamp fittings. Local free-stone was used in construction, the cut stone being clamped together with reinforced iron supports. By October 1737, work on the new Louisbourg lighthouse was well advanced with the masonry finished, although delay occurred in the completion of the ironwork because of a shortage of skilled artificers in the colony. The new lighthouse was completed in July 1738.[7] The tower was 45 feet 6 inches high, with the lantern adding another 23 feet. By 1751, the lantern was fitted with reflectors to focus and hence improve the light derived from 32 lamp wicks.[8] The whole installation was subject to monthly inspection.

The accounts for the year 1739 showed a net revenue from light dues directed to the upkeep of the Louisbourg lighthouse of 2,882 *livres*, 11 *deniers*. The light's operating expense for that year came to 2,349 *livres*, 1 *sol*, 10 *deniers*, but there was a surplus of 2,446 *livres*, 7 *sols*, and 9 *deniers* left over from 1738.[9] In that year the light duty for ships plying the high seas was 5 *sols* per ton, schooners and local coasters 6 *livres* per annum, and smaller craft 3 *livres* annually.[10]

Canada's first lighthouse was not fated to survive the second British siege. On 9 June 1758, between nine and ten in the evening, British batteries and naval vessels opened a heavy bombardment which continued throughout the night.[11] The lighthouse was damaged and after the fall of the fortress, the victors allowed the structure to continue to disintegrate, presumably because it was deemed beyond repair. It was not replaced until 1842.

Sambro Island

Sambro Island lighthouse, the construction of which in 1758 was financed partly by a tax on spirits and partly by the proceeds of a lottery, is the oldest lighthouse extant on Canadian shores. The Sambro light was built on a small island of granite rock commanding the outer approaches to Halifax Harbour; at one time the island was fortified and several abandoned cannon are to be seen on a rocky prominence to this day.

In 1758, the Nova Scotia legislative council provided for construction costs by means of a tax on spirits. This is probably the only lighthouse in Canada to have been financed, at least in part, by means of a lottery; 1,000 tickets were sold at £3 apiece with prizes ranging as high as £500.[12] According to the governor in a despatch to the Colonial Office on 20 April 1759,
This I am to observe to your Lordships, will put the public to no expense, the charge attending it to be paid out of the savings of the duties on past imported and retailed spirituous liquors.... Out of the same fund, we are now finishing the inside of the Church.[13]
The Sambro lighthouse, originally 62 feet in height and solidly built of stone, was completed on a promontory 72 feet above the water in 1760.[14]

At first considerable satisfaction was expressed by ships' masters concerning the new facility, but by 1769 complaints reached the floor of the legislature that the light money was detrimental to the trade of the colony and that some of the proceeds were misappropriated.[15] A little later, complaints concerning the quality of the light found their way into official correspondence. The loss of the sloop

Granby off Halifax on 12 May 1771 brought matters to a head.
Having received a letter from Captain Gambier, Commander in Chief of his Majesty's ships in North America, dated the 12th. of last month, at Boston, giving an account of the loss of the Granby *sloop off Halifax owing as is believed, to the want of a light being kept in the Lighthouse at that place; that the Captains of His Majesty's ships are frequently obliged to fire at the Lighthouse to make them shew a light; and that the masters of merchant ships complain heavily at being forced to contribute to the support of a thing from which they receive no benefit; and which is moreover a great annual expense to Government.*[16]

Regarding the financial upkeep of the light, the governor in a despatch of 28 September 1771 stated that a light duty of sixpence per ton on all shipping entering the harbour of Halifax provided an operating revenue averaging £184 sterling annually; that the annual operating expense was calculated at £142, and the balance went to the contractor, under an arrangement whereby "The person who manages this Light has undertaken to bear all expenses in consideration of receiving all the duties laid on shipping for the support of it."[17] This arrangement had been in effect for the previous two years, based on a recommendation of the legislature dating from 6 November 1769. The governor contended that charges of mismanagement on this score were without foundation.

Complaints concerning the effectiveness of the light were attributable to the smoking of the sperm oil lamp, depositing a layer of carbon on the

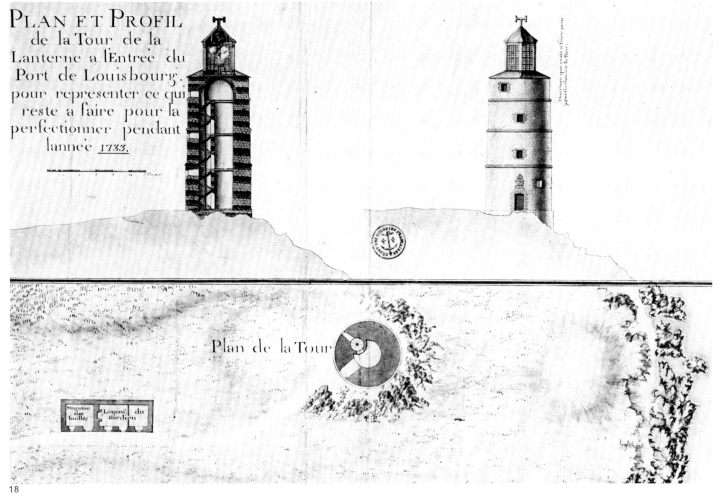

18

lantern glazing. This was a common failing, due to insufficient combustion, of all oil lights before the advent of the Argand burner in 1782. The credit for overcoming this condition went to a Henry Newton,

one of His Majesty's Council, and collector of the customs here. He has constructed fountain lamps, that give a strong and clear light, without snuffing, or any supply of oil, during the longest winter night, with flues that carry off the smoke, which heretofore darkened the glasses, and almost obscured the light at times.[18]

The trouble basically had been due to insufficient lantern ventilation, which no doubt Newton's modification did much to improve. Complaints continued, however, concerning the upkeep of the light. Finally in 1774, the legislature levied light duty on all shipping which passed "from the Westward to Canso, and other Places to the Eastward of the Harbour of Halifax," regardless of whether Halifax was a port of call.[19]

19 Sambro Island lighthouse, oldest extant in Canada. (*Photo by author.*)

20 East Ironbound lighthouse, south coast of Nova Scotia. (*Canada. Department of Transport.*)

19

20

The Sambro tower was increased to its present 80-foot height at an unknown date. In 1969, the original cast-iron lantern was replaced with one of aluminum, and the elaborate dioptric apparatus, made up of finely ground lenses and prisms of French manufacture with a simple airport-type rotating beacon, was fitted with a bulldog lens and a 500-watt incandescent light. The current establishment on Sambro Island includes a 40-watt radio beacon,

diaphone, and three neat, well-kept dwellings, each supplied with a cistern and water purifier. The shingling on the tapering sides of the tower must be renewed at regular intervals and the concrete lantern platform is of recent installation.

In all likelihood, the largest vessel to meet with disaster off Sambro was the Leyland line *Bohemian*, of 8,855 tons register, outbound from Boston to Liverpool, which went aground on Broad Breaker one mile to the east of the light shortly before three in the morning of 1 March 1920. Fortunately

only six lives were lost. No fault was found with the light or its keeper, but rather with inadequate precautions on the bridge of the liner. The captain doubted the accuracy of a radio bearing on Chebucto Head and neglected to take adequate soundings.[20]

McNutt Island

The third lighthouse to be built on the Nova Scotian outer coast, one of the many long since replaced with newer structures, was on McNutt Island near Shelburne in 1788. The governor, in a despatch of 18 July 1792, stated that "a large expense has been incurred" in the construction of an "excellent Lighthouse" at this location, but that due to a misunderstanding, the light had not seen service until September 1791. The governor boasted that the McNutt Island light was the finest on the continent and that Captain George of HMS *Hussar* had rated it equal to any in the English Channel and that the light had been seen at a distance of fully seven leagues at sea (i.e., about 25 miles).[21]

Seal Island

The Seal Island lighthouse, built in 1830 on a small island covered with stunted conifers some 18 miles off the southwestern extremity of Nova Scotia, constituted an important landfall light for vessels making for the Bay of Fundy.

Originally, two married couples, the Edward Crowells and the Richard Hickens, settled on the island to provide aid to distressed mariners. Such was the frequency of distress in the vicinity that the Crowells and the Hickens appealed to the governor, Sir

21 **Seal Island lighthouse, off the southwestern extremity of Nova Scotia.** (*Canada. Department of
Transport.*)

21

James Kempt, for the erection of a lighthouse, whose design has been described as "of massive timbers and pinned with hardwood trenails." This octagonal tower of very solid frame construction with its circular cast-iron lantern is in good condition, and apart from the shingling on the exterior, very much in its original shape. Four straight flights of stairs connect the three landings and ground floor within the tower. Crowell and Hickens were the first keepers, at a salary of £30 per annum.[22]

The powerful 2d Order lenticular light, electrified in 1959, is still fitted with the complex and intricately designed optic made up of lenses and prisms required before the advent of electricity. No doubt the Seal Island light has witnessed the whole gamut of progression from seal oil, mineral oil and petroleum vapour to electricity.

The Seal Island lighthouse should be counted as one of the best surviving examples of frame construction dating from colonial times. It is well worth a visit, but the helicopter is recommended for anyone not sure of his sea legs. The 1½-hour run aboard a shallow-draught diesel-powered lifeboat is not for the peckish or squeamish.

Bay of Fundy

The frequently fog-ridden Bay of Fundy, as a glance at a map would suggest, became the responsibility of the contiguous colonies of Nova Scotia and New Brunswick and their respective lighthouse commissioners. Undoubtedly the first lighthouse in the

22 Yarmouth or Cape Fourchu lighthouse of modern
reinforced concrete design. (*Canada. Department of
Transport.*)
23 Typical harbour light, Dalhousie, N.B. (*Public
Archives of Canada.*)

region was that on Partridge Island in Saint John Harbour, built in 1791 on the site of a former fort. This lighthouse, which must be counted the oldest in New Brunswick, disappeared at a date not determined at the time of writing. The present concrete tower on the site probably dates from as recently as 1961. Lighthouse construction along the Fundy shore (under the direction of the New Brunswick lighthouse commissioners) followed at Campobello Island in 1829, Gannet Rock and Point Lepreau in 1831, Machias Seal Island in 1832, and Quaco further up the bay in 1835 ; of these the only one to survive in its original form is that on Gannet Rock.

Gannet Rock

Constructed on a mere rock islet 7 to 8 miles south of Grand Manan Island, Gannet Rock lighthouse was a sturdy octagonal frame tower of substantial hand-hewn timbers after the manner of Seal Island light. It was six-storeyed, shingled on the outside and set on a stone foundation later covered with cement. The interior of the tower was lined with matched lumber. The original brick dwelling attached to the tower has been replaced with a two-storey concrete house.

   This 91-foot structure might almost be classed as a wave-swept tower, and no doubt there are many times when the islet is inundated by high seas. A gale of unprecedented severity on 18 February 1842 so shook the foundations as to warrant the building of a granite retaining wall in

22

23

1845. The exposed location called for special measures for the safeguarding of life.

The keepers have a retreat from the upper part of their residence over the wall into the lighthouse in case of emergency and consider themselves as secure as they can be in such an exposed situation.[23]

Until recent years families used to accompany keepers to this storm-swept, hazardous location, but now the station is manned by the two duty keepers only who are relieved each month. The installation of a dioptric light of the 2d Order indicates that Gannet Rock was considered on a par with Seal Island.

Demolition was set about in 1967, but with the removal of the leaking lantern and lantern deck, the tower was found to be in sound condition. Hence the decision was made to replace the light and optic with a simple rotating beacon, as at Sambro Island, but without the shelter of a lantern.

Machias Seal Island

Machias Seal Island lighthouse in the same region dates from 1832. It has been replaced with a reinforced concrete tower, probably in 1915. The original lighthouse was of frame and similar in shape to that at Gannet Rock. It stood 36 feet in height and showed its light 48 feet above the high-water mark with a claimed range of 15 miles.[24] The reflector-type catoptric apparatus installed at Machias Seal Island, a cumbersome, less than satisfactory installation, may well have been typical of the mid-19th century. Within its 7-foot diameter it held 8 parabolic 23-inch reflectors set in a 16-foot circle, each reflector lighted by one large Argand lamp. Pipes from

these lamps led to a common oil reservoir which was heated in winter by an Argand lamp burning under it. Not only did the keeper find it difficult to work within this cramped space, but the lamps were so near the outer frame that the glass was constantly covered with mist. Captain W. F. W. Owen, R.N., author of the above report, recommended that one good and sufficient compound Argand lamp properly fitted with chimney and several concentric wicks would serve much better.[25]

Brier Island

In 1807 the legislature voted the sum of £500, to which New Brunswick added a further £100, for the erection of a lighthouse on Brier Island, at the extremity of a narrow peninsula known as Digby Neck enclosing St. Mary's Bay. This light went into service in 1809, and along with Gannet Rock and Machias Seal Island of later date stood sentinel at the entrance to the frequently fog-enshrouded Bay of Fundy. The original Brier Island lighthouse was replaced in 1944 with a reinforced concrete tower.

St. Paul Island

The rugged fog-bound shores of Cape Breton Island, particularly on the eastern or seaward side, claimed many an unfortunate vessel in the days of sail. Irregular currents, fog, sudden snow and rain squalls posed a mariner's nightmare. St. Paul Island and Scatarie Island, the former lying off the North Cape far out in the Cabot Strait and the latter off the eastern extremity of Cape Breton Island, were the most pressing sites for lighthouse construction.

The hazards of the Cape Breton shore were forcefully put by J. H. Tidmarsh, a Nova Scotia lighthouse commissioner, in 1833.

As our route from Main a Dieu to Louisbourg on our return lay chiefly on the seashore taking nearly the course of the beaches, it gave us a melancholy view of the numerous wrecks with which the shore is strewed, the whole coast is covered with pieces of the wreck of ships and in some coves there is an accumulation of shipwreck nearly sufficient to rebuild smaller ones.

The number of graves bore strong testimony also that some guide or land mark was wanting in the quarter to guard and direct the approach of strangers to this boisterous rugged shore.[26]

In the same year a total of 10 ships had been lost on the outer shore of Cape Breton Island at a cost of 603 lives.[27] One of the worst disasters of the period was the loss of the *Astrea*, inbound from Limerick, on Lorraine Head in March, 1834; there were but three survivors of the 240 souls on board.[28]

The year 1839 saw the establishment of two sorely needed lighthouses on St. Paul Island, a bleak location well out in the passage known as the Cabot Strait. The need for a light at this dangerous locality had been recognized by the Quebec Trinity House as early as 1817. The board had garnered some preliminary information on the site; the island consisted of irregular rock covered lightly with soil on which grew scrubby cedar, pine and spruce. Stone and fine sand were available,

24

but apparently the former was considered inferior for building purposes for wood construction was resorted to, despite the advice tendered by the imperial Trinity House. The Canadian authorities considered that a lighthouse at this point in conjunction with one on Anticosti Island would do much to alleviate the navigational hazards of the region.[29] Since St. Paul Island at this time lay outside the jurisdiction of all the Atlantic colonies, the initiative at the outset lay with the home government. Lord Dalhousie, governor of Lower Canada, put the matter before imperial authority in a despatch of 24 March 1826.

As the undertaking is one of great importance to the whole of British Shipping which resorts to the shores of the Gulph of St. Lawrence, to the number of more than 100 sail annually, I entertain a hope that His Majesty's Government will view the measure as in some degree one of National concern.[30]

The imperial treasury concurred in June 1829 in sharing the cost of the project with the colonies concerned, but ruled that Newfoundland be excused a contribution.[31] Whereupon the Lower Canada House of Assembly on 17 March of the following spring (1830) resolved that a sum of up to £2,000 be authorized as the province's share in construction, and that one-half the annual cost of upkeep be met from the funds of the Quebec Trinity House.[32] The Nova Scotia treasury administered the funds, rendering annual accounts through the legislature to each of the contributing provinces. The Nova Scotia lighthouse commissioners took charge of construction, both at St. Paul Island and at Scatarie. Six commissioners were appointed in 1836 from the participating colonies to determine the site; Samuel Cunard (founder of the celebrated Cunard Line) and Edmund M. Dodd from Nova Scotia, Augustin N. Morin from Lower Canada, Thomas Owen from Prince Edward Island, and Alexander Rankin and William Abrams from New Brunswick. In addition to the selection of suitable sites at the two locations, the commissioners were to determine the type of structures to be built and to reach agreement on shared maintenance costs.[33] Lower Canada headed the list with a £500 annual commitment. New Brunswick offered £250, Prince Edward Island £30, and Nova Scotia £250 for the first year's operation and thereafter sufficient to make up the total sum of £1,030.[34]

"Two good and sufficient lighthouses, with bells and guns" were ordered for St. Paul Island in August 1836.[35] The establishment was to include a life-saving station consisting of six men with boats and full provisions. The need for the humane establishment had been tragically demonstrated in the light of the frequency of disaster in the recent past; to such a degree, indeed, as to affect immigration. As recently as 1834, the immigrant ship *Sibylle*, bound from Cromarty to Quebec, foundered off St. Paul Island with the loss of all 316 passengers aboard. In its issue of 23 September 1834, the *Royal Gazette* published in Charlottetown could scarcely have put the case for a light in stronger terms.

Good God! can nothing be done to erect a lighthouse on that fatal island? Surely means should be taken if possible to prevent such dreadful shipwrecks.[36]

The *Sibylle* was one of a numerous and ill-fated company to meet her end on St. Paul Island. Nonetheless, five more years were to pass before the long-sought lights were finally in service.

Bayfield and the lighthouse commissioners appointed by the colonies agreed on the sites for the two St. Paul Island lighthouses in the summer of 1837, but felt that the lights at either end of the island should be so dissimilar as to preclude the possibility of mistaking one for the other. The Admiralty, which was shouldering the main burden of the construction costs, insisted that one of the lights should be made either a flashing or revolving one.[37] The site was a difficult one for construction, there being no harbour and only two beaches available for the discharge of heavy stores. Fog was

25 Grand Harbour lighthouse, Grand Manan Island, N.B., a tower with an attached dwelling, a common design. (*Public Archives of Canada.*)

26 Walton Harbour lighthouse. (*Canada. Department of Transport.*)

26

prevalent. Although a report printed in the Lower Canada *Journals of the Legislative Assembly* of 1830 described granite found on the island as suitable building material, the officer commanding the Royal Engineers in his report recommended the use of 40-foot wooden towers resting on 5-foot foundations.[38] The two lighthouses were finished in 1839; one was built on a rock off the north point of the island and the other on the south point, about 150 feet above the water. The estimates were exceeded on several occasions, and the imperial treasury was approached for additional funds. Since the St. Paul Island installations were included with the Scatarie Island project in the estimates, it has not been

27 St. Paul Island lighthouse, although which of the two originally built on the island has not been determined. (*Canada. Department of Transport.*)

27

28 St. Paul Island, southwest point, short circular iron tower. (*Canada. Department of Transport.*)

possible to determine individual construction costs. One considerable difficulty was the supply of labour for such a relatively isolated location. Once built, the lighthouses were to be maintained by the four colonies themselves, but in the event of their loss, Britain would share the cost of reconstruction.

A statement submitted by the Nova Scotia commissioners in 1847 records the contributions of the four colonies toward the maintenance of the St. Paul Island and Scatarie establishments for that year.[39]

Canada	£601	4s.	10d.
New Bunswick	250	0s.	0d.
Nova Scotia	351	4s.	11d.
Prince Edward Island	36	1s.	6d.
Total	£1,238	11s.	3d.

An annual report of the Department of Marine and Fisheries for the season 1873-74 described the lanterns in both lighthouses as of iron, 10½ feet in diameter, fitted with plate glass of dimensions 20 by 24 inches. By this date lenticular apparatus had replaced

28

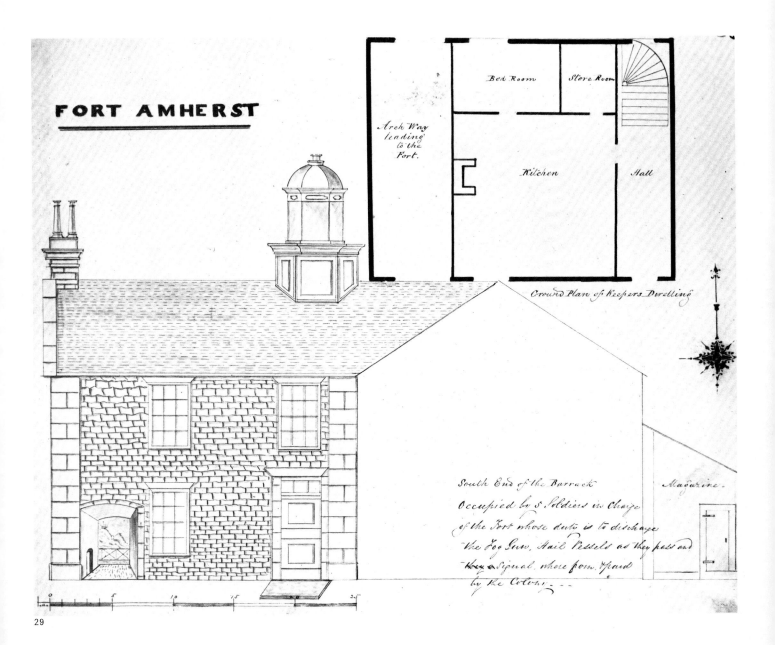

FORT AMHERST

Arch Way leading to the Fort.

Bed Room

Store Room

Kitchen

Hall

Ground Plan of Keepers Dwelling

South End of the Barrack Occupied by 5 Soldiers in Charge of the Fort whose duty is to discharge the Fog Gun, Hail Vessels as they pass and they a Signal, where from, & paid by the Colony.

Magazine.

29

30 Cape Spear lighthouse. This is a good example of the lantern mounted on the roof, common among the older structures in Newfoundland. (*Canada. Department of Transport.*)

30 Cape Spear lighthouse. This is a good example of the lantern mounted on the roof, common among the older structures in Newfoundland. (*Canada. Department of Transport.*)

30

the catoptric first installed, and presumably the lamps were burning a vegetable oil in place of sperm oil. Complaint was made of the lights themselves, of a pattern which failed to do justice to the fine optical apparatus provided.[40] By 1889 the St. Paul Island lighthouses had been re-furnished with 12-foot iron lanterns which enabled "new pressure lamps sent to the island two years ago" to be installed, producing a much better light.[41]

The lighthouse at the southern end of St. Paul Island together with its adjoining dwelling was destroyed by fire in December 1914. Replacement with a new, short cast-iron tower designed and built at the Dominion Lighthouse Depot in Prescott was taken in hand at once. Transported from Prescott in sections, the 12-foot tower was assembled at Halifax. The short round tower supported a 10-foot-high lantern with octagonal outer gallery. Total height of the structure base to vane was 27 feet 6 inches. The 4th Order flashing petroleum vapour light produced 35,000 candlepower. This light was scheduled for service on 1 March 1916.[42] With good visibility the light had a range of 16 miles. Total cost of construction, materials, labour and optical apparatus amounted to $9,175;[43] with final revision for incidentals to $10,340.16. This lighthouse, an excellent photograph of which is shown in Figure 28, stands today, but its companion at the north end of the island has been replaced by a concrete tower with aluminum lantern within the past decade.

Scatarie Island

Scatarie Island was the principal landfall for ships making for Sydney, Pictou, Miramichi and Quebec. In 1833, the Nova Scotia legislature granted £500 as its share in the cost of establishing a light at this point. The project, in conjunction with that on St. Paul Island, was to be a joint undertaking on the part of Nova Scotia, New Brunswick, Lower Canada and the imperial government.[44] The project had been the subject of a merchants' petition to the Admiralty, possibly following the loss of the transport *Leonidas* on the island of Scatarie in 1832, in which both troops and crew were lost along with a consignment of gold.[45]

As were the structures on St. Paul Island, the lighthouse on Scatarie was of wooden construction, contrary to the counsel of the British Trinity House, on the grounds that stone would be too difficult and costly to transport to the two sites. The Scatarie Island light was exhibited for the first time on 1 December 1839, the establishment to be maintained by a keeper and one assistant.[46]

The first lighthouse on Scatarie Island has been replaced in recent years by a 13-foot steel skeleton tower. The catoptric light listed in the 1970 *List of Lights, Buoys and Fog Signals* is one of the few purely reflector-type lights, apart from range lights, still in service.

Newfoundland
Britain's oldest colony until recent years, by reason of its command of the two entrances to the Gulf of St. Lawrence and its proximity to one of the richest fishing grounds in the world on the Grand Banks, was very much a seafaring dependency. Lighthouses, therefore, were among the early projects of Newfoundland enterprise. A number of the more important lights on her shores served the interests of the Canadas and the maritime dependencies more than those of Newfoundland, and for this reason a number were built and maintained by imperial and later by Canadian authority.

Fort Amherst
The first lighthouse in Newfoundland (save for the possibility of one at Placentia early in the 18th century) was established at Fort Amherst at the entrance to the harbour of St.

John's. The Quebec Trinity House minutes record that a light was first exhibited here in 1811,[47] but the rare and beautiful though unpublished work of Robert Oke, Newfoundland lighthouse inspector, dates the establishment of the Fort Amherst lighthouse from 1813.[48] The lantern in the form of a cupola rose from the house roof, a common design in early Newfoundland lighthouses. The walls of the house, fully two feet thick, were of stone set in Portland cement. Voluntary contributions maintained the Fort Amherst light until the establishment of the colonial legislature in 1832. In 1852, a triple-wick Argand burner fitted with an annular lens provided Newfoundland with its first dioptric light.

Cape Spear
In 1836, a lighthouse of similar design was built at Cape Spear on the approaches to St. John's Harbour. The lighting apparatus, transferred from the Inchkeith lighthouse on the Scottish coast, consisted of seven Argand burners fitted with reflectors for which a range in clear weather of 36 miles was claimed. A concrete tower replaced the original Cape Spear lighthouse in 1963 which, however, is being preserved by the crown.

Harbour Grace Island
The third lighthouse to grace Newfoundland's shores was built on Harbour Grace Island, first seeing service on 21 November 1837. Like its predecessors, the Harbour Grace lighthouse essentially was a house with the light showing from a cupola on the roof. A despatch from Government House dated 27 November 1837 stated,

31

32

33 Cape Pine lighthouse, a 50-foot cast-iron tower, a controversial design in Newfoundland. The light was fully 300 feet above the sea. (*Canada. Department of Transport.*)
34 Cape Race lighthouse. (*Canada. Department of Transport.*)

I have the honor to inform your Lordship that on the 21st. Inst. a powerful fixed light extending eastwardly, or seaward, from N to SW by compass was exhibited, and will continue to be exhibited, from sunset to sunrise on Harbour Grace Island in Conception Bay.[49]

Again a Newfoundland lighthouse was to benefit from the conversion to improved apparatus in the British Isles. The catoptric apparatus, consisting of 15 Argand burners and silver reflectors, was shipped out from England, where it had served in the Isle of May lighthouse, for use in the Harbour Grace structure.[50] In 1865 the lighthouse, threatened by coastal erosion, was moved back 65 feet from the shore.[51] The old Harbour Grace lighthouse was replaced in 1961 with a graceless, open-frame galvanized tower.

Cape Bonavista

The fourth of these early Newfoundland lighthouses, of similar design to the preceding three, was built at Cape Bonavista in 1843. The cost of construction, complete with light, was £3,024 10s., and its annual upkeep was established at £375.[52] The revolving light exhibited both a white and a red characteristic from an overall height of 150 feet above high water. The anticipated range from all quarters seaward was 30 miles.[53] In 1966, after nearly a century and a quarter in service, the old Cape Bonavista lighthouse was replaced by a tower of skeleton steel. The province is preserving the old lighthouse (*see* Fig.

32) complete with the original lighting apparatus made up of 16 Argand burners with reflectors transferred from the famous Bell Rock lighthouse on the east coast of Scotland.

With the completion of the Cape Bonavista lighthouse in 1843, four lighthouses were maintained by Newfoundland on her east coast. For a colony of more slender resources than either Nova Scotia or New Brunswick, Newfoundland had made a commendable effort. The first four lighthouses served the St. John's trade, but there were as yet no lights on the perilous south coast so subject to fog off the Grand Banks. Navigational facilities here, however, were of more significance to the St. Lawrence trade than to that of Newfoundland.

Cape Pine

Particularly was the lack of a light felt on the southern coast of the Avalon Peninsula, lying as it did nigh the shipping lane for vessels bound for the St. Lawrence. A number of vessels had met with disaster along this rocky, indented and frequently fog-bound coast. In a despatch to the Colonial Office dated 7 November 1840, the governor of Newfoundland, Sir John Harvey, had enclosed the legislature's petition for the erection of a lighthouse on Cape Pine at the southernmost extremity of the Avalon Peninsula. The mounting toll of ships and lives had been a matter of concern since 1837.[54] The colony's slender resources frequently necessitated appeals to the mother country for such projects. In this instance, the imperial government responded, but Newfoundland's neighbours did not. In 1843 the governor of Newfoundland sounded out the Canadian authorities for the con-

33

34

struction of a lighthouse at Cape Pine. The Montreal Trinity House concurred in Canada's assuming a share of the expense, but the Quebec authority contended that other sites in the region would better serve Canada's interests, and so advised against Canadian participation in the project. The executive council so advised the Newfoundland governor.[55] The colony had found ready support, however, in London, Parliament appropriating the sum of £2,000 sterling for the construction and outfitting of a lighthouse on the south coast of Newfoundland, to be maintained by the colony once completed. The contractor's tender[56] for £6,514 9s. 6d. comprised the following items:

Cast-iron tower, with gallery and railing stairs, ventilators, windows, doors, etc.	£2,192	5s.	0d.
lantern	2,330	0s.	0d.
freight, shipping insurance, landing, hoisting up cliff, inland transport, foundation, resident engineer & workmen from England	400	0s.	0d.
	700	0s.	0d.
screaming apparatus (fog alarm)	300	0s.	0d.
contingencies	594	4s.	6d.

The Cape Pine lighthouse, still standing today, was a circular 50-foot cast-iron tower (a type to be frequently resorted to in Newfoundland) whose revolving light scanned the sea from a height of fully 300 feet. The catoptric light originally incorporated 16 burners and reflectors but these later were reduced to 12.

The Cape Pine lighthouse went into service on New Year's Day, 1851. The installation was at once handed

35

over to the Newfoundland Board of Works, which maintained it thenceforth at a cost of about £395 per annum. The tower at first included living quarters, but the damp quickly rendered these uninhabitable, and so a separate dwelling had to be built.[57] In

its report for 1851, the Newfoundland Board of Works reflected critically on the refusal of the neighbouring Atlantic colonies to share in an endeavour as

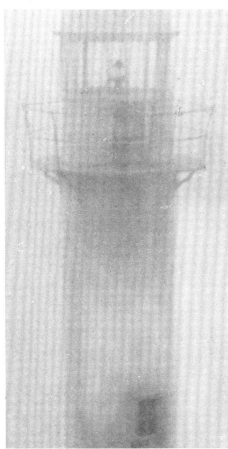

36

much in their interests as in those of Newfoundland.[58] In light of this it is perhaps not surprising that Newfoundland a few years later withheld contributions for the Cape Race light.

Cape Race

By all odds the famous Cape Race lighthouse, commanding the busiest shipping lanes on the approaches to British North America, was the most important landfall light ever established on our shores. As early as 1838, the Elder Brethren of Trinity House selected Cape Race as the best site for a lighthouse by which ships making for the gulf could take their bearings. With the installation of the efficient lights on St. Paul Island, a suggested site at Cape Ray on the Newfoundland shore of the Cabot Strait was thought less important.[59] No doubt the Elder Brethren considered at this early date that the St. Paul Island lights were sufficient for the 75-mile-wide strait, and in fact a light appeared on the Newfoundland side only in 1871. The designer of the Cape Race lighthouse, as well as of its predecessor at Cape Pine, was the civil engineer Alexander Gordon.

The Cape Race project got under way in the spring of 1855, like Cape Pine entirely under imperial authority. At the request, however, of the Newfoundland lighthouse commissioners, who had had misgivings concerning the utility of iron in such a climate as theirs, stone construction was resorted to rather than cast iron. The circular 68-foot tower was built on a site 178 feet above the sea. A red circular iron lantern originally housed a catoptric light (fixed) made up of 13 Argand burners with reflectors; the light was visible from northeast by east through south to west.[60] The Cape Race tower was provided with living quarters consisting of a circular shelter built about the tower's base; the two apartments fronting seaward were used only as

storerooms, and the other four accommodated the keepers and their families. This accommodation would not be forgotten by those who initially used it. A leaking roof, condensation and hoarfrost lining the walls and smoking chimneys dictated the early provision of a separate dwelling for the keepers and their families. The Cape Race lighthouse was finished in October, 1856, and went into operation on 15 December of the same year, with an initial supply of 350 gallons of seal oil.[61] With an anticipated consumption of 600 gallons per annum, operating costs were estimated at £130 annually. A light duty of one-sixteenth of a penny per ton was levied by the imperial government in March 1857 on all transatlantic shipping bound for or departing the gulf.[62] Tolls were to be collected at ports of clearance, and the governor of Newfoundland was to render accounts quarterly to the Board of Trade in London covering the cost to the colony of maintaining and operating the light.[63] The total maintenance costs of the Cape Race lighthouse for the year 1860 stood at £471 10s. 0d., of which Canada's share was £169 15s. 1d.[64]

The first Cape Race light, destined to become the most powerful on our shores, was not satisfactory. The trouble was that each of the 13 Argand lamps and reflectors illuminated too broad an arc (14 degrees); however, in order to concentrate the beams for optimum effect calling for an arc of no more than 5 degrees per lamp, no fewer than 68 reflectors would have been required, an installation which even the largest lantern could in no way accommodate.[65] The ultimate solution was the substitution of a 1st Order lenticular apparatus, but this was not resorted to until much later.

The Cape Race light had not been a fortnight in operation when the first of several ships foundered within hailing distance, yet unable to see the new facility. On Christmas night 1856, the *Welsford*, of 1,293 tons register outbound from Saint John for Liverpool, ran aground within two miles of Cape Race with the loss of her captain and most of her crew. Had it not been for the strenuous and valiant efforts of the lighthouse crew, the four survivors would have perished in the surf. The mate testified that the light had been completely obscured in the fog and suggested the provision of a signal gun to be used in such thick weather.[66] A few years later on the night of 12 October 1863, the passenger liner *Africa* foundered off Cape Race ; so thick was the weather on this occasion that even the ship's officers testified that no light regardless of brilliance could have saved the *Africa*.[67]

Notwithstanding these extenuating circumstances, it was recognized that the Cape Race light left something to be desired. In 1864 Robert Oke, the well-known Newfoundland lighthouse inspector under whose direction eight of the twelve Newfoundland lighthouses had been built, recommended that in the interest of readier identification, the Cape Race light be changed from a fixed to a revolving one. The new catoptric apparatus comprised nine burners and reflectors.[68] The governor accepted the recommendation.

The London firm of DeVille & Company supplied the new light, complete with "gun metal wheels enclosed in a mahogany case and provided with the necessary cord, weights and pulley," cast-iron and gun-metal lantern.[69] The conversion of the Cape Race light was carried through in 1866, and simultaneously the Cape Pine light, again on the recommendation of Robert Oke, was changed to a fixed light.

In 1886, 30 years after its construction, the Cape Race lighthouse was transferred to Canadian jurisdiction, taking effect on Dominion Day of that same summer, together with the sum of $100,151.50 in light dues, on the sole condition that Canada maintain it henceforth without the imposition of light duty.[70]

In 1906 work began on a new lighthouse at Cape Race which is still in service, very close to the original site (the difference being 12" of latitude and 1'39" longitude). The new circular stone and concrete tower rose 68 feet from the base to the lantern platform, 96 feet overall base to vane. The three-foot thick wall was 20 feet in diameter, rising perpendicularly to the lantern platform or balcony.[71] A lantern 17 feet 1½ inches in diameter, larger than any hitherto mounted on our shores, housed the single-flash petroleum vapour light, described as hyperradial (beyond the dimensions of a 1st Order light). This massive lenticular apparatus rotating effortlessly on its mercury float produced a flash of more than one million candlepower. The new light, manufactured by the well-known Birmingham firm of Chance Brothers, went into service in the spring of 1907.

37

The Cape Race light was electrified sometime in 1926-27, fed by a Delco generator in a nearby power house. The lenticular apparatus installed in 1907 was retained, however, and to our knowledge at time of writing is still in use.[72] Cape Race is still a manned light station, one of the few on Canada's coasts.

38

Cape St. Mary's

In 1860, Newfoundland added a third light to her rugged south coast on the lofty promontory known as Cape St. Mary's 325 feet above the sea. Construction was of brick with separate dwellings for the staff. The revolving light on the catoptric principle employing a dozen burners was pronounced by a parliamentary commission to be second to none of its type in the British Isles. Great difficulty was experienced in landing this weighty and delicate apparatus on the rocky shore and hauling it up to the site; nonetheless, the light was ready for service on the night of 20 December 1860. A range of 14 leagues (about 42 miles) was claimed for it in good weather.[73] The old St. Mary's lighthouse has been demolished and replaced with a new structure within recent years.

Cape Ray and Channel Head

Cape Ray, built by the Canadian government in 1871, and Channel Head, erected by Newfoundland in 1875, provided lights complementary to those on St. Paul Island on the Cape Breton side of the strait. Cape Ray was replaced with a new lighthouse in 1960.

Unfortunately information is skimpy on the origins of the Channel Head lighthouse a dozen miles or so southeast of Cape Ray. Construction of a light on this site was recommended by a Captain John Orlebar, R.N., in 1864. It is not clear from information presently on hand whether the Canadian government shared the construction costs or not. In any case, a lighthouse of circular iron construction was completed in 1875 on Channel Head, 40 miles from St. Paul Island.[74]

The Gulf, Northumberland Strait and the Lower St. Lawrence

Access to the gulf is gained by the Strait of Belle Isle and the Cabot Strait to the north and south of Newfoundland respectively. The northern route, an ice-beset channel until well into mid-summer, offers the shorter passage to the British Isles from Quebec and Montreal. In the days of sail Belle Isle was avoided, but with the coming of the steamer by mid-century, the 15- to 20-mile-wide channel between the inhospitable Labrador and Newfoundland coasts attracted more shipping. The advent of the 17- to 18-knot subsidized mail steamer by the year 1905 accelerated this trend. A light did not mark this northerly passage until 1858, and as will be recalled from the previous chapter, only in 1839 had the mariner in the Cabot Strait the benefit of the two lights on St. Paul Island. Inasmuch as the bulk of the shipping used (and yet does) the southern route, it received the first attention.

The increased steaming speeds in the latter half of the 19th century demanded a substantial improvement in navigational aids. The president of the veteran Allan Line, the principal steamship company in the Canadian service, put the issue bluntly to the Canadian government in 1869. Among the measures mandatory if Canadian aspirations for a fast mail service operating to the St. Lawrence were to be realized, the following lighthouse projects must have high priority:

Bird Rocks estimate	$13,000
Anticosti Island, South Point	10,000
Magdalen Islands (Dead Man's Rock)	6,500
Cape Ray	11,000
River Magdalene	6,000
Cap Chat	6,000
Ferolle Point	22,000
Cape Norman (Strait of Belle Isle)	22,000
Seven Islands (north shore)	6,000
Red Island Reef (lightship)	14,000

Construction at these sites was authorized by an order in council dated 14 January 1870.[1] Short of such an outlay, aggregating $95,000, the chimerical "Canadian Fast Line" would never be feasible.

Belle Isle

Over a period of a half-century, three very important lighthouses were built at the Atlantic entrance to the Strait of Belle Isle on the long tapering island of rugged contour bearing the same name. Undertaken by the Canadian Board of Works, the first of these was constructed on a highly inaccessible site at the south end of Belle Isle, 470 feet above the sea. An access road approximately a mile in length had first to be built from the beach to the site. At some points the gradient approached 40 degrees. The cliffs fell away precipitately to the shingle, and no cove or harbour lay within 20 miles. The extreme difficulty experienced in landing and hauling bulky and delicate apparatus under such conditions may be readily appreciated.[2]

The 62-foot stone tower was one of four undertaken simultaneously by the Canadian commissioners of Public Works. The stone was faced externally with firebrick of a light colour. The solidly built circular tower and lantern may still be seen at this lonely spot basically as it was in 1858, although no doubt the firebrick has been renewed and replaced several times. The first light was a fixed one fitted with dioptric apparatus of the 1st Order.[3] In the photograph in Figure 38, the aerial for the radio installations, put up at a much later date, is visible on the left.

In 1880 this lighthouse was joined by a companion, to be known as the "lower light." As may be seen from Figure 39, the circular lantern was mounted directly on the stone foundation near the edge of a cliff 125 feet above the sea. The lower light was fitted with dioptric apparatus of the

39

2d Order, to serve in conjunction with the "upper light."

A third lighthouse was built at the north end of Belle Isle in 1905. This 90-foot cylindrical iron tower was later reinforced with concrete and exterior supporting buttresses. The lantern was fitted with dioptric apparatus of the 2d Order, employing a kerosene pressure lamp with a 50-mm. mantle.[4] This light went into service with the opening of navigation in 1905, in time for the new 17-knot Allan liners *Virginian* and *Victorian*, to be joined during the season of 1906 by the celebrated CPR liners, the *Empress of Britain* and her ill-fated sister, the *Empress of Ireland*. Until the construc-

40 Point Amour lighthouse. (*Canada. Department of Transport.*)

41 Bird Rocks lighthouse in the middle of the Gulf of St. Lawrence, one of the most difficult construction sites. (*Canada. Department of Transport.*)

40

41

tion of the Triple Island lighthouse on the Pacific coast, the lighthouse on the northern end of Belle Isle was the most northerly in Canada.

All three Belle Isle lighthouses are basically in their original state today, although only the two at the south end of the island are old enough to be of historical interest.

Point Amour

A very fine and impressive lighthouse which was built in 1857 at the western entrance to the Strait of Belle Isle by the Canadian Board of Works is still in good condition today. Situated on the bleak Labrador shore, the Point Amour lighthouse, fully 109 feet in height, is a particularly handsome structure. The slightly tapered circular tower was built of stone, faced with firebrick and surmounted by a round lantern mounted on a circular, railed lantern deck or observation platform. Dioptric apparatus of the 2d Order signifies the importance of this light at the western entrance to the strait.[5]

The Point Amour lighthouse was the scene of a near disaster on the afternoon of 16 September 1889 when a British naval vessel, HMS *Lily*, went ashore in a dense fog. One officer and 30 of the crew made shore. The lightkeeper, Thomas Wyatt, was credited with saving four lives.[6]

Point Amour was one in a series of lighthouses built and maintained by the Canadian government on the Newfoundland and Labrador shore to serve ships on the St. Lawrence route. By the turn of the century Canada maintained a total of 10 light stations in Newfoundland and Labrador.[7]

Belle Isle (2)	Flower Island
Cape Bauld	Greenly Island
Cape Norman	Point Rich
Cape Race	Point Amour
Cape Ray	

With the exception of Cape Race, it will be noticed that all these lighthouses were in the Strait of Belle Isle or along the west or gulf coast of Newfoundland.

Bird Rocks
Construction of a lighthouse at the remote mid-gulf Bird Rocks location, hard on the main fairway of shipping inbound from the Cabot Strait, presented one of the most arduous projects attempted in Canadian waters. As the department's chief engineer, John Page, commented in his 1860 report, *I beg to remark, that so far as my knowledge of the place and locality goes, it appears to me that the construction of a light house on this islet will be one of the most difficult pieces of work that has ever been undertaken by this Department.*[8]

A notation of the difficulties faced may be had from a glance at Figures 41 and 42. Captain Bayfield, Admiralty hydrographer, had aptly described these islets consisting of soft red sandstone or conglomerate in his survey of the gulf some 30 years previously. The islets presented near-perpendicular cliffs well over 100 feet in height on

every hand. Access to the top could be gained in only one or two places, and that with no little difficulty; the device used by the construction engineers is shown in Figure 42. Bayfield concluded by stating that the landing of men and materials could only be effected in the calmest of seas.[9] The largest of the islets, and presumably the one chosen for construction, was 1,800 feet in length by 300 in width, with sheer cliffs some 140 feet above the shingle. The site could be approached only during the settled mid-summer months of July and August.[10] Carried out by contract let by the Department of Public Works, the 51-foot timber and frame tower "of a substantial description thoroughly bolted and fastened similar to the one recently erected on Machias Seal Island" was completed in 1870 and fitted with a powerful 2d Order lenticular light of French make.[11]

Pointe-des-Monts
Based on the 1827 hydrographic survey conducted by Commander H. W. Bayfield, R.N., Anticosti Island, the head of the Gaspé peninsula and the broad reaches of the estuary became desirable sites for lighthouse construction.[12] According to surveys carried out at the behest of the Lower Canada House of Assembly, a light at Pointe-des-Monts on the north shore would benefit vessels both in- and outbound. Anticosti Island, the scene of so many disasters, should have lighthouses established at both its eastern and western extremities. Cap-des-Rosiers, at the head of the Gaspé peninsula, would also be a desirable location, but Bayfield considered that this could be dispensed with if a lighthouse were

42

built at the eastern end (Heath Point) of Anticosti. He offered the further opinion that the Green Island light would have been more effective on the neighbouring Red Islet, but that it was not worthwhile to move it. Bicquette Island was another favourable site, but because of its relative propinquity to Green Island, this project might be considered less urgent.[13]

The crying need for lighthouses on the St. Lawrence in 1828 was further emphasized by Captain Edward Boxer of HMS *Hussar* who had been engaged in survey work along its shores. *I found the greatest want of them, the navigation being so very dangerous, from the currents being so very strong and irregular, and the very great dif-*

ficulty in getting good observations, the horizon at all times being subject to so great an elevation and depression, and there not being even one in the whole Gulph.

It was truly lamentable Sir, the number of wrecks we saw on the different parts of the coast; . . . for the number of lives lost must be very great, and property incalculable.[14]

Admiral Sir Charles Ogle was yet more emphatic in his description of the hazards encountered along the coast for the want of lights.

The shores of Newfoundland, Anticosti, and the continent, are covered with wrecks, occasioned chiefly by the want of Lighthouses, and the longitude of the places being incorrectly laid down on the charts, and in the books; under these circumstances I venture to recommend to your Excellency, that Lighthouses should be erected on some of the principal points — perhaps on St. Paul's Island, east end of Anticosti, Cape Rosier, and Cape Deamon, which I conceive might be kept up by a Tax levied on all ships entering the St. Lawrence, or the adjacent ports, and would be cheerfully paid by the Shipowners who reap the advantage.[15]

In the main, Ogle's recommendations concurred with Bayfield's except that Bayfield preferred Cape Gaspé to Cap-des-Rosiers, and West Point of Anticosti Island to Southwest Point on the basis that the former would be visible from more points of the compass. But he feared that Lower Canada would lack the money for so extensive a program.[16]

It was true enough that lack of money had put off necessary lighthouse construction for a number of years, but in the 1828-29 session, the Lower Canada legislature appropriated the sum of £12,000 for this purpose. The total appropriation in 1831 reached £25,212 10s. 0d. local currency.[17] The special committee on lighthouses appointed by the House of Assembly selected the east and west points of Anticosti Island and Pointe-des-Monts as sites; they further resolved to contribute toward the building of lighthouses on St. Paul Island and Cape Ray, two points vital to the navigation of the Cabot Strait giving access to the gulf. These projects had to wait the concurrence of the maritime colonies.[18]

The Pointe-des-Monts site had already been selected by the Quebec Trinity House in 1826 as a good location to serve as a point of departure for outbound vessels in order that they keep well clear of Anticosti Island and as a checkpoint for inbound shipping. The Trinity House board concluded its recommendations to the governor that the utility of a light at Pointe-des-Monts was supported by "all Masters of Vessels trading to this Country."[19]

The original Pointe-des-Monts lighthouse, a 90-foot circular stone tower, has been replaced in recent years with a skeleton steel tower of contemporary design, though the stone tower is still standing and reported in good shape. The first lighthouse, completed in 1830, had walls six feet thick at the base, tapering to two feet at the lantern deck.[20] The polygonal copper lantern was of the same dimensions as that installed at Green Island, measuring 10 feet 6

inches in diameter and 6 feet in height. It was fitted with glazing of "polished Plate Glass of double substance as made for the use of lighthouses."[21] The catoptric light consisted of 13 Argand burners of brass fitted with copper tubes and "thirteen improved strong Silver plated, high polished parabola reflectors on improved principles," the estimate for the whole lantern assembly coming to £960.[22] Unfortunately, as is so often the case, this estimate was very much on the low side, the final bill being £1,766 3s. 8d.[23] This handsome structure (*see* Fig. 44) stood sentinel at this point for more than a century. The original optic was replaced with a more effective lenticular apparatus sometime in the eighties or nineties or after the turn of the century.

Anticosti Island

The next lighthouse to be built in this region was that on Southwest Point of Anticosti Island, guarding the approaches of the broad estuary from the gulf. Originally Captain Bayfield had favoured West Point, but on consideration, Southwest Point offered the twin advantages of closer proximity to the shipping lanes and suitable building materials (limestone and sand) were available on the site.[24] The 75-foot lighthouse of stone construction went into service in 1831, the first on Canadian shores to display a revolving light. The annual upkeep of this lighthouse was estimated at £525, a figure which included the cost of 600 gallons of sperm oil for the light at the rate of 10 shillings per gallon. The keeper was paid £130 per annum. The tower, 36 feet in diameter at the base, was com-

43 Bird Rocks lighthouse. This is a good example of
  the very short, squat tower used on elevated locations. (*Canada. Department of Transport.*)
44 Pointe-des-Monts lighthouse. (*Canada. Department
  of Transport.*)

pleted by the contractor for the sum of £3,350 local currency and the lantern with the optic was supplied for £2,800. The revolving light swept the horizon from a height of 100 feet above high water with a range of 15 miles.[25]

A second lighthouse at the eastern extremity of Anticosti Island was established in 1835, and a third on English Head in 1858 at the western extremity. This 109-foot circular stone tower on West Point was constructed under the aegis of the Canadian Department of Public Works. Completed in 1858, the West Point lighthouse was of similar dimensions, design and apparatus to the Point Amour installation, but unlike the latter, the West Point structure was replaced in 1967.

None of this trio has survived to the present; indeed of all those cited so far, only the Green Island and Pointe-des-Monts lighthouses are extant today.

Point Escuminac

In 1841, the New Brunswick lighthouse commissioners established an important coastal light at Point Escuminac at the northern entrance to the Northumberland Strait. A quarter-century later a twin sentinel joined it on the North Point of Prince Edward Island, on the opposite shore. Described as an octagonal wooden building 58 feet in height, the focal plane of its fixed light shone 78 feet above the sea and was visible 14 miles in clear weather.[26] A measure of the importance of the Point Escuminac light to ships entering or leaving the Northumberland Strait was its subsequent equipment with a lenticular light of the 3rd Order. The old lighthouse was replaced with a steel tower installation in 1963.

Miscou Island

Another fine old lighthouse, largely built of hand-hewn timbers, 80 feet in height and eight-sided, was constructed under the authority of the Quebec Trinity House on Miscou Island in 1856. This one has survived to the present and is said to be in good condition. Eventually it, too, was fitted with a powerful dioptric light of the 3rd Order, and early this century, with a diaphone fog alarm. Situated off Birch Point, the Miscou Island light is a major coastal aid standing at the southern entrance to Chaleur Bay.[27]

Point Prim

The oldest lighthouse to grace the verdant shores of Prince Edward Island, Point Prim, built in 1846 and still in service today, stands sentinel at the southern end of Hillsborough Bay on the outer approaches to Charlottetown Harbour. The 60-foot circular brick tower topped by a polygonal lantern is still in its original condition, complete with a central weight shaft dating from the days of mechanically actuated rotary mechanisms. This feature is simply a relic of the past, for the light source and rotary machinery has long since been electrified. The Point Prim lighthouse is now fully automated, in common with an ever increasing number of lights. The lantern platform is gained by four flights of stairs. Apart from the mercury vapour electric light source and the lantern platform railing, the Point Prim light and optic are the original installation. It is quite a handsome structure on a commanding site, and one of the showplaces of the island.

43

44

Cap-des-Rosiers

The Cap-des-Rosiers lighthouse, completed in 1858 on Gaspé Cape, is the fourth in the handsome series of Public Works lighthouses and today is considered the showpiece of the Quebec agency. One hundred twelve feet in height, its circular lantern housed a 1st Order dioptric light, indicative that the Cap-des-Rosiers installation was considered a major coastal light.

Fortunately the journals of the Canadian legislature record considerable detail on this lighthouse, which is shortly to be removed from service. The foundation, set 50 feet back from the cliff edge, extended 8 feet below the surface. The masonry walls of the 112-foot tower tapered from a thickness of 7 feet 3 inches at the base to an even 3 feet at the top; similarly, the base diameter narrowed from 25½ feet at ground level to only 17 feet at the lantern platform. The tower contained nine storeys including a basement and the light room directly below the lantern. Windows were set at each storey or landing in an alternate pattern.[28]

The masonry called for was of top quality. To consist generally of good sized, flat, well-shaped stones, not less than 5 inches in thickness, laid on their natural and broadest beds in full mortar, properly bonded over and with each other throughout the wall, and to have their inner faces hammered or scrabbled off to a line corresponding to the position they are to occupy in the work, one third of the arch of each course to be laid as headers, that is to say: To have their greatest length extending into the wall, the depth of these headers for the first 30 feet in height of the Tower to be at least 3½ feet, for the next 30 feet in height to be not less than 3 feet in depth, thence upwards they may be from 2 feet 9 inches to 2 feet in depth midway between the headers of the inner face, must be other of a like length extending inwards from the exterior brick facing, especially in the lower 50 feet of the building.

All the brick used in the exterior of the work to be of the best quality of English Fire Brick laid throughout in horizontal courses, except arches in English bond well flushed up at every course with mortar . . . The brick facings of the Tower as before stated is to be one brick (or 9 inches) in depth, with headers extending into the wall at every fourth or fifth course.[29]

The windows were to be arched with stone, and the door with stone on the inside and brick on the exterior. There were to be two doors to the tower, the outer of which was to be 7 feet by 3 feet.[30] The exterior was to receive three coats of white lead and oil paint; the interior surface of the walls was to be finished with two coats of plaster.

It is not surprising that so carefully and soundly built a structure should have lasted over a century and still be reported in excellent condition. In the near future the Cap-des-Rosiers lighthouse may be offered to the crown for possible preservation, since a light is no longer needed at this point. It is a handsome and impressive structure, somewhat similar in form and design to the series built on Lake Huron and Georgian Bay at the same time. Cap-des-Rosiers is readily accessible by motor, in contrast to Belle Isle or Point Amour, for which the services of a helicopter or supply vessel would be required.

Father Point

Transatlantic travellers of a few years ago, when the steamship lines retained more custom, will remember Father Point some 180 miles below Quebec where the pilot was dropped on the outbound voyage. The first lighthouse at Father Point, according to the light lists, was put in service in 1859, although one rather obscure source under the signature of a Raoul Lachance speaks as early as 1800 of a lantern on the roof of a house 45 feet in height, the light consisting of five oil lamps fitted with 21-inch reflectors.[31] The first lighthouse cited in the light lists (Admiralty 1864) is described simply as octagonal with the focal plane of the light 43 feet above high water. This lighthouse was destroyed by fire on 13 April 1867; plans were at once set afoot for its replacement at an estimated cost of $1,600 to $2,000.[32] This lighthouse in turn was replaced with a 97-foot, eight-sided reinforced concrete tower in 1909 in order that a more powerful light and hence larger lantern might be installed. The Father Point lighthouse was fitted with external buttresses in similar manner to that at the north end of Belle Isle. As a major coastal light Father Point rated dioptric apparatus of the 3rd Order, manufactured by the Parisian firm of Barbier and Turenne. It is understood that this optic with a mercury vapour light is still in service at Father Point.

Green Island

The first lighthouse built on the shores of the St. Lawrence and still standing today was that on Green Island in 1809. This is the third oldest lighthouse in Canada, being pre-dated only by the Sambro light off Halifax, and Gibraltar Point, no longer in use, on Toronto Island.

As early as 1787 one Peter Fraser, who had been working 15 years for the improvement of St. Lawrence navigation, went to London to raise funds

45 Cap Chat lighthouse, short tower with attached
dwelling. Short towers are often sited on lofty headlands where the light is already at a considerable
elevation above the sea. (*Canada. Department of
Transport.*)

46 Anticosti Island, Southwest Point. (*Canada.
Department of Transport.*)

46

among city merchants trading to Canada. Fraser estimated that fully 8,000
tons of shipping passed Green Island
off the mouth of the Saguenay River
in the course of a year. A light duty of
9d. per ton would finance the Green
Island project.[33] Fraser's recommendation was supported by Commodore
Sawyer, R.N., in a report written aboard
the *Leander* in the harbour of Quebec,
9 October 1787.

*I have seen the estimates and the plan
of a lighthouse meant to be erected
on Green Island; also the plan of a
Dwelling House. In regard to the ex-
pediency of the former, I am clearly
of opinion that it is absolutely necessary as I look upon that part of the
River to be most dangerous owing to*

45

the situation of Red Island, and the setting of the Currents from the Saguenay River, which are so very irregular that Vessels are frequently deceived as to their Situation, and I am credibly informed that several have been Ship wrecked on Red Island, that would have been saved if there had been a light on Green Island.[34]

But it was not until the spring of 1806, more than 18 years later, that the executive council of Lower Canada took the matter in hand. By late November of that same year, the masonry work on the 56-foot circular stone tower was finished. A further sum of £875 local currency was needed in addition to the original £500 grant to complete the project. The lantern was supplied by George Robinson of London, and the lamps and reflectors by the London firm of Brickwood and Daniel at a cost of £388 sterling. The stone tower was topped by a double flooring of three-inch oak plank sheathed with copper, on which was mounted the lantern.[35]

An early inspection by the deputy master of the Quebec Trinity House on the night of 13 September 1810 found all in good order.
We arrived at half past two o'clock in the morning of Thursday the thirteenth instant, and found the lantern illuminated with thirteen lamps, set in an equal number of reflectors, these with the other apparatus in it were in high order. At day-light, we again examined the lantern and tower; the former is erected in a master-like solid manner, the latter is also a piece of good mason-work. The rough casting par-

ticularly attracted our notice, it being exceedingly hard and durable.[36]

The first keeper of the Green Island lighthouse was Charles Hambledon, who was instructed to be in continuous attendance from 15 April to 15 December. His duties included the care of the lamps, reflectors and the lantern glazing, for which he was paid £100 per annum. The keeper must be "careful, sober and intelligent."[37] He was required to keep a daily journal, "of all occurrences and observations" to be forwarded to Quebec once a quarter.[38]

Late in 1811, the following supplies were ordered for the Green Island lighthouse:
2 caldrons of coal
20 lbs. soap for washing
polishing leather and cloths (for the reflectors of polished silver)
1000 board nails
100 boards
1 lb. polishing powder for the reflectors
24 gross fine cotton wick for the lamps[39]
The Green Island structure remained the sole light on the shores of the mighty river for a full 21 years.

Stone Pillar and Red Islet
The 1840s saw the establishment of three lighthouses below Quebec. Two of these, Stone Pillar and Red Islet, were of similar design — circular, grey stone towers, each 52 feet high with circular lanterns. A distinctive feature of these two towers was the three string courses spaced at equidistant intervals, mainly a decorative embellishment. The Stone Pillar lighthouse was built in 1843, and the Red Islet structure in 1848. According to local authority, stone for the latter was brought out from Scotland. Both lighthouses are standing today.[40] As re-

47

48

cently as 1966 the Red Islet light was described as catoptric long focus, of which there must be very few left in service.

Bicquette Island
The third of this trio and farthest downstream of the three was Bicquette Island, built in 1843 by the Quebec Trinity House in the broadening reaches of the river below Quebec. Shipowners and mariners had been petitioning for a light at this point as early as 1828.
It frequently happens that vessels running up in a dark night give to the Island of Bicquet so wide a birth that the North Shore of Portneuf or Mille Vaches will frequently bring them up. Vessels navigating the River St. Lawrence are never certain of their distances, for where the channel is very narrow and the current strong without any safe anchorage ground, vessels are often at a loss which course to steer to a place of safety. A Light House upon Bicquet Island would in such a case prove of great advantage, inasmuch as a vessel would then make boldly towards the light, knowing that from thence she could direct her course for Green Island, and if the weather was clear she would possess the further advantage of obtaining a view of one Light while losing sight of the other.[41]

Sir John Barrow, secretary to the commissioners of the Admiralty, recommended in 1838 the installation of a strong light on Bicquette Island, but with a characteristic to distinguish it from the fixed light on Green Island.[42] The Quebec Trinity House, on the other hand, expressed a preference for

closely adjacent Bic Island on the grounds that fuel and fresh water were more readily available; but in the sequel, Bicquette Island was the chosen site. Construction estimates stood at a minimum £6,000.[43] The circular stone tower 74 feet in height was completed with a revolving light in 1844. The first fog alarm was a gun, to be fired hourly in thick weather. The Bicquette lighthouse is another survivor from the colonial past. It is understood that the fog signal gun is still on the site, though replaced by more effective devices many years ago.

This construction in the 1840s notwithstanding, at mid-century the words of Beaufort's report to the Admiralty prepared in 1834 were still basically true.
Thus in a seaboard of about 400 leagues, as there are at present 20 lights, or an average one to about every 20 leagues, very few more can be wanted for the general purposes of navigation — but those few would be of most essential benefit.[44]
These were to be forthcoming in the next few decades.

The Great Lakes Region and the Upper St. Lawrence
Around the beach the sea gulls scream;
Their dismal notes prolong,
They're chanting forth a requiem,
A saddened funeral song.
They skim along the waters blue
And then aloft they soar
In memory of the sailing men
Lost off Lake Huron's shore!

(popular lake song composed on the loss of the schooner *Persia* with all hands in November, 1869)

In order to describe early developments on the Great Lakes, it is necessary to return to the early years of the 19th century when the Province of Upper

49

Canada was very much of a backwoods wilderness. Pioneer settlements existed at such places as York, Newark and Niagara, with Kingston only presenting a finished aspect.

These vast freshwater inland seas, the Great Lakes, ravaged frequently by savage storms, offered a challenge to the mariner comparable to the ocean itself. Seas on the lakes were shorter and sharper, and at the same time the

50 Plan drawings of the Cap-des-Rosiers lighthouse on the Gaspé coast. (*Public Archives of Canada.*)

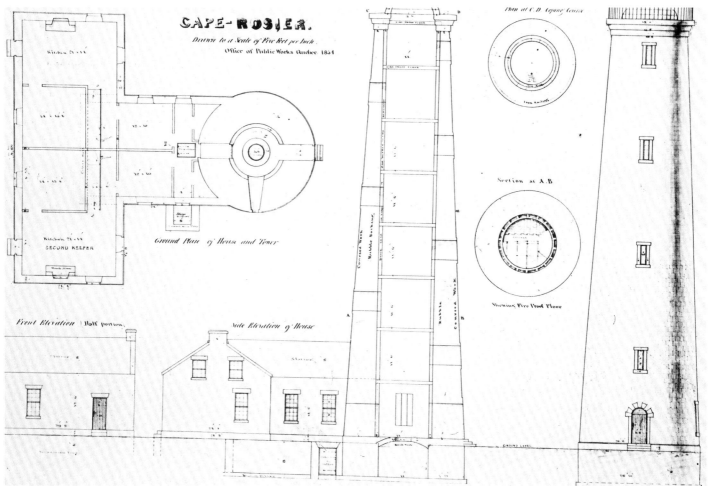

50 Plan drawings of the Cap-des-Rosiers lighthouse on the Gaspé coast. (*Public Archives of Canada.*)

navigator was ever within range of the perils posed by off-shore navigation — rocks, shoals and sandbars. Lighthouses, therefore, were as much a necessity to the Great Lakes mariner as to his contemporary on the high seas. And, in fact, lighthouse development on Lake Ontario was coincident with that on the lower St. Lawrence as well

as with many of the early installations on the Atlantic coast.

In a more or less chronological account of early lighthouse construction on the Great Lakes, the trend of settlement will be followed, from Lake Ontario, over the steep Niagara escarpment to the shallow reaches of Lake Erie, thence through Lake St. Clair to the broader expanse of Lake Huron, and finally to the frigid, rockbound waters of Lake Superior, more

than 600 feet above sea level. (Lake Michigan, lying wholly within American territory, is not included in this treatment.) With the first settlements and resultant waterborne trade, safeguards to navigation soon followed.

Lake Ontario
The journals of the House of Assembly for Upper Canada record the passing

51

of an Act dated 5 March 1803 "to establish a fund for the erection and maintaining of lighthouses."[1] Lighthouse commissioners were appointed who were directly responsible to the governor; later, in 1833, the inspector general took over this responsibility.[2] With the Act of Union in 1841, lighthouses and divers aids to navigation came under the jurisdiction of the Department of Public Works, although until Confederation, those below Montreal remained the charge of the Montreal and Quebec Trinity Houses.

Mississauga Point
The first lighthouse to grace the shores of Lake Ontario was built at Mississauga Point at the mouth of the turbulent Niagara River, a site recommended by the Board of Lighthouse Commissioners on 17 April 1804.[3] James Green, the Niagara customs collector, was given charge of the work and the contractor was a John Symington. When the project was completed, the officer commanding at Fort George was to appoint "a careful non-commissioned officer or soldier

52 Red Islet lighthouse, built in 1848. The stone for this lighthouse is said to have been brought out from Scotland. (*Canada. Department of Transport.*)

52

to keep the lights lighted during the season for which he will receive from the commissary at the post one shilling Halifax currency per day."[4] Military masons of the 49th Regiment of Foot were engaged at civilian rates. The resultant labour cost became the subject of official correspondence in which an ambitious young officer, Lieutenant Colonel Isaac Brock, found it advisable to render his superiors an explanation, dated 15 November 1804. *To the statements therein given I verily subscribe requesting at the same time to be allowed to add that, in giving my consent to the masons of the 49th. Regiment assisting in building the Light house at Mississauga point, I had no idea they would be employed longer than two or three days, as they were then under orders to proceed to Amherstburg in the* Canadian, *which was momentarily expected, but her arrival having been delayed a fortnight or three weeks, beyond his usual time, they were in consequence, enabled to finish the building. I embarked soon after giving my consent, for Kingston, without once supposing it possible the masons would have time to earn so many dollars.*[5]

It transpired that the resultant cost, using military labour, ran to £9 7s. 6d. The total outlay came to £178 3s. 8d. Halifax currency.[6] The hexagonal tower, an artist's attractive sketch of which appears in Figure 53, was completed in 1804 preceding by five years Green Island lighthouse, the first on the lower St. Lawrence. Research to date has not elucidated the type of apparatus used on this first lighthouse on the Great Lakes; the light may have been derived from tallow candles, or more likely from one or more Argand lamps fitted with reflectors and burning sperm oil. In any case, the Mississauga lighthouse stood for only 10 years, giving place to fortifications in 1814 following the American sack of Niagara.

Gibraltar Point

Authorization for the construction of the Gibraltar Point lighthouse on the crescent-shaped island enclosing what was to be one day the busy port of Toronto was given on 1 May 1808, the project to be directed by William Allan whose commission read: *You are hereby authorized and directed to provide such materials as may be required for the purpose of erecting a Light House on Gibraltar Point, under the authority of an Act passed in the Third Session of the Third Parliament of this Province, and also to pay the workmen employed thereon.*[7] Constructed solidly of limestone by artificers of the 41st Regiment, the tower was originally built to a height of approximately 67 feet, with a 15-foot extension added in 1832. The hexagonal tower, as may be readily seen in Figure 56, has vertical sides for the first 10 feet or so, after which the walls assume a slight taper up to the extension, of slightly different stonework, which again assumes the vertical. The tower door, recessed slightly into the four-foot-thick wall, has a pleasing rounded arch. The original lock is in place, to be opened by means of an enormous, outsize key. The polygonal lantern and platform are not the originals, being of a design more frequently seen in the later 19th century. The lantern deck was sheathed with copper as a precaution against fire.[8] The lantern is gained by a spiral staircase, in the centre of which rises the original weight shaft, a revolving light replacing the former fixed one in 1832.

Figure 55 depicts the Gibraltar Point lighthouse as it appeared in the early days of "muddy York," and Figure 56 as it stands today in quiet, spacious and well-tended parkland, across the bay from the maelstrom of downtown Toronto.

53

Leaking lanterns have always been a problem with lighthouses, and Gibraltar Point was no exception. By 1822, the lantern stood in obvious need of repair, the rain beating in to such a degree that frequently the light was extinguished. In the words of its builder, William Allan, reporting to the executive council that year,

The roof leaks so much that whenever there is any Rain, with the least Wind, it beated in all round it so much that the Lamps are frequently extinguished and it is not possible to keep the lights in during any Storms which generally happens at Night. The Wet is also gradually rotting the Floors above and the Stairs . . . . I don't think the expense can exceed £15 or £20.[9]

"Haunted" lighthouses are most likely as common as allegedly ghost-ridden old houses. Apparently the first keeper of the Gibraltar Point light died suddenly in 1815 under mysterious circumstances; the subsequent discovery of a human skeleton near the site gave rise to the legend that the lighthouse was haunted.

The Gibraltar Point lighthouse is the oldest extant in the Great Lakes region and second only to Sambro Island in the whole of Canada.

False Ducks Island

Lighthouse construction in Upper Canada proceeded slowly in these early years. The establishment of a Trinity House for the region, suggested by Lord Bathurst in 1816, was never implemented.[10] In its session of 1832-33, the legislature observed that to date, besides the Gibraltar Point light, only two additional lighthouses had been built in the area – Long Point on Lake Erie and False Ducks Island at the eastern end of Lake Ontario.[11]

The latter, an early installation built in May 1828, was quite recently demolished. J. W. Macaulay, lighthouse commissioner, complained of "the scantiness of the appropriation" and the lack of suitable sand and stone on the site. Nonetheless the commissioners addressed themselves to their task.

We have an idea of building a round tower, nearly in the proportion of a Tuscan column, and as small in its diameter as may be consistent with its solidity, in order to save materials.[12]

In June 1828, Macaulay was able to report the making of "a very advantageous contract" for a 60-foot stone tower with stairs and lantern platform for the modest sum of £546.[13] The lighthouse was fitted with a polygonal lantern, and its four-foot-thick rubble masonry walls were in fair condition nearly a century later. The district engineer in 1924 recommended "the scabbling of the entire surface," repointing with the best quality mortar, and the entire tower to be whitewashed, the results of which may be

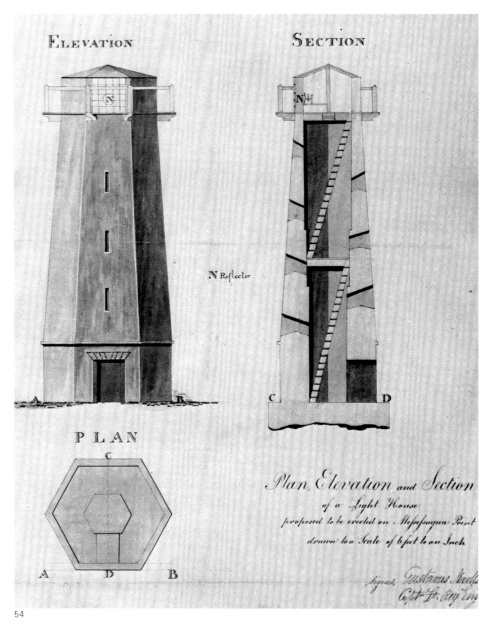

ELEVATION

SECTION

N Reflector

PLAN

*Plan, Elevation and Section
of a Light House
proposed to be erected on Mississauga Point
drawn to a Scale of 6 feet to an Inch*

*Signed, Gustavus Nicolls
Captn. R. Roy. Eng.*

54

55 Sketch of the Gibraltar Point lighthouse as it once was. This is the second oldest lighthouse extant in Canada, located on Toronto Island. It is no longer in use but is preserved by the city in excellent condition. (*Public Archives of Canada.*)

56 Gibraltar Point lighthouse, as it is today. (*Photo by author's son.*)

57 False Ducks Island lighthouse, Lake Ontario, before renovation. (*Canada. Department of Transport.*)

55

56

57

seen in Figure 57.[14] This lighthouse, unlike some of its contemporaries in these early years, maintained a high reputation for the quality of its light, apparently derived from three Argand lamps with reflectors which in the words of the inspector general "are kept in a more cleanly state than any which are to be found on the opposite shores of Lake Ontario."[15]

Point Petre

The Point Petre lighthouse was built under contract by the firm of Matthews and Scott for the sum of £398. Located on the southwest extremity of Prince Edward Peninsula, the Point Petre lighthouse, no longer in use, stands about 12 miles from Picton. The 62-foot circular and slightly tapered tower of "even coursed rubble" was "topped by a cornice of stepped corbelling," on which was set the 12-sided lantern on a platform of the same configuration. Neither the lantern nor the platform is original.[16] The original lantern was supplied by a blacksmith, Thomas Masson, for £164 10s., and the chandelier, reflectors, lamps and lantern glazing were ordered from Boston. The commissioners were well pleased with the work.

The Commissioners have indeed great satisfaction in speaking favourably of the work of the Contractors, who are most respectable persons, and have performed their engagements in a very creditable manner. The tower is built

58

in the most substantial manner, and cannot fail to endure for ages. . . . The frame work of the Lantern fits together with uncommon neatness, and is secured in every respect better than any other Lantern that the Commission has seen.[17]

The commissioners considered the Point Petre tower to be of sounder construction than that at False Ducks. The light consisted of 11 Argand lamps with 16-inch reflectors set in an iron chandelier and complemented with 11 copper oil heaters, the whole supplied by Winslow Lewis of Boston for the sum of $522.65.[18] The Point Petre light was said to have a range of 25 miles in clear weather.

Nine Mile Point

The Nine Mile Point lighthouse located on the western point of Simcoe Island, a landfall light for vessels making for the St. Lawrence from Lake Ontario, is of identical design to the Point Petre structure but only 45 feet in height. The Nine Mile Point lighthouse is still in use today. The old weight shaft and weights are still in place, though the lantern is thought to have been replaced at a later date. This lighthouse is one of the few, other than range lights, equipped with the reflector or catoptric type light, the apparatus consisting of three parabolic copper reflectors lined with quicksilver. Built in 1833 it is not surprising that the mortar is now soft, and so this tower may require considerable maintenance to preserve it. The site is accessible to motor by means of two ferries.

Presqu'Ile

Another important lighthouse, built in 1840 in the eastern waters of Lake Ontario and still in use today, is that of Presqu'Ile. Located three miles from Brighton, the Presqu'Ile lighthouse is an octagonal stone structure, shingled throughout on the exterior and set on a stone base cemented over at a more recent date.[19] The cornice, as indicated in Figure 58, exhibits a pronounced flare noticeable from the ground. There are five landings within connected by steep straight runs of stairs with an almost ladder-like ascent. Originally the lighthouse was fitted with a polygonal lantern with guard rail around the observation platform, but recently the lantern has been replaced with a rotating beacon mounted on a buoy structure. The Gothic arch of the door is of rather an ecclesiastical outline.

Burlington

At Burlington, located at the western extremity of Lake Ontario, two lighthouses were built at an early date, the first in 1838; this one is still standing, although removed from service in 1961. Overtaken by highway construction in recent years, the old Burlington light, situated on a canal known as the Burlington Cut by which shipping enters the bay from the lake, found itself overshadowed by the Burlington Skyway and cheek-by-jowl with a lift bridge. The present light is shown from a reinforced concrete tower, complete with a radio beacon and Airchine fog alarm on the end of the jetty. The old lighthouse, as may be seen in Figure 59, is a tall graceful structure in stone, the tapering tower rising to a height of approximately 55 feet[20] with narrow rectangular windows at each of the four landings giving ample evidence of the thickness of the walls. The lantern is believed to be of more recent date. The department had decided upon its demolition, since in this location the light was manifestly useless. Strenuous protests from a local historical society have to date, however, saved the old structure from the wrecker's hammer.

Queen's Wharf

A curious but pleasing survival from Toronto's early days is the diminutive Queen's Wharf lighthouse, whose construction date in the 1864 Admiralty list of lights is cited as 1838 and as 1861 according to the Toronto Historical Society. It is a square frame, two-storey structure with angles at each corner sheared off. It has widely

projecting eaves, and its height, base
to vane, is not over 20 feet. This little
lighthouse was moved about 500
yards from its original location on
Queen's Wharf when the city undertook a large-scale reclamation of land
along the waterfront in 1911 ; its present position within a street car loop is
at the intersection of Fleet Street and
Lakeshore Boulevard, a good distance
from the harbour. The light has not
been in use since this time but the
well-built little structure has been kept
in excellent condition by the Toronto
Historical Society. The only renovation
has been the replacement of some of
the sheathing boards and the exterior
siding, although the original style has
been faithfully maintained.[21]

Port Dalhousie
Port Dalhousie Harbour on the south
shore of Lake Ontario features two
fairly old frame range lights. The main
light, built in 1879, is of the common,
square tapered design with an octagonal lantern. The doorway on the
south side projects from the wall and
has an attractive gabled roof, more or
less creating a porch effect, with a
transom above the door. John R. Stevens, architect, reported this old range
light to be in good condition.[22]

  The inner range light at Port Dalhousie, built in 1852, consists of a
four-storeyed octagonal tower with
a 12-sided lantern. The gently tapered
walls are shingled. Stevens doubts
that this lighthouse dated from 1852,
considering that its general configuration and design are attributable to the
1870s rather than mid-century.[23]

59

Lake Erie
Long Point
Moving over the Niagara escarpment
to the shallow waters of Lake Erie, one
finds an obvious place for the first
lighthouse to grace its shores at Long
Point, a sand spit running at an oblique
angle some 20 miles out into the lake.
As early as 1817, the lieutenant governor of the province cited the need of
a lighthouse at this point. The completion of the Welland Canal in 1829
gave added impetus to the project, as
a landfall for shipping making for the
canal entrance.

The shallow waters of Lake Erie
were frequently whipped to fury by
sudden and violent storms. Long Point,
judging from American representations to the British minister in Washington, was the scene of many
mishaps.

60

61

The navigating and commercial interests on Lake Erie sustain serious losses from the want of a Lighthouse on Long Point, in Upper Canada. This point stretches so far into the Lake that in violent storms vessels are unavoidably driven on to it in the night, and not only property, but the lives of mariners are lost. I understood last fall, that four of our vessels were driven onto this point in one storm; that a part of them went to pieces, and that the hands on board those wrecked perished.[24]

The gist of the matter reached the Foreign Office and eventually Government House. In March 1829, the sum of £1,000 was appropriated for the project, undertaken by Joseph Van Norman and Brothers who contracted to build the lighthouse equipped with lighting apparatus for £925 local currency.

The first in a series of three lighthouses on Long Point went into service on 3 November 1830. A circular stone tower 50 feet in height whose walls tapered from a thickness of five feet at the base to two at the top, was set on a seemingly solid foundation 30 feet square, made up of two tiers of squared oak and pine.[25] The care so taken, however, was not proof against the continual erosion, which by 1838 had thoroughly undermined the structure. The inherent difficulties of the site were expressed by G. I. Ryerse, customs collector at Port Dover, who undertook the rebuilding of the lighthouse for the sum of $1,212, in a letter to the inspector general on 22 February 1839.

Agreeable to your request I lay before you the state of the light house on Long Point. I suppose you are aware that . . . concerning the precarious state in which the light house was situated almost the whole time surrounded with water, partly undermined, entirely useless in stormy times, being unapproachable, and almost certain of falling in the lake in the spring, it being impossible to protect it with piles, it being founded on deep moveable sand, at the edge of deep water, the beach having disappeared and the water becoming deep for more than eighty yards after it was built.[26]

The second Long Point lighthouse was begun on 10 April 1843 and completed ready for service on 16 September of that year. The structure was an octagonal wooden tower 60 feet in height, and the original light was a fixed one employing 16 Argand lamps. The lamps were later reduced to six on the revolving principle and fitted with silver-plated copper reflectors.[27] To complete the story of Long Point, one may mention that the third in the succession of lighthouses, a reinforced concrete tower 102 feet high, went into service in May 1916, and is still in use at the present time.[28]

But before leaving Long Point, now a popular summer resort, one should note yet a fourth lighthouse built in 1879 on the neck of land separating the lake from Long Point Bay (Fig. 61). The square tower with attached dwelling is of frame construction plastered on the inside and shingled on the exterior. The tower has two landings leading to what is now a sunroom, for the light was removed from service sometime between 1915 and 1920 and the structure has since served as a residence. The verandah

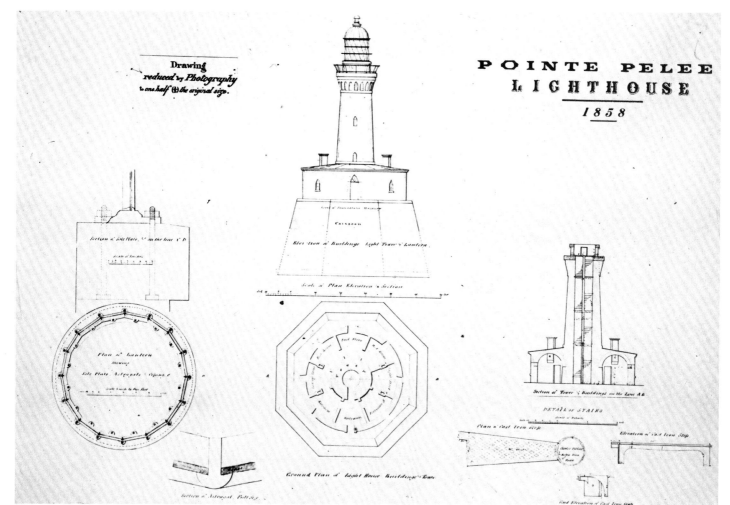

Drawing *reduced by Photography to one half (½) the original size.*

POINTE PELEE
LIGHTHOUSE
1858

62

and kitchen are additions to the original structure. The lantern has been removed and, it is surmised, replaced with the sunroom. At present this one-time lighthouse serves as an outsize summer cottage which can accommodate comfortably several families at a time.

Pelee Island
The second lighthouse to be built on the Canadian shore of Lake Erie was that on the northeast point of Pelee Island. Built in 1833 and situated in the hazardous Pelee Passage by which shipping passed in increasing tonnage to the upper lakes, the Pelee Island lighthouse exhibited a fixed light for which a range of 9 miles was claimed.

The round stone tower was 40 feet in height.[29] Despite the importance of this light to navigation, the early one was neglected. The light was destroyed by the rebels in 1837 and was not

63 River Thames range light. (*Canada. Department of Transport.*)

64 Goderich lighthouse, the first on Lake Huron, 1847. (*Photo by author's son.*)

65 Point Clark lighthouse. (*Photo by author's son.*)

63

64

65

relit the following spring. A complaint on the neglected state of the Pelee Island light appeared in official correspondence that summer. "The want of attention to the Lights upon this shore is a source of complaint among our traders, as they still pay the dues without reaping the benefit."[30] The following year the quality of the light was still unsatisfactory, the result of negligence on the part of an absentee keeper. By 1845, however, the Board of Works had secured the services of a conscientious keeper, a retired German sailor.[31]

Despite the manifest improvement in the Pelee Island light by this date, it had become apparent that a much stronger one was required to keep shipping clear of the dangerous shoal. The poor condition of the foundation precluded modifications to the present tower. J. McIntyre's *Report on Lighthouses for 1845* stressed the pressing need for an improved facility in this critical passage:

This Channel is becoming of more importance every year; all vessels take it that are bound for the Upper Lakes. To make it navigable at all times a revolving light would be required on the outer end of Pointe aux Pelee not less than 70 feet high. . . .

The improvement of the Channel is of the greatest importance and I would beg to call the attention of the Board to it, at as early a day as possible.[32]

Only in 1861, however, was a considerably improved lighthouse established on Pelee Spit, the foundation for which was a stone-filled caisson well offshore. The 61-foot wooden tower was constructed on shore and transported to the site. On 3 November 1861, the new coal-oil light, made up of nine flat-wick lamps and six reflectors, went into service.[33] In 1902 a new cone-shaped lighthouse was constructed of steel plates set upon a steel caisson filled with concrete and masonry. This structure exhibited a powerful dioptric light of the 3rd Order for the first time on 4 July. The establishment included a steam fog siren, indicative of the importance of this light station in the Pelee Passage.[34]

River Thames

Before proceeding to the upper lakes, we should mention a curiously shaped lighthouse built in 1845 where the meandering Thames empties into Lake St. Clair. The original coursed rubble tower was circular in shape and had a slight taper; it was heightened considerably at a later date. The tower is in very poor shape having developed an inclination, and the masonry is disintegrating; the whole structure indeed is due for demolition.[35] This old lighthouse forms one of a pair of range lights designed to guide vessels on a safe course over a dangerous sandbar. Its companion, built in 1837, has been replaced recently by a steel tower visible in the right background of the photograph in Figure 63. Although local representations have been made for its preservation on historical grounds, by all accounts the old lighthouse is beyond restoration.

Lake Huron
Goderich

The first lighthouse to be built on the shores of Lake Huron in 1847, the Goderich lighthouse, stands on a cliff over 100 feet above the lake level. Standing in what is now a park, this square and rather squat stone tower faced with smooth, even-coursed stone still serves, with its mercury vapour light, as a principal beacon along Huron's shore. In 1896, the original stone lantern deck was replaced with a reinforced concrete slab; the lantern too is new.[36]

Imperial Towers

In 1859, the Department of Public Works completed a series of six very tall tapering lighthouses of graceful proportions on the shores of Lake Huron and contiguous Georgian Bay. These circular stone towers, all of which have lasted well to the present day, are known locally and within the department as "imperial towers." The derivation of this term has not been traced. Certainly all were built under Canadian authority. It may have been that the design originated in England, and local lore in several instances traces the building material to Britain, but this seems highly unlikely. Dwellings, storage sheds and out-buildings of the same material originally formed one complex at each of these locations, but at several sites only the lighthouse remains. The six lighthouses are Point Clark and Chantry Island on the eastern shore of Lake Huron; Cove Island off Tobermory at the entrance to Georgian Bay; Griffith Island at the entrance to Owen Sound, and Nottawasaga and Christian Island in southern Georgian Bay.

With the exception of the Christian Island lighthouse which is but 60 feet in height, the other five towers all exceed 85 feet. All six are fitted with red

66 Southampton Harbour lighthouse. (*Canada. Department of Transport.*)

67 Cove Island lighthouse. (*Canada. Department of Transport.*)

68 Nottawasaga Island lighthouse. (*Canada. Department of Transport.*)

66

67

68

cast-iron polygonal lanterns, and the towers are whitewashed. The powerful 2d Order light at Nottawasaga Island has been replaced in recent years with an acetylene AGA-type beacon fitted into the original optic; the light produced is a feeble one compared with its predecessor. Apparently a light of such brilliance is no longer required at the entrance to Collingwood Harbour.

The most southerly of the series, at Point Clark about 20 miles to the north of Goderich, is situated on a low-lying shore and was so located to warn mariners off a dangerous shoal about two miles offshore. The Point Clark tower, containing nine storeys or landings leading to the lantern, has tapering limestone walls fully 5 feet thick at ground level and 2 feet thick at the top, with a total height of 87 feet from base to vane. The exterior stonework is laid in 19-inch courses, while the interior is lined with stone of smaller dimensions. One cannot do better than quote the Stokes report in paying tribute to the craftsmanship of these impressive structures.

The rugged stone walls are simple expressions of the idea of solidity and durability — the functional tradition of the nineteenth century being worked out in picturesque forms.[37]

Another feature, invisible from the ground but mentioned by Stokes, is that of an artistically designed gutter drain in the form of a lion's head, an example of careful craftsmanship dating from a time less utilitarian than our own.

69 Griffith Island lighthouse. (*Canada. Department of Transport.*)
70 Red Rock Point lighthouse, marking the entrance to the Killarney Channel. (*Photo by author's son.*)

69

70

Unlike so many older lighthouses, this one, and perhaps the others in the series as well, has retained its original lantern. All six lighthouses were fitted with dioptric apparatus of the latest design ranging from the 2d Order for Point Clark, Chantry Island, Cove Island, and Nottawasaga to the 3rd Order for Griffith Island and 4th for Christian Island.[38]

A few miles to the north on Chantry Island, just to the south of the town of Southampton, stands a similar lighthouse again to safeguard ships from running aground on a dangerous shoal.[39] Chantry Island is uninhabited and so has been the scene of considerable vandalism; the dwelling is in derelict condition. Department engineers are considering the lighthouse's demolition because of the high cost of maintenance, and the replacement of it with a simple steel tower. The Chantry Island lighthouse, though a handsome and impressive structure, is one of a type and difficult of access.

The reader will perhaps notice a structural similarity between this series of six lighthouses on Lake Huron with those built under the auspices of the same authority in the Gulf of St. Lawrence and Strait of Belle Isle region, completed about the same time (1858) – Point Amour, West Point of Anticosti and Cap-des-Rosiers, all of which exceeded 100 feet in height.

Killarney Channel
The two little frame structures, square with sloping sides in the configuration of a pepper-shaker, built at the entrance to the Killarney Channel in northern Georgian Bay were probably the first lights to go into service in the early days of the new dominion: their revolving lights were lit for the first time on 27 July 1867.[40] Of identical design, the one illustrated in Figure 70 is located at Red Rock Point at the eastern entrance to the channel. The little tower has a half-landing below the lantern deck, which flares out considerably to form a cornice at the platform. The lantern is of the familiar polygonal shape. At some later date, the two were converted to range lights to mark the proper course to enter the Killarney Channel.

Lonely Island
There are three more lighthouses of sufficient age to merit attention in the Lake Huron region, although all three are of a common design. The Lonely Island lighthouse, no doubt aptly named, was built in 1870 in northern Georgian Bay. An eight-sided frame tower with sloping sides and fitted with a red circular lantern, this otherwise unremarkable structure is at time of writing just a century old and is situated in what appears to be a very exposed location.[41]

Gore Bay and Strawberry Island
The Gore Bay and Strawberry Island lighthouses (illustrated in Figs. 73 and 74) date from 1879 and 1881 respectively. Both take the familiar form of square, slightly tapering towers with attached dwellings and are set on stone foundations. Strawberry Island lighthouse, 40 feet in height, has two

landings within the tower whereas the somewhat lower tower at Gore Bay has but one. In each case, polygonal lanterns are mounted on square projecting lantern platforms.

Lake Superior

Quebec Harbour and Porphyry Island The most northerly and most extensive of the five Great Lakes and credited with being the largest body of fresh water in the world, Lake Superior has few lighthouses of any historic interest, and those in generally offshore, inaccessible locations. The first lighthouse was built in 1872 at Quebec Harbour on Michipicoten Island. As may be seen from Figure 75, this structure consisted of a one-storey frame house with a range light shining from a dormer window. The present facility at Quebec Harbour still answers this description in the current list of lights.[42] The second lighthouse to be built on Superior's shores was on Porphyry Island in 1873, at the entrance to Black Bay in the vicinity of Port Arthur (Thunder Bay). This lighthouse has been replaced.

The bulk of lighthouse construction on Lake Superior has been carried out over the course of the past 30 to 40 years: open-work steel towers, mast and pole lights predominate.

Upper St. Lawrence River

Since lighthouse construction in the upper St. Lawrence got under way so much later than on Lake Ontario, its description follows that on the Great Lakes. In point of fact, early lighthouse construction on the upper St. Lawrence was contemporaneous with that on Lake Huron.

The first of the upper St. Lawrence lighthouses on the low-lying shore of placid Lake St. Francis was that at Lancaster Bar, built in 1844. This lighthouse, according to information furnished by the Dominion Lighthouse Depot, was a 20-ft square frame tower of a type frequently seen on inland waters. It is still standing, though no longer in use. A lighthouse of similar design but twice the height was built on Cherry Island in 1847; this light is no longer listed. A square wooden tower appeared on Magee Island in 1848, and a lantern was installed on the roof of a house at Coteau Landing the same year.[43]

By the mid-1850s, the advent of the river steamer and its increasing use by night called for the lighting of the intricate channels threading their way among the scenic Thousand Islands. A series of nine small lighthouses following the familiar design of square frame and sloping sides was built at Cole's Shoal, Grenadier Island, Fiddler's Elbow, Lindoe Island, Jack Straw Shoal, Spectacle Island, Red Horse Rock, Burnt Island and Gananoque Island. An official report compiled in 1855 boasted that this stretch of the river "is now lighted as a street."[44]

Of all these small river lighthouses, only Cole's Shoal is still standing though it is no longer in use. The Red Horse Rock lighthouse, which may be taken as one of typical design on inland waterways, survived until 1968. This lighthouse was built in 1855, set on a foundation of piers in the river. The 26-foot frame tower, 12 feet to a side and with a slight taper, was lined with narrow clapboarding and capped with a plain cornice. The octagonal lantern rested on a four-foot square box. The cupola was described as ogee in configuration; that is, embodying a double continuous curve.[45] Although reported in good condition, the little lighthouse, then over a century old, has since given place to one of the economical and utterly functional circular steel towers which are appearing in ever greater profusion on our inland waterways.

A surviving example of one of these small river lighthouses, dating from 1874 and believed to be the original, is located at Knapp Point on the north shore of Wolf Island. Its lantern has been removed and replaced with a steel buoy structure on which is mounted a rotating beacon.

A considerable need was felt for a light in the Prescott area in the years following Confederation. In 1873, the Department of Marine purchased a former windmill located a mile below Prescott which they converted to a lighthouse for the sum of $3,266.27. The lantern atop the 62-foot stone tower originally housed four flat-wick coal oil lamps fitted with 16-inch reflectors exhibiting a fixed white light.[46] The Windmill Point lighthouse is still in use, showing a dioptric light of the 5th Order.

Although the lighthouse per se is now nearly a century old, the principal interest in this structure is rather related to its function before conversion to serve the interests of river navigation. It was this windmill which gave its name to the decisive action, fought on a cold and dark November day in

71

72

73

74

75

1838, in which an American filibustering force under the command of a Polish "nobleman" met decisive defeat at the hands of a mixed force of British regulars, marines and Canadian militia. The Americans took refuge in the windmill, from which they defied the besiegers until guns brought down from Kingston forced their surrender. A plaque affixed to the lighthouse wall donated by a Polish-American patriotic association in memory of the unfortunate Von Schoulz is a fitting tribute to the amicable relations which have for so long existed along the undefended border.

76 Windmill Point lighthouse. (*Canada. Department of Transport.*)

77 Fisgard Island lighthouse. (*Canada. Department of Transport.*)

78 Race Rocks lighthouse, Strait of Juan de Fuca. (*Canada. Department of Transport.*)

76

77

78

The Pacific Coast

The colonization of the rugged and picturesque Pacific coast came much later in time than that along our Atlantic shores. The celebrated navigator Captain James Cook landed on Vancouver Island in 1778. It was not, however, until the year 1850 that there was sufficient settlement for the island to be proclaimed a crown colony. The Fraser River gold-rush of 1858 brought in its train the first influx of white settlement, much of it of a transient character, to the mainland. It is hardly surprising, therefore, that lighthouse development, as with the multiple other phases of colonization and settlement, followed at a much later date than was the case along the Atlantic coast, the St. Lawrence and the Great Lakes. At the time of her entry into Canadian federation in 1871, British Columbia's mountainous coast boasted but two lighthouses and one lightship, the latter at the mouth of the Fraser River. The Race Rocks and Fisgard lighthouses, both of which entered service in 1860, are still in use today although the latter is now property of the crown.

Fisgard Island

The Fisgard Island lighthouse at the entrance to Esquimalt Harbour is a circular brick tower 56 feet high with attached dwelling. It was fitted with a dioptric apparatus of the 4th Order and a coal-oil light.[1] By 1872, the tower stood in need of extensive repairs, the bricks used in construction having been of an inferior quality. The solution found for this unsatisfactory condition was the coating of the whole tower with a generous layer of Portland cement followed by three coats of "best white paint." New windows were also installed. The following season, 1873, these repairs which have stood the structure in good stead for nearly a century were well advanced.[2]

Race Rocks

For a number of years, indeed until the construction of the important landfall light at Carmanah Point in 1891, the 102-foot Race Rocks lighthouse commanding the Strait of Juan de Fuca from the southern tip of Vancouver Island was considered the most important in the province. The original light burned colza oil and subsequently (1898) dog fish liver oil in conjunction with catoptric long focus apparatus — apparatus which according to the latest list of lights, is still in service employing an electric light source. This rather old-fashioned optic was not the original one used, however, for the revolving light of the 2d Order was described as dioptric in the annual report for 1871-72.[3] This presumably was replaced after the installation of the Carmanah Point light at a later date.

Again, however, as with the case of the Fisgard structure, economies in initial construction were paid for in subsequent maintenance. Built of sandstone, the Race Rocks tower within 20 years gave serious cause for concern. The sandstone had been quarried, at the least cost to the contractor, from locations below high tide resulting in an inferior quality of stone. One consultant in 1878 considered the whole tower unsound and recommended that it should be demolished and re-built.[4] This expedient did not prove necessary; whatever measures were taken with the Race Rocks tower were effective for the structure stands today, more than a century later.

Point Atkinson

With only the two original lighthouses of pre-Confederation vintage on its shores in 1872 and little taken in hand in the course of the first year, the agent for British Columbia sourly concluded in his report for that year that the policy of the Department of Marine, insofar as the Pacific coast was concerned, must be one of frugal economy.[5] Although the Race Rocks light had won the approbation of mariners, the same could not be said of its contemporary on Fisgard Island.

In 1875, the third lighthouse on the Pacific coast was completed at Point Atkinson at the northern entrance to Burrard Inlet on the outer approaches to Vancouver Harbour. This structure was replaced in 1912 by the present lighthouse. The contract was let to an Arthur Fenny for the sum of $4,250. The 60-foot hexagonal tower with six exterior buttresses exhibited from its circular lantern a powerful lenticular light of the 3rd Order, at an elevation of 108 feet above high water. Local authority advises that the lighthouse is still very much in its original condition.

Berens Island and Entrance Island

The following year, 1876, two more lighthouses went into service : Berens Island at the entrance to Victoria Harbour on 5 March and Entrance Island in the vicinity of Nanaimo on 8 June.

The Berens Island lighthouse, a 30-foot, square wooden structure equipped with catoptric apparatus, exhibited a fixed blue light; the total cost of this installation, complete with dwelling, was $3,218.38.[6] The Berens Island lighthouse is no longer in existence having been replaced by a pole light serving the same purpose. The Entrance Island lighthouse, on the other hand, consisting of an eight-sided lantern mounted on the roof of a square frame house,[7] according to current advice still stands and is, therefore, one of a trio of lighthouses more than 90 years of age on this coast.

With the construction of the latter two, there were now, including the Fraser River lightship, a total of seven lights on the Pacific coast. With the exception of the Fisgard and Race Rocks installations, kerosene was the favourite illuminant on this coast.

Cape Beale
The outer coast of Vancouver Island fronting on the open Pacific had not been neglected. On the eighth anniversary of Dominion Day, 1874, the Cape Beale lighthouse went into service showing a revolving catoptric light atop a square tower. The focal plane of this light was 160 feet above the sea and it was visible at a range of 19 miles in good weather. The first Cape Beale lightkeeper, Robert Westmoreland, received $700 per annum.[8] The department's engineers contended that the Cape Beale light, about 100 miles north of Victoria, was superior to the important American landfall light at

79

Cape Flattery, installed in 1857[9] at the southern entrance to the Strait of Juan de Fuca. The original Cape Beale lighthouse has been replaced with an open-work steel tower.

The landing of materials, supplies and apparatus on the rugged outer coast, often through pounding surf, posed a hazardous operation frequently entrusted, as at Cape Beale, to the traditional skill of the local Indians. These boatmen exacted a good price for their services, and rightly so! The Victoria agent, in his report for 1874, reveals both the high cost of construction and labour on the coast, but still more his, and no doubt the current, attitude toward the Indians.

I apprehend that the custom of this country and the emoluments paid to individuals for their services contrast more strangely with that of similar services in the Eastern Provinces. Even the natives are imbued with a notion of their own value, and as this paragraph more particularly refers to Cape Beale . . . I must beg permission to relate a circumstance that actually transpired in Barclay Sound in the month of June, 1874. . . . The landing at the lighthouse is nearly always bad, and sometimes dangerous, but the sea-coast Indians are very expert in handling their canoes, and it is considered safer to entrust property or life to the care and management of the natives than to risk the same in frequently very inferior boats. . . . The Indian trader being on board, I requested him to find out what they expected for the service, and he informed me that each man in either of the two canoes must be paid six dollars, and three dollars for each canoe. This ap-

peared to me simply extortionate, and in an angry moment I threatened to take the schooner through the surf and land it myself. This they knew to be almost a physical impossibility, and quietly retorted that they thought I could not do that but I might try if I liked. I remonstrated, and tried to reason with them but all to no purpose; they knew that I was more or less dependent on them, and were sharp enough to know how to make me pay for it. . . . I also explained to them that the Government would be writing angrily to me for paying such exorbitant sums. Well, they replied, can't you write back and ask them how could you help it? I ultimately agreed to pay them each $4.50 and $3.00 each for the two canoes, and after some considerable time had passed they consented to my terms.[10]

Sand Heads

By 1879, the hull of the Fraser River lightship had been damaged beyond repair by dry rot, whereupon the decision was taken to replace the vessel with an offshore lighthouse set on an iron-screw pile foundation. The tender was awarded to a Thomas McKay of New Westminster for $9,500. Slow progress was made because of the difficulty in securing a firm foundation. Begun in 1882, the project was finally completed and the light in service by May 1884. The six-sided frame shingled tower 49 feet in height, was fitted with a dioptric light of the 3rd Order and a fog alarm bell to be rung in thick weather.[11] This curiously shaped lighthouse, one of the earlier offshore in-

80

stallations and the first on the Pacific coast, did not survive 1956. In that year a rectangular aluminum building on a steel pile pier replaced the earlier structure.

By the year 1890, 11 lighthouses had been installed on the Pacific coast and steam fog alarms were supplied at Race Rocks, Discovery Island and Point Atkinson.[12]

Carmanah Point

An important landfall light for vessels inbound from the Orient was projected for Carmanah Point on the southwest coast of Vancouver Island, to be completed under contract by December 1890. The 46-foot wooden or frame tower with an attached dwelling built on a high headland first showed a light on 15 September 1891, 173 feet above the sea. This light station included a ship-to-shore wireless installation (commonly known as a "coast station"), with telephone connection with Cape Beale further up the coast. The total cost of the project came to $15,220.89.[13] The original lighthouse has been replaced.

At the turn of the century, with new installations at Pointer Island, Fitz Hugh Sound and Dryad Point late in 1899, the Pacific coast establishment numbered 26 lighthouses and six steam fog-alarms.[14] Wooden towers with attached dwellings were a common type along the Pacific coast, no doubt because of the abundance of lumber and the proliferation of sawmills along those heavily wooded shores.

Brockton Point

The Brockton Point lighthouse in Vancouver Harbour, a 42-foot square tower which was built in 1890, is of interest more from the personal than the technical aspect. The first keeper, Captain W. D. Jones, was faithful to his trust but still managed to conduct a considerable business of his own on the property. This was quite permissible, provided the keeper's tendance of his light was in no way affected. Jones' successor, John H. Walsh, in an effort to have this humble harbour light upgraded (and hence his pay increased), carried on a protracted feud by post with his immediate superior in Victoria in which the keeper did not scruple to go over the head of local authority. In a letter addressed to the Civil Service Commission in 1926

appears a detailed description of the enterprise displayed by his predecessor.

Capt. Jones was mostly concerned with his farm, a good parcel of land in Stanley Park which was always a perquisite of his office. At one time he kept horses, cattle and goats; at another he bred rabbits, chickens, ducks, pheasants, pidgeons etc. In recent time he cultivated roses and various kinds of flowers, and his income from this source was up to $1500 a year. He also had trees, canes, bushes and brambles which produced a great variety of fruit, including apples, pears, cherries, plums and six different sorts of berries and currants.

For a long time the Vancouver Board of Park Commissioners coveted this parcel of lighthouse ground – the perquisite of the lightkeeper who was getting a small salary; and about 8 years ago the Government of the day actually agreed to give it to the city, together with $15,000 to pull down all the out-buildings and put the place in shape. However, Capt. Jones protested so effectively that the transfer of the property was cancelled and he continued in possession.[15]

Jones seems also to have been an amateur winemaker of note. Finally Jones secured the office of park commissioner, and thereafter had the benefit of the park horticulturist's service, not to mention an increased variety of shrubs and plants. His successor concluded, "Capt. Jones was an oldtimer, a very good sort, and he was able to take a great many liberties which would not be tolerated in my case."[16]

The first keeper of the Brockton Point light must not, however, be taken as a mere colourful eccentric. By 1907

he was credited with having saved the lives of no fewer than 16 persons, including the engineer of the steamer *Chehalis* which collided with the CPR *Princess Victoria*. On retirement, Captain Jones received the Imperial Service Medal from the hands of the king in 1925.[17] In his courage and devotion to duty, Jones was typical of many lightkeepers.

Cape St. James

Early in 1913 the Department of Marine undertook a difficult project at Cape St. James, at the southern extremity of the Queen Charlotte Islands. As this was a remote location several hundred miles from settlements, the department decided early in 1913 to undertake the project itself rather than by contract. The cost was not to exceed $26,500. In addition to the 44-foot octagonal reinforced concrete tower at an elevation of 279 feet above high water, the station was to include a wooden or frame dwelling with out-buildings, an oil storage shed and a boathouse.[18] The 3rd Order dioptric light of 100,000 candlepower had a range of 24 miles and was scheduled to go into service "on or about 15 February 1914."[19]

Triple Island

The Triple Island lighthouse (Fig. 81) in the vicinity of Prince Rupert was surely the most hazardous construction site ever attempted in Canada, rivaling in over-all difficulty that of Bird Rocks. The first contractor, Snider Brothers and Brethour of Vancouver, gave up the contract, convinced that the project was impractical. J. H. Hildritch of Prince Rupert then submitted

81

a tender for $33,500 in the summer of 1919, which was accepted by the Department of Marine. On closer acquaintance with the site the contractor charged the department with ignorance concerning the perils attending a construction crew on this exposed and tiny islet. Whenever a strong westerly wind coincided with spring and fall flood tides, the sea inundated the rock, carrying all before it. In the contractor's words, "the two westerly islands are so fiercely swept that nothing of a temporary nature could stand against it."[20] Continuing his letter to the department's marine agent at Victoria, he said,

Had the storms of 1919 been of the same nature and direction as were the storms of November, 1920, seventeen men and myself would have been swept off the rock without even a fighting chance for our lives....Three times in October and November the seas broke in the end of the cook house, once while we were eating breakfast; pouring in about eighteen inches above the height of the table, sweeping everything before it and drenching the men.[21]

The savage weather in October 1919 swept away 19,000 board feet of lumber, and at the end of the month a scow loaded with provisions, hardware and gravel was lost. In addition to the rising cost of labour, endemic along the Pacific coast, the contractor understandably had difficulty in keeping men at any price under such conditions. Many of the men he employed at Triple Island were recently repatriated veterans from the trenches of France, some of whom rated the Triple Island project as the greater ordeal. Be that as it may, it is to the contractor's lasting credit that he lost not a single life on

the job, begun on 4 August 1919 and completed two days before Christmas 1920. The 76-foot reinforced concrete tower, rising from a corner of the rectangular building which housed the fog alarm and keeper's quarters, exhibited a dioptric light of the 3rd Order. Rated at 400,000 candlepower, the beam of this powerful light swept the horizon 97 feet above high water. The 55 millimeter oil vapour light was scheduled to be lit for the first time on New Year's Day 1921.[22]

Hildritch lost money on the contract, although he was partially reimbursed at a later date. He had the satisfaction, however, of having completed successfully a hazardous feat in which he felt justifiable pride.

But what seemed at one time an almost impossible job is completed, and from reports I have received from sea-going men who visited it the work will compare favorably with any light station on the Pacific Ocean. It is a structure worthy of your Department and a monument to myself and employees.[23]

In latitude 54° N., the Triple Island lighthouse is one of the most northerly in Canada, other than open-work steel and aluminum towers found in higher latitudes in Hudson Strait and along the Mackenzie River system. These installations serve the same function, but are not lighthouses in the true sense of the word.

Sub-Arctic Waters: Hudson Strait and Hudson Bay

Commercial navigation came late to the lonely sub-Arctic waters of Hudson Bay and Strait, so long the preserve of the exploratory and the company supply vessel. For this reason, visual aids to navigation have assumed a secondary role to electronic ones.

The lighthouse per se—a solid stone, masonry or wooden tower or simply a house with lantern mounted thereon—has not made its appearance in these northerly latitudes. The transportation of stone or lumber to these remote locations would be uneconomical and in any case, the presence of permafrost poses a major foundation problem. In the place of the conventional lighthouse first pole lights, then open-work steel and aluminum towers have performed the function in sub-polar regions. Although these visual aids are of scant, if any, historical interest, a brief account is required to complete a descriptive survey across Canada.

Initial Aids in Hudson Strait

The opening of commercial navigation by this northerly route, longer by about 200 miles than the traditional St. Lawrence, hung upon the long-deferred completion of the Hudson Bay Railway to Churchill, a project undertaken in 1911 and completed only in 1931. From this port wheat grown on the Canadian prairies could be shipped to the British Isles during the short two-month navigation season. In premature anticipation of the railway's completion across more than 500 miles of muskeg and rock, the Department of Marine, during the season 1913-14, installed ten AGA-type acetylene pole lights along the shores of Hudson Strait at a cost little short of $69,000. These lights could be left untended during the short navigational season.[1] Although these beacons were mounted only five or six feet above the ground, many were swept away by the frequent gales which ravaged the region. This initial attempt to facilitate passage in the Hudson Strait was not considered a success.

Radio Aids

As mentioned in an earlier context, radio assumed a role of major importance between the two world wars. Radio beacons and direction-finding stations won an early preference over the traditional visual aids in these northern waters. This was in part due to the considerable distances to be covered initially in the Hudson Strait region, and in part because of the few specialized supply vessels using the route, all of which were adequately equipped with radio. In line with this policy, a department memorandum drawn up in January 1928 recommended that the provision of lights and fog signals should await the advent of commercial navigation.[2] The priority given radio aids was illustrated in a departmental letter of the following summer in which the point is made that the installation of a radio direction-finding station at the terminal port of Churchill rendered the employment of a lightkeeper superfluous.[3]

This policy was confirmed by the lighthouse board at a meeting held in December 1929, at which the trend for the future was clearly enunciated by the chief engineer.

I am of opinion that any lights which may be established in Hudson Strait should be electric, and suggest the use of steel towers with lanterns to enclose apparatus and a hut below to contain the machinery which should be in duplicate. I think we should have in mind a visibility of thirty miles.[4]

Herewith was formulated the policy for the future which was carried out over the course of the next four decades with little variation; electric lights powered by diesel generators were to become the order of the day in the far north, as part of the electrification program which followed hard on the Second World War. Most of the earlier lights in the northern regions had been acetylene.

In December 1929 Resolution Island, lying off the southeastern tip of Baffin Island, was chosen as a site for a landfall light to guide shipping inbound to the Hudson Strait. A similar light at the opposite end of the strait was recommended for Carys Swan Nest on Coats Island.[5] Three years later, in 1932, a powerful light was established on Resolution Island on Hatton Headland, 200 feet above the

82 Brockton Point lighthouse, Vancouver Harbour.
(*Canada. Department of Transport.*)

82

sea, in latitude 61°N.[6] A frame skeleton base supported a square frame lantern.

During the 1932 season, seven lights were established in Hudson Strait: those at Resolution Island and at Cape Hopes Advance were electric, in association with radio stations. In addition, lights were installed at the eastern end of Wales Island and at both ends of Charles Island, lying along the southern shore of the strait. Other lights appeared on the south shore of Nottingham Island, at the western entrance to Hudson Strait and on Coate's Island, in the northernmost reaches of Hudson Bay. With the exception of the electric lights installed on Resolution Island and Cape Hopes Advance, all these initial light stations employed acetylene lights. The commentary of ships' captains was mixed, some contending that the lights should be of greater power; a range of from 15 to 18 miles was claimed for some.[7]

Experience indicated that steel and aluminum open-work towers of the type installed at Cape Pembroke in 1964 were best suited to the region. At some stations, care of the light devolved upon the radio operators, but at many, the lights were entirely automatic—a trend now becoming rapidly general throughout Canada.

To a considerable degree, this northerly region, bypassing the colourful era of the lighthouse, moved directly into that of electronics.

Selected Inland Waterways

Lighthouses per se, other than on the Great Lakes and the upper St. Lawrence and Ottawa rivers, are rarely encountered on Canada's inland waterways. Mast and pole lights serve this function. Of the few bona fide lighthouses in this vast inland region of innumerable freshwater lakes and their connecting river systems, few are old enough or distinctive enough to be of historical interest; Black Bear Island lighthouse on Lake Winnipeg and several frame structures on the Ottawa River are possible exceptions.

Ottawa River
The first lighthouses to be built on the Ottawa were at Green Shoal opposite Templeton, lit for the first time on 27 October 1860, and at Point Valois, which went into service on the sixth of the same month. The latter was a floating light mounted on an iron barge which was discontinued a number of years ago. The reflector apparatus used employed flat-wick coal oil lamps.[1] The Green Shoal structure, now over a century old, consists of a square tower 21 feet in height from base to vane, its timbers and lumber of oak and pine. The total estimate for the project came to $3,985.[2]

On the upper Ottawa, three surviving structures claim our attention, one of which is of rather unusual height. Both follow the familiar configuration of square towers, with sloping sides (pepper-pot style) and square wooden lanterns, and both first saw service in 1873. One was built on Morris Island at the lower end of broad and placid Lake Chats, and the other at Deep River Islet (Fig. 83), a 24-foot square frame tower with a pronounced slope to its shingled sides, located above Allumette Island on the upper Ottawa.[3]

The 26-foot Arnprior Island lighthouse, built in 1885 a half-mile offshore from the thriving lumber town of the same name, is an unusually tall structure for a river lighthouse. Built on a small rocky islet in Lake Chats, this graceful structure is set on a square stone foundation. Two straight flights of stairs of almost ladder-like pitch lead to the square lantern platform, which has a pronounced overhang and is supported by eight brackets. The lantern, as may be seen in Figure 84, is square and set upon a pedestal of similar shape.

Lake Nipigon
In 1938, the uninhabited and closely wooded shores of Lake Nipigon lying just to the north of Lake Superior witnessed the installation of their first light. To date, a total of 10 pole lights have been put in service, including one at Tichnor Island which is mounted on a tree stump.[4]

Lake Winnipeg
The broad but shallow waters of Lake Winnipeg are frequently the scene of squalls, making for hazardous navigation for all but the stoutest vessels. In 1898, Lake Winnipeg's lonely shores witnessed the installation of their first two lighthouses at Gull Harbour and Black Bear Island. The latter, simply a light showing from the cupola of a frame house, is still the original installation, but a steel skeleton tower now serves at Gull Harbour.[5] Pipe towers and pole lights predominate at light installations on Lake Winnipeg as upon sundry other inland waterways.

Mackenzie River System
Moving to the north of the sixtieth parallel and following the Mackenzie River system on its 1,500-mile progress from the headwaters of the Liard and Lake Athabasca to the Arctic Ocean, we may note that the first light to be established on Great Slave Lake was at Outpost Island in 1932. Most of the lights in this northerly region have been mounted on aluminum tripod towers in the period since the last war.[6] Indeed river traffic on this northward-flowing sub-Arctic waterway has so

83

85

84

86

increased since the war that in 1956 the establishment of a new marine agency at Forth Smith, N.W.T., with jurisdiction over the whole Great Slave Lake–Mackenzie River system, was effected.

Finally, on the shores of the Beaufort Sea, well within the Arctic Circle, are the range lights of Tuktoyaktuk (popularly known as "Tuk-Tuk"), in latitude 69°N. The lights in this remote Arctic region are mounted on 20- to 40-foot aluminum open-work tripod towers, the first of which was installed in 1956.[7]

Appendix: Regional Agencies and their pre-1880 Lighthouses
In the following appendix under the headings of the various regional agencies will be found brief tabular data on lighthouses built before 1880 and still substantially in their original condition. By this is primarily meant the tower, or in some cases, the house or attached dwelling; lanterns have more often than not been replaced as has been the original optical apparatus, particularly in the case of those lights originally fitted with catoptric (C) or reflector type (D) apparatus.

St. John's Agency

Baccalieu Island
(northeast)
48°09'N., 52°48'W.
built 1859

tower : circular, cast-iron, height unknown likely original, poor condition

light : D., gas

area : Conception Bay

Belle Isle, South End
lower 51°53'N., 55°23'W.
built 1880

tower : masonry foundation on cliff, circular steel tower, height 23 ft.

light : D., 2d Order

Belle Isle, South End
upper 51°53'N., 55°23'W.
built 1858

tower : circular, stone, height 59 ft., clapboarded attached dwelling (both original) dwelling renovated

light : D., electric

Belleoram
47°31'N., 55°25'W.
built 1873

tower : may be original ; original circular iron ; re-built slightly in new location 1931 ; present tower circular steel

light : acetylene

Cape Pine
46°37'N., 53°32'W.
built 1861

tower : circular, iron, red and white bands ; lower 10 ft. encased in concrete (hexagonal) ; said to be in good condition ; height not known

light : D., electric

Point Amour
51°27'N., 56°52'W.
built 1855

tower : circular, stone, height 104 ft., attached dwelling, masonry strapped and shingled exterior ; repaired in 1957

light : D., 2d Order

Rocky Point
47°29'N., 55°48'W.
built 1873

tower : iron, circular, height 20 ft., concrete foundation

light : acetylene (harbour light)

Dartmouth Agency

Cape Negro
43°30'N., 65°21'W.
built 1872

tower : octagonal, height 44 ft., local authority not sure this is the original

light : C., long focus

Cape North
47°02'N., 60°24'W.
built 1876

tower : cylindrical iron, painted red ; height 47 ft. ; regional authority not sure whether this is the original

light : D., 3rd Order

Ciboux Island (Cape Breton)
46°23'N., 60°22'W.
built 1863

structure : rectangular house, polygonal lantern on roof ; original

light : D., 7th Order

East Ironbound
44°26'N., 64°05'W.
built 1867

tower : unusual structure ; square wooden tower rising steeple-like from front end, oblong dwelling ; tower 40 ft., shingled exterior ; houses fog alarm & storage batteries : ground floor originally kitchen ; second storey originally bedrooms ; four straight flights of stairs ; interior walls lined with matched lumber

lantern : polygonal, iron

light : electric

Guysborough
45°28'N., 61°29'W.
built 1846

tower : square, frame, height 35 ft., rises from roof of dwelling ; may be the original

light : D., electric (M.V.)

Sambro Island
44°26'N., 63°34'W.
built 1758 (oldest extant in Canada)

tower : octagonal, stone with reinforcing cement ; shingled exterior ; height 82 ft. ; spiral stairway in tower renewed but with original configuration

lantern : new (aluminium) : lantern deck or platform consisting of 2-3 ft. thick concrete base ; new ; lantern installed 1969

light : airport-type rotating beacon ; original dioptic apparatus now on display, local museum

Charlottetown Agency

Big Shippegan
47°43'N., 64°40'W.
built 1872

tower : wood, octagonal, height 54 ft. ; square cribwork foundation

lantern : round with octagonal lantern platform

Blockhouse Point
46°11'N., 63°08'W.
built 1851

structure : tower combined with dwelling ; frame ; tongue & groove wallboarding interior ; tower square with slight taper ; height 40 ft. ; dwelling original except for roof and chimney ; ground floor : parlour, kitchen & 2 bedrooms ; second floor : bathroom, 4 bedrooms

lantern : octagonal, cast-iron ; lantern platform may be more recent

Cape Jourimain
46°09'N., 63°48'W.
built 1870

tower : frame, octagonal, height 51 ft.

light : D., 4th Order
This may be the original ; in any case, has been moved several times

East Point
46°27'N., 61°58'W.
built 1867 (moved 1885)

tower : octagonal, frame, height 64 ft. ; not sure that this the original but informed timbers hand-hewn ; shingled exterior

light : electric

North Point
47°03'N., 63°59'W.
built 1866

tower : wood, octagonal, height 62 ft.

light : C., long focus ; changed to D., electric 1970. Agency states this likely the original ; has been moved several times

Panmure Head
46°09'N., 62°28'W.
built 1853

tower : octagonal, frame, shingled ; hand-hewn timbers ; 3 landings, straight flights of stairs ; reshingled in 1956 ; in foundation original masonry replaced with concrete

lantern : polygonal ; new lantern platform in 1950s

light : dioptric apparatus made in Charlottetown

Point Prim
46°03'N., 63°02'W.
built : 1846 (oldest in P.E.I.)

tower : circular, brick, shingled exterior, height 60 ft ; central weight shaft ; 4 landings

lantern : polygonal, original lantern platform thought original ; pipe railing, exterior gallery, later addition

light : D., electric (M.V.)

Seacow Head
46°19'N., 63°49'W.
built 1863

tower : wood, octagonal, stone foundation faced with cement (later date), weight shaft intact ; 3 landings with straight flights of stairs ; ladder leading to lantern ; 3 cast-iron tie rods at each landing running horizontally across tower for bracing

lantern : polygonal (12-sided) ; lined interior with tongue & groove lumber to waist height

light : D., electric

Souris East
46°21'N., 62°15'W.
built 1880

tower : frame, square, sloping sides, shingled with gabled windows ; 2 interior landings, straight runs of stairs ; central weight shaft

lantern : round with 3 panels obscured (light not required in that quarter) ; lantern interior lined with tongue & groove lumber to waist height

dwelling : originally attached to tower, now separate

West Point
46°37'N., 64°23'W.
built 1876

tower : grey sandstone foundation on cribwork of cedar logs ; stone from N.B. ; frame with sloping sides, shingled exterior ; very heavy timbers ; height about 80 ft. ; 26 ft. square at base ; 3 landings with straight flights of stairs ; inner walls plastered ; originally bedrooms located ground floor and first landing ; original attached dwelling now demolished

lantern : polygonal, cast-iron ; light oil vapour until 1963 when converted to electricity
Legend that Captain Kidd buried treasure in the dunes north of the lighthouse ; also that a mysterious burning ship visible offshore at times

Wood Island
45°57'N., 62°44'W.
built 1876

tower : square, frame, sloping sides, shingled, attached dwelling ; height 50 ft. ; 2 interior landings, straight flights of stairs ; windows at each landing

lantern : octagonal ; lantern platform & railing appear comparatively new
light : D.

Saint John Agency
Church Point
44°20'N., 66°08'W.
built 1874

tower : wood, square, height 20 ft. ; dwelling attached

light : D., 4th Order

Gannet Rock
44°31'N., 66°47'W.
built 1831

tower : stone foundation cemented over ; octagonal frame with attached dwelling ; exterior shingling ; windows each face ; 6 storeys in tower ; some timbers apparently handhewn

dwelling : 2 storeys, with kitchen, parlour, bedroom

lantern : removed in 1967 ; substitution rotating beacon

Fanjoy Point
45°54'N., 66°01'W.
built 1873

tower : square, frame, height 20 ft.
light : D., 7th Order

Mark Point
45°10'N., 67°13'W.
built 1876

tower : frame, sloping sides, square

lantern : square, frame
The Mark Point, Church Point and Walton lighthouses are of similar design, built in the 1870s

Seal Island
43°24'N., 66°01'W.
built 1830

tower : octagonal, wood, height 67 ft. ; shingled ; 4 landings, straight flights of stairs

light : oil vapour until 1959 ; since D., 2nd Order
Structure appears very much in its original condition

Sissiboo
44°26'N., 66°01'W.
built 1870

tower : square, frame, height 33 ft.

lantern : apparently square, presumably of wood ; regional authority states only minor repairs effected

Swallow Tail
44°46'N., 66°44'W.
built 1860

tower : frame, octagonal, shingled, height 53 ft. ; interior plastered ; 2 main landings and a half landing ; straight flights of stairs

lantern : new (aluminum) also lantern platform since 1969

light : original Barbier & Turenne optic now fitted with 500 w. ; D., 4th Order

Walton Harbour
45°14'N., 65°01'W.
built 1873

tower : square, wood, height 31 ft.

lantern : polygonal, apparently frame, with copper roof ; square lantern platform with wooden railing

Quebec Agency
Bicquette Island
48°25'N., 68°54'W.
built 1844

tower : circular, stone, boarded ; height 74 ft.

lantern : circular

light : D., electric

Bon Ami Point
48°04'N., 66°21'W.
built 1870

tower : square, wood, height 33 ft. Repaired in 1965, regional authority believes this to be the original

Brandypot
47°53'N., 69°48'W.
built 1862

tower : circular, brick, painted white and rising from middle of roof of frame house ; height 39 ft.

light : D., 4th Order

Cap-des-Rosiers
48°52'N., 64°12'W.
built 1858

tower : circular, limestone, height 112 ft. (base to vane) ; exterior lined with firebrick, interior coated with plaster ; walls 7 ft. 3 in. thick at base and 3 ft.

at top; base diameter 25 ft., top diameter 17 ft.; nine storey; new enamel brick on exterior of recent date

lantern: likely the original (round)

light: D., 1st Order; optic the original Barbier & Turenne

Grand Ile Kamouraska
47°37'N., 69°52'W.
built 1862

tower: square, frame height 39 ft., attached dwelling dating from 1913

light: D., gas

Green Island
48°03'N., 69°25'W.
built 1809

tower: circular, stone, clapboarded; height 56 ft.

light: D., 4th Order

Long Pilgrim
47°43'N., 69°45'W.
built 1862

tower: circular, brick on square dwelling; height 39 ft.

light: D., gas.

Maquereau Point
48°12'N., 64°46'W.
built 1874

tower: octagonal, wood, height 51 ft.

light: D., gas

Red Islet
48°04'N., 69°33'W.
built 1848

tower: stone, circular, painted grey, height 64 ft.

lantern: iron, circular, painted red

light: C., long focus

Stone Pillar
47°12'N., 70°22'W.
built 1843

tower: 52 ft.

lantern: polygonal

Similar to Red Islet lighthouse

Prescott Agency
Burlington Bay
43°18'N., 79°48'W.
built 1838

tower: circular, stone, height 79 ft., with slight taper; 4 landings and spiral stairs

lantern: cast-iron, polygonal; concrete platform
Removed from service in 1961

Deep River Islet
46°00'N., 77°16'W.
built 1873

tower: square, wood, height 27 ft.

light: D., 6th Order

Gibraltar Point
43°37'N., 79°23'W.
built 1808

tower: hexagonal, stone, present height 82 ft. (original 67 ft.) spiral staircase; door with rounded arch; central weight shaft

lantern: not the original (probably dates from 1870s or 1880s)
Informed at the location that the original height of the tower was 52 ft., extended in 1832 to 82 ft., differing slightly from figures culled from light lists

Knapp Point
44°14'N., 76°23'W.
built 1847

tower: square, wood, height 20 ft.

lantern: removed, replaced with buoy structure and rotating beacon

Morris Island
45°27'N., 76°16'W.
built 1873

tower: square, wood, height 29 ft.; one landing with straight stairs

lantern: hexagonal frame with conical roof; no glazing

Nine Mile Point
44°09'N., 76°33'W.
built 1833

tower: circular, stone, height 40 ft.; 4 landings and 5 straight runs of stairs, walls 2½ ft. to 3 ft. thick; structure unfortunately not in good condition due to deteriorating mortar

lantern: polygonal, iron, with external gallery

light: C., 3 parabolic reflectors of copper lined with quicksilver

Point Petre
44°50'N., 77°09'W.
built 1833

tower: circular, stone height 60 ft.

lantern: removed; light no longer in use; Point Petre and Nine Mile Point very similar in structure and design except that Point Petre was considerably higher

Port Dalhousie, back range
43°13'N., 79°16'W.
built 1852

tower: wood, octagonal, painted white

lantern: polygonal, red, platform same shape

River Thames, back range
42°19'N., 82°27'W.
built 1845

tower: circular, stone (coursed rubble), precarious condition

Scotch Bonnet
43°54'N., 77°33'W.
built 1855

tower: circular, stone, height 54 ft. (base to vane), slight taper
Taken out of service probably in 1959

Windmill Point
44°43'N., 75°29'W.
built prior to 1838; converted to lighthouse, 1873

tower: circular, stone, height 92 ft.

lantern: polygonal

light: D., 5th Order

Wolf Island
44°14'N., 76°11'W.
built 1861

tower: square, wood, height 33 ft.

lantern: removed, buoy structure in its place

Parry Sound Agency
Chantry Island
44°29'N., 81°24'W.
built 1859

tower: circular, stone, whitewashed, height 86 ft., slight taper

lantern: removed

Clapperton Island
46°03'N., 82°14'W.
built 1866

tower: wood, square, pronounced taper

lantern: platform square, lantern polygonal

light: D., 6th Order

Gereux Island
45°45'N., 80°40'W.
built 1870

tower: square, wood, sloping sides, attached dwelling; height 48 ft.

light: D., 4th Order
The dwelling is deteriorating and will most likely be pulled down in the near future

Goderich
43°45'N., 81°44'W.
built 1847

tower: stone, square, height 20 ft.; walls about 1½ ft. to 2 ft. thick, perpendicular; one landing

lantern: square lantern platform with slight overhang; pipe railing; polygonal lantern

light: D., electric

Gore Bay
45°57'N., 82°29'W.
built 1879

tower: square, wood, height 30 ft.; dwelling attached
This and the Strawberry Island lighthouse are of similar design

Griffith Island
44°51'N., 80°53'W.
built 1859

tower: circular, stone, slight taper, height 61 ft.; one of the so-called "imperial" series

light: D., 5th Order

Killarney East
45°58'N., 81°29'W.
built 1866

tower: wood, square, pronounced taper, height 20 ft.; half landing within

lantern: platform with pronounced overhang; polygonal lantern; pipe railing round exterior gallery
The west light is almost identical and built the same year

Kincardine
44°11'N., 81°39'W.
built 1881

tower: hexagonal, frame, sloping sides; 3 landings in tower with straight flights of stairs; attached 2-winged dwelling

lantern: polygonal

Lonely Island
45°34'N., 81°28'W.
built 1870

tower: wood, octagonal, height 54 ft.

Mississagi Strait
45°54'N., 83°13'W.

built 1873

tower : square, wood, slight taper, height 37 ft. ; attached dwelling

lantern : octagonal with square platform

No longer in use, with new tower built ; no plans (at time of writing) for disposal

Nottawasaga Island
44°32'N., 80°08'W.

built 1859

tower : circular, stone, height 82 ft. ; slight taper with walls 6 ft. to 7 ft. thick at base and 2 ft. at top, whitewashed ; stone thought to be limestone or granite (local legend states brought out from Scotland in ballast) ; 6 landings and straight flights of stairs ; weight shaft on inner wall and weights still stored in light room ; windows at each landing

lantern : polygonal, iron, presently using an AGA acetylene beacon controlled by AGA sun switch. Photo taken on lantern platform or outer gallery ; railing may be original

Point Clark
44°04'N., 81°46'W.

built 1859

tower : circular, stone, (stone reported from Inverhuron & Kingston) ; whitewashed

height 87 ft. ; walls about 7 ft. thick at base

light : D., 4th Order

Pointe aux Pins (Main Light)
46°28'N., 84°28'W.

built 1873

tower : square, wood, height 23 ft.

light : D., 4th Order

Quebec Harbour
47°43'N., 85°48'W.

built 1872

structure : house with light in dormer window

Several similar structures on Lake Superior

Southampton Harbour
44°28'N., 81°24'W.

built 1877

tower : square, wood, pronounced taper, height 28 ft.

lantern : square

Victoria Agency
Entrance Island (Nanaimo)
49°13'N., 123°48'W.

built 1876

structure : square frame house, painted white, red roof

lantern : square lantern platform with railed external gallery and polygonal lantern mounted centre of roof ; height 44 ft.

light : C., electric
(Photo answers this description, but at time of writing not sure that it is indeed the Entrance Island lighthouse. Intended demolition in near future)

Fisgard
48°26'N., 123°27'W.

built 1860

tower : circular, brick, height 56 ft. ; red brick house attached
Custody of the crown but, still in service as a navigational aid

Race Rocks
48°18'N., 123°32'W.

built 1860

tower : circular, stone, black & white bands, height 105 ft. ; dwelling attached ; minor repairs top of tower

light : C., long focus
Dwelling may be pulled down

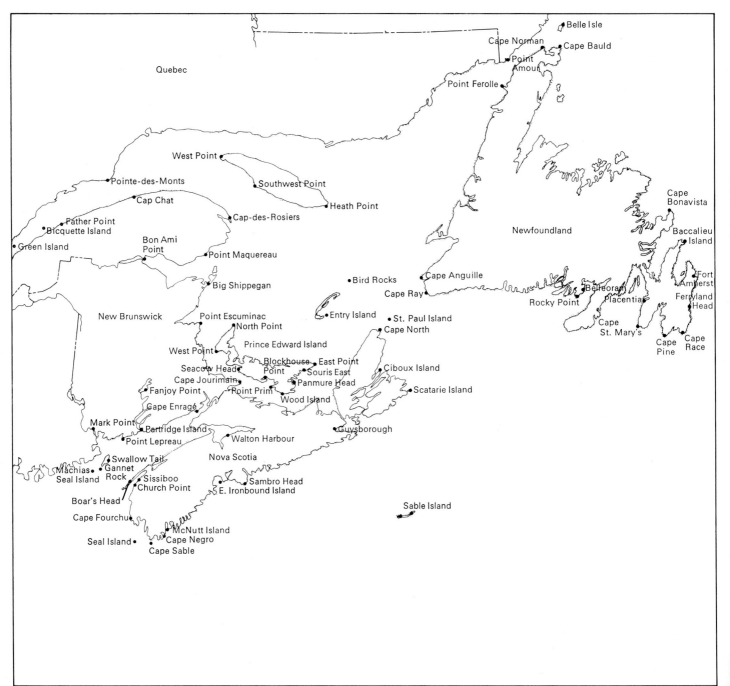

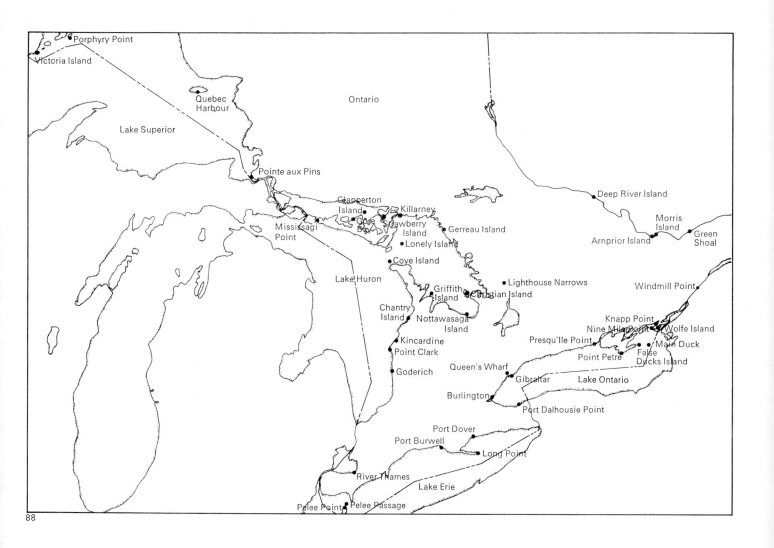

Porphyry Point

Victoria Island

Quebec Harbour

Ontario

Lake Superior

Pointe aux Pins

Deep River Island

Clapperton Island

Killarney

Morris Island

Gore Bay

Strawberry Island

Gerreau Island

Green Shoal

Mississagi Point

Arnprior Island

Lonely Island

Cove Island

Lake Huron

Griffith Island

Lighthouse Narrows

Christian Island

Windmill Point

Chantry Island

Nottawasaga Island

Knapp Point

Nine Mile Point

Wolfe Island

Presqu'Ile Point

Kincardine

Main Duck

Point Clark

Point Petre

False Ducks Island

Goderich

Queen's Wharf

Gibraltar

Lake Ontario

Burlington

Port Dalhousie Point

Port Dover

Port Burwell

Long Point

River Thames

Lake Erie

Pelee Point

Pelee Passage

88

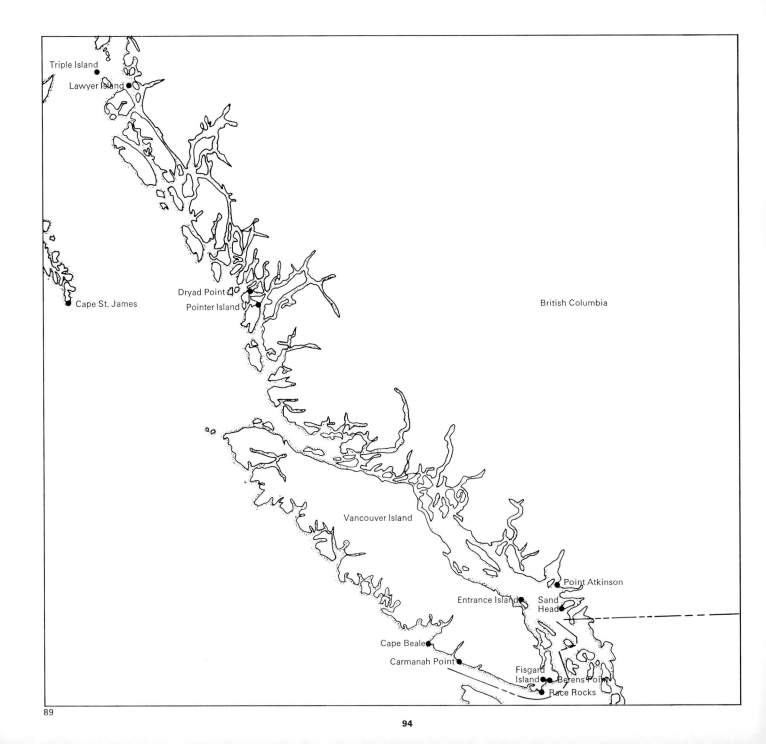

89

Introduction

1 Encyclopaedia Britannica, 14th ed., (1929), Vol. 22, pp. 480-1, "Trinity House."

Lighthouse Structures

1 Ibid., (1960), Vol. 14, p. 85.
2 U.S. Coast Guard, The Significance of Aids to Marine Navigation (Washington: U.S. Government Printing Office, 1943), p. 7.
3 Canada. Public Archives (hereafter cited as PAC), MG11, Nova Scotia A, Vol. A.133, pp. 211, 213, Capt. Jones Fawson to Sir John Wentworth, Halifax, 18 Oct. 1801.
4 PAC, MG11, Q Series, Vol. Q.218, p. 33, Francis Beaufort report, 29 July 1832.
5 Encyclopaedia Britannica, (1960), Vol. 14, pp. 85-6, "Lighthouses."
6 Ibid., p. 87.
7 PAC, MG11, Nova Scotia A, Vol. 187-1, pp. 265-7, Campbell to Glenelg, Halifax, 23 March 1838.
8 PAC, MG9, A1, Vol. 44, pp. 372-3, I. Woodward to Provincial Secretary, Saint John, 7 Oct. 1851.
9 Newfoundland. House of Assembly, Journals, 1856, App. 82, despatch, 26 Sept. 1855.
10 PAC, MG11, CO194, Vol. 150, pp. 37-8, Report of Robert Oke, Inspector of Lighthouses, St. John's, 22 Dec. 1856 (hereafter cited as Robert Oke).
11 PAC, RG11, Series III, subject 227, Vol. 82, file 78040, G. F. Baillarge, 11 Dec. 1865.
12 PAC, MG11, CO194, Vol. 151, p. 103, Bannerman to Labouchère, 22 Dec. 1857.
13 Newfoundland. House of Assembly, Journals, 1879 App., p. 589, Report of the Inspector of Lighthouses and Public Buildings, 1878, St. John's, 1 Jan. 1879.
14 PAC, RG11, Series III, subject 227, Vol. 82, file 45797, pp. 43-5, John Page Report, 28 Feb. 1860.
15 Ibid., file 78040, pp. 453-4.
16 Ibid., subject 303, file 7446.
17 Great Britain. Admiralty Hydrographic Office, List of the Lights on the Coasts and Lakes of British North America Corrected to January 1864 (London: Eyre & Spottiswoode, 1864).
18 Canada. Department of Public Works, Report of the Commissioner of Public Works for the Year Ending 30 June 1867 (Ottawa: Hunter Rose, 1868), App. 10, "Tabular Statement of the Light Houses in Canada."
19 PAC, RG42, file 20995C, p. 80, 184.
20 Canada. Parliament, Sessional Papers, 1904, No. 21, p. 48.
21 Ibid., 1919, No. 21, pp. 31-5, Report of Chief Engineer.
22 PAC, RG42, Marine Records, file 20395R.
23 Canada. Parliament, Sessional Papers, 1906-07, No. 21, App. 2, Report of the Commissioner of Lights, p. 58.
24 Canada. Department of Transport, Annual Report, 1952-53, p. 62.
25 Ibid., 1954-55, p. 67.

Apparatus: Lights and Optics

1 D. Alan Stevenson, The World's Lighthouses Before 1820 (London: Oxford Univ. Press, 1959), p. 63.
2 John P. Bowen, British Lighthouses (London: Longmans Green, 1947), pp. 17-19.
3 D. Alan Stevenson, op. cit., p. 46.
4 Ibid., p. 77.
5 PAC, MG9, A1, Vol. 44, pp. 252-3, Report, Capt. W. F. W. Owen, R.N., to lieutenant governor, 29 May 1846.
6 Henry J. Powell, Glass-making in England (Cambridge: Cambridge Univ. Press, 1923), pp. 108-10.

7 PAC, RG11, Series III, Vol. 82, subject 227, file 45797, p. 49, John Page Report to Commissioner of Public Works, 28 Feb. 1860.
8 Ibid., Vol. 80, file 50974, enclosing Tariff of Dioptric or Lenticular Apparatus for Lighthouses, p. 2.
9 Ibid., pp. 1-2.
10 PAC, RG11, Series III, Vol. 82, subject 225, Vol. 79, file 3354, "List of Various Appurtenances supplied by Chance Bros. & Co.," pp. 240-1.

Dioptric Apparatus

	Internal Diameter	
First Order	72½ in.	sea light
Second Order	55	" "
Third Order	39⅜	" " "
Fourth Order	19⅝	harb. light
Fifth Order	14½	" "
Sixth Order	11¾	" "

11 PAC, RG11, Series III, Vol. 82, subject 227, file 45797, Page Report to the Commissioner of Public Works, 28 Feb. 1860, p. 51.
12 Encyclopedia Canadiana, centennial ed., Vol 4, p. 362, "Gesner, Abraham."
13 PAC, RG11, Series III, Vol. 80, subject 225, file 50497 of 1860, 21 Nov. 1860.
14 Ibid., file 56626.
15 Ibid., Vol. 82, subject 227, file 63053, pp. 342-3, John Page Report, 9 Feb. 1863.
16 John P. Bowen, op. cit.
17 PAC, RG42, file 29156, pt. 1, p. 237.
18 PAC, RG2, 1, Orders in Council, Vol. 1011, docket 1447, P.C. 1295, 5 July 1906, p. 13.
19 Canada. Parliament, Sessional Papers, 1910, No. 21, App. 2, Report of the Commissioner of Lights, p. 74.
20 Ibid., 1903, No. 21, Report of the Chief Engineer, p. 45.
21 Ibid., 1904, No. 21, Report of the Deputy Minister, pp. 32-3.
22 Ibid., 1906-07, No. 21, Report of the Commissioner of Lights. App. 2, pp. 57-8.
23 Thomas Corwin, Report on the Trade and Commerce of the British North American Colonies with the United States and Other Countries (Washington: Printers to the Senate, 1851), p. 100.
24 PAC, RG11, Series III, Vol. 80, file 50974, enclosing Tariff of Dioptric and Lenticular Apparatus for Lighthouses, p. 8.
25 Encyclopaedia Britannica, 1960 ed., Vol. 14, "Lighthouses."
26 Canada. Parliament, Sessional Papers, 1903, No. 21, Report of the Chief Engineer, pp. 59-60.
27 Ibid., 1916, No. 21, App. 2, Report of the Commissioner of Lights, p. 65.
28 Canada. Department of Marine and Fisheries, Annual Report, 1930-31 (Ottawa: King's Printer, 1931), p. 31, Report of the Deputy Minister.
29 Canada. Department of Transport, Annual Report, 1947-48 (Ottawa: King's Printer, 1949), p. 10.
30 Ibid., 1950-51, p. 58.
31 Ibid., 1962-63, p. 27.
32 Ibid., 1954-55, p. 68.
33 Ibid., 1952-53, p. 63.
34 Ibid., 1960-61, p. 24.
35 PAC, RG11, Series III, subject 227, Vol. 82, file 54777, James Keefer to Joseph Cauchon, Quebec, 30 Aug. 1861.
36 Canada. Parliament, Sessional Papers, 1900, No. 11, p. 48, Report of the Chief Engineer.

37 Encyclopaedia Britannica, 11th ed., Vol. 16, p. 647, "Lighthouses."
38 PAC, RG42, file 28261, pp. 17-18, Chief Engineer, 30 Dec. 1910.
39 Canada. Department of Transport, Annual Report, 1966-67, pp. 35-6.
40 Canada. Parliament, Sessional Papers, 1905, No. 21, App. 2, Report of the Commissioner of Lights, pp. 64-5.
41 Ibid., pp. 69-70.
42 Ibid., 1916, No. 21, App. 3, p. 101, Report of the Superintendent, St. Lawrence Ship Channel, 28 July 1915.
43 PAC, RG2, 1, Orders in Council, Vol. 1712, docket 743, p. 1, P.C. 1048, 12 June 1923.
44 PAC, RG42, file 1-0-8-A; United States. Department of Commerce, Lighthouse Service Bulletin (Washington, 1927).
45 Ibid., Marine Records, file 600-0-33, Liverpool Journal of Commerce, 13 July 1929, p. 34.
46 Canada. Department of Marine and Fisheries, Annual Report, 1929-30 (Ottawa: King's Printer, 1930), Report of the Deputy Minister, p. 155.
47 PAC, RG42, Marine Records, file 600-9-33, Liverpool Journal of Commerce, pt. 1.

Administration

1 Lower Canada, Statutes, 45 Geo. III, cap. 12.
2 PAC, MG11, Q series, Vol. Q.117-2, pp. 237-8.
3 2 Will. IV, cap. 24; PAC, MG11, CO42, Vol. 238, p. 232.
4 PAC, MG11, CO 217, Vol. 143, p. 109, (fol. 241), Wallace to Bathurst, Halifax, 14 Sept. 1824.
5 PAC, MG11, Q series, Vol. Q.218, p. 27, Beaufort Report, 29 July 1834.
6 PAC, MG11, CO 188, Vol. 45, pp. 13-15, James A. Hanshaw to Campbell, Saint Andrews, 15 Nov. 1832.
7 Ibid., Vol. 69, p. 133, lighthouse commissioners to Provincial Secretary, Saint John, 24 Aug. 1840.
8 PAC, MG9, A1, Vol. 44, pp. 280; Vol. 45, pp. 423-4.
9 PAC, MG11, CO 188, Vol. 99, pp. 135-6.
10 PAC, MG9, A1, Vol. 44, p. 245, Report of the Secretary of the lighthouse commissioners, 18 Feb. 1846.
11 Ibid., pp. 339-40, New Brunswick Commissioners to Nova Scotia Commissioners, Saint John, 15 Jan. 1848.
12 Ibid., pp. 204-6, Saint John Lighthouse Commissioners to Lieut. Gov., 21 June 1843.
13 18 & 19 Vic. Cap. 7; ibid., Vol. 147, pp. 54-55, Darling to Labouchère, St. John's, 8 Jan. 1856.
14 PAC, RG7, G1, Vol. 93, pp. 321-322, letter, Capt. Sandom of Niagara to Charles Wood, 18 June 1839.
15 PAC, RG1, E3, Vol. 102, pp. 210-12, J. W. Macaulay to S. B. Harrison, 2 Aug. 1839.
16 PAC, MG11, Q Series, Vol. Q.431A-3, p. 516.
17 PAC, RG11, Public Works, Series II, Vol. 34, No. 187.
18 Ibid., Vol. 23, file 6642, J. McIntyre to S. Keefer, Windsor, 31 March 1845.
19 Ibid., Vol. 29, file 8836.
20 Ibid., pp. 14-15.
21 Ibid.

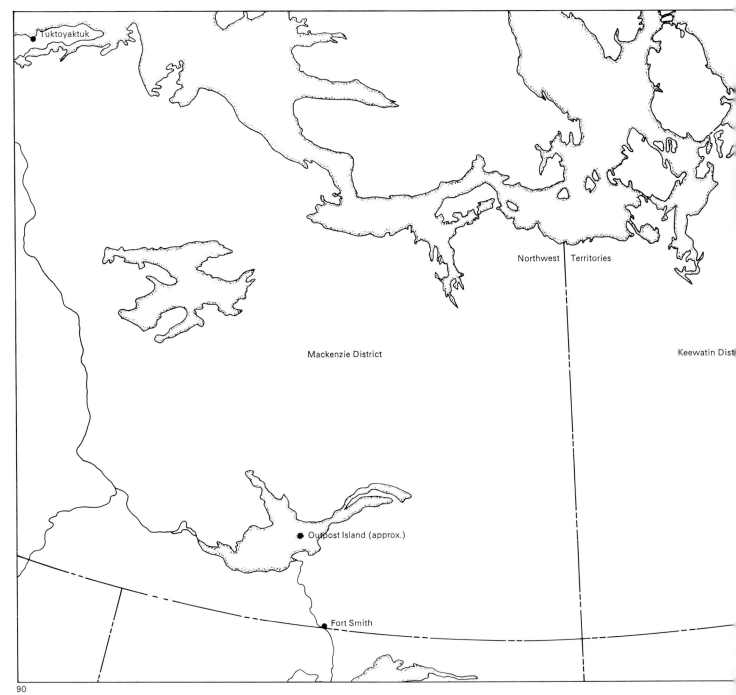

Tuktoyaktuk

Northwest Territories

Mackenzie District

Keewatin Dist

Outpost Island (approx.)

Fort Smith

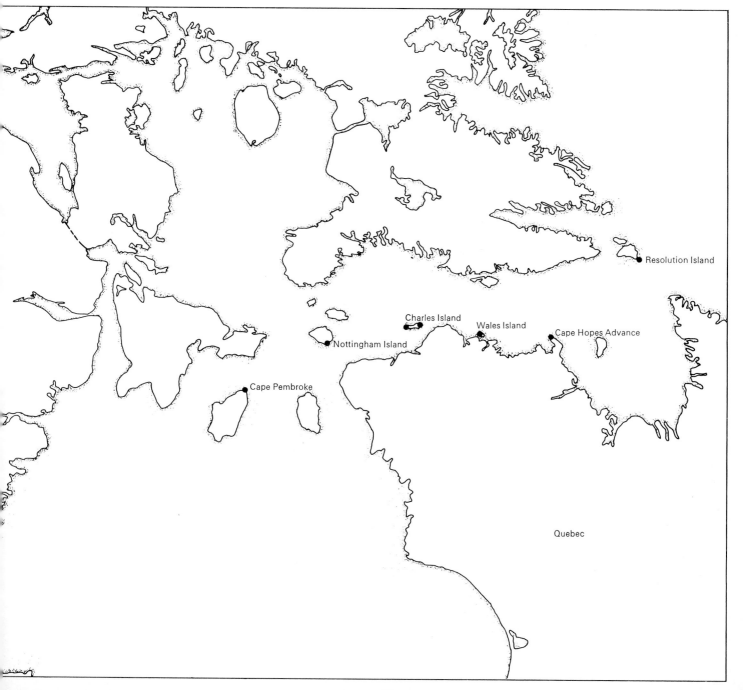

Resolution Island

Charles Island

Wales Island

Cape Hopes Advance

Nottingham Island

Cape Pembroke

Quebec

22 Canada. Parliament, *Sessional Papers, 1874*, No. 4, pp. 7-8.
23 Canada. Department of Public Works, op. cit., p. 98.
24 Canada. Parliament, *Sessional Papers, 1873*, No. 8, p. 29.
25 Ibid., App. 37, p. 361.
26 PAC, RG11, Series III, subject 227, Vol. 82, file 9728, encl. P.C. of 28 Feb. 1870.
27 Canada. Parliament, *Sessional Papers, 1873*, No. 8, pp. 28-9.
28 Ibid., *1877*, No. 5, Report of the Minister, p. x.
29 57-58 Vic. cap. 41 ; PAC, RG2, 1, Orders in Council, Vol. 949, docket 881, P.C. 349, p. 4, 26 Feb. 1904.
30 Ibid., Vol. 1158, docket 215, P.C. 88, 20 Jan. 1911.
31 PAC, RG2, 1, Orders in Council, Vol. 1085, docket 1976, P.C. 2122a, Schedule of Classification of Lights and Fog Alarm Stations.
32 Ibid.
33 Ibid.
34 Canada. Parliament, *Sessional Papers, 1916*, No. 21, p. 4, Report of Deputy Minister.
35 PAC, RG2, 1, Orders in Council, Vol. 1519, docket 2193, P.C. 2682.
36 Canada. Department of Transport, *Annual Report, 1936-37* (Ottawa : King's Printer, 1937), p. 78.
37 Ibid., p. 97.

Lighthouses along the Atlantic Coast

1 U.S. Coast Guard, *Historically Famous Lighthouses* (Washington : U.S. Government Printing Office, 1957), p. 33.
2 PAC, MG1, C¹¹B, Vol. 9, fol. 27, despatch, 24 Nov. 1727 ; PAC, MG1, 2B, Vol. 53-3, fol. 603 (transcript pp. 590-1), despatch, 22 May 1729.
3 PAC, MG1, C¹¹B, Vol. 24, fol. 316 (transcript pp. 251-2), despatch, 26 June 1732.
4 PAC, MG1, C¹¹B, Vol. 15, fol. 68, pp. 146-7, St. Ovide de Brouillan to Minister, Louisbourg, 21 Oct. 1734.
5 Ibid., Vol. 18, fol. 89, pp. 94-6, Lenormant to Minister, Louisbourg, 10 Nov. 1736.
6 Ibid., fol. 149, Lenormant to Minister, Louisbourg, 27 Dec. 1736.
7 Ibid., Vol. 20, fol. 115, pp. 88-9, Lenormant to Minister, Louisbourg, 15 Oct. 1738.
8 PAC, MG1, C¹¹C, Vol. 15-2, fol. 259.
9 Ibid., C¹¹B, Vol. 24, fol. 155, (transcript p. 171), Bigot to Minister, 1 Oct. 1740.
10 PAC, MG1, C¹¹C, Vol. 15-2, fol. 259.
11 Ibid., Vol. 16-2, p. 271, despatch from Prévost, Louisbourg, 10 June 1758.
12 Will R. Bird, op. cit., pp. 94-96.
13 PAC, MG11, Nova Scotia A, Vol. A.63, p. 33, Lawrence to C.O., Halifax, 20 April 1759.
14 Ibid., Vol. A.87, pp. 114-5 (Col. Cor. N.S. Vol. 6, fol. 61), Campbell to C.O., Halifax, 28 Sept. 1771.
15 PAC, MG11, CO 220, Vol. 11, p. 85.
16 PAC, MG11, Nova Scotia A, Vol. A.87, p. 81 (Col. Cor. N.S. Vol. 6, p. 32), Admiralty to Hillsborough, London, 20 June 1771.
17 Ibid., pp. 114-5, (Col. Cor. N. S., Vol. 6, fol. 61), Campbell to C.O., Halifax, 28 Sept. 1771.
18 Ibid., pp. 147-8, (Col. Cor. N.S., Vol. 6, p. 68), Campbell to C.O., Halifax, 16 Oct. 1771.
19 PAC, MG11, CO 220, Vol. 11, p. 156, Journals and Votes of the House of Assembly for the Province of Nova Scotia, 13 Oct. 1774.
20 PAC, RG42, file 51, 203.
21 PAC, MG11, Nova Scotia A, Vol. A.117, pp. 245-6, (Col. Cor. N.S., Vol. 21, p. 469), Wentworth to Dundas, 18 July 1792.
22 Will R. Bird, op. cit., pp. 93-4.
23 PAC, MG9, A1, Vol. 44, pp. 373 & 375.
24 Thomas Corwin, op. cit., pp. 106-7.
25 PAC, MG9, A1, Vol. 44, pp. 252-4, Report, Capt. W. F. W. Owen, R.N., to the Lieut. Gov., 29 May 1846.
26 PAC, MG11, Nova Scotia A, Vol. A.177-1, pp. 317-8.
27 Ibid., Vol. A.178-1, p. 257 (CO 217, Vol. 156-1, p. 257).
28 Ibid., Vol. A.179, p. 43, J. Bainbridge to Hay, 18 June 1834 (CO 217, Vol. 157, p. 43).
29 PAC, RG7, G14, Vol. 33, first file, Board of Trinity House Report, 28 March 1817.
30 PAC, MG11, Q Series, Vol. Q.176-1, pp. 44-45, Dalhousie to Bathurst, 24 March 1826.
31 Ibid., Vol. Q.191-1, p. 168, 19 June 1829.
32 Canada. *Legislative Assembly Journals, Lower Canada*, Vol. 39, p. 342, 17 March 1830.
33 Ibid., *1841*, App. A.
34 PAC, MG11, Nova Scotia A, Vol. 184, p. 109.
35 PAC, MG11, Q Series, Vol. Q.229-1, pp. 50-53.
36 PAC, MG11, CO 226, Vol. 51, Prince Edward Island A, Vol. 51, p. 525.
37 PAC, RG4, A1, S, Vol. 384, p. 67.
38 PAC, MG11, Nova Scotia A, Vol. 181, pp. 199-203.
39 PAC, RG7, G7, Vol. 11, Statement of Expenditure by the Commissioners of Light Houses, Nova Scotia, for the Support of the Light Houses and Humane Establishments on the islands of St. Paul and Scatarie for the year 1847.
40 Canada. Parliament, *Sessional Papers, 1875*, No. 5, App. No. 4, p. 125.
41 Ibid., *1889*, No. 7, p. 13, Report of the Deputy Minister.
42 PAC, RG42, B1, Vol. 1, file 21026C, p. 59, memorandum 18 Jan. 1916.
43 Ibid., p. 16.
44 PAC, MG11, Q Series, Vol. 177-1, p. 309, Jeffery to Stanley, Halifax, 23 Sept. 1833 (CO 217, Vol. 155-1, p. 309).
45 Ibid., Vol. 178-1, p. 259, address, Nova Scotia House of Assembly, 4 April 1834 (CO 217, Vol. 156-1, p. 259).
46 PAC, MG11, Nova Scotia A, Vol. A.193, p. 629 (CO 217, Vol. 171-2, p. 629), Lighthouse Commissioners to Provincial Secretary, Halifax, 21 Dec. 1839.
47 PAC, MG8, A18, vol. 2-1, fol. 67, 5 July 1811.
48 Robert Oke, op. cit.
49 PAC, MG11, CO 194, Vol. 98, pp. 199-200, Prescott to Glenelg, St. John's, 27 Nov. 1837.
50 D. Allan Stevenson, op. cit., p. 295.
51 PAC, RG11, Public Works, Series III, subject 227, Vol. 82, file 78,088, Report of the Board of Works for the year 1864.
52 Robert Oke, op. cit.
53 PAC, MG11, CO 194, Vol. 117, p. 305.
54 PAC, MG11, CO 194, Vol. III, pp. 181-2.
55 PAC, RG4, C1, P.S.O. Corresp., Vol. 78, No. 706 of 1843, Report of Executive Council, Kingston, 14-20 Dec. 1843.
56 PAC, MG11, CO 194, Vol. 132, p. 252.
57 Robert Oke, op. cit., pp. 13-13a.
58 Newfoundland, *Journals of the House of Assembly, 1851*, App., p. 138.
59 PAC, MG11, Nova Scotia A, Vol. 189, pp. 271-3, (alt. ref. CO 217, Vol. 167-1).
60 Robert Oke, op. cit.
61 PAC, MG11, CO 194, Vol. 148, pp. 402-3, 559.
62 Ibid., Vol. 150, p. 56.
63 PAC, RG7, Series G2, Vol. 6, Office of Committee of Privy Council for Trade, Whitehall, 22 Aug. 1857.
64 PAC, MG11, CO 42, Vol. 628, pp. 121-2, despatch, Monck to Newcastle, Quebec, 26 Nov. 1861.
65 PAC, MG11, CO 194, pp. 229-30, Report, Robert Oke, St. John's, Dec. 1863.
66 PAC, MG9, A1, Vol. 44, pp. 378-83.
67 PAC, MG11, CO 194, Vol. 172, pp. 189-90.
68 Ibid., Vol. 174, pp. 9-11.
69 Ibid., Vol. 173, pp. 237-9.
70 49 Vic. cap. 20 ; PAC, RG2, 2, Vol. 186, docket 1157, p. 10 (P.C. 1293).
71 Department of Transport records, file 7952-821, data sheet dated 11 March 1968.
72 *Sixtieth Annual Report, Department of Marine and Fisheries, 1926-27* (Ottawa : Queen's Printer), Report of the Deputy Minister, p. 67, 21.
73 Newfoundland. House of Assembly, *Journal*, 1860, Appendix, p. 245.
74 PAC, RG11, Public Works, Series III, subject 227, Vol. 82, file 4337, pp. 648-51.

The Gulf, Northumberland Strait and the Lower St. Lawrence

1 PAC, RG11, Series III, subject 227, Vol. 82, file 9,171.
2 Canada. *Journals of the Legislative Assembly, 1855*, App. JJJ, Return to an Address from the Legislative Assembly, 29 March 1855.
3 PAC, MG11, CO 43, Vol. 613, p. 78.
4 Canada. Parliament, *Sessional Papers, 1906*, No. 21, App. 1, Report Department of Marine & Fisheries, 1905.
5 PAC, MG11, CO 42, Vol. 613, p. 78.
6 PAC, RG42, Marine Records, file 7956 — F 1, Vol. 1.
7 Ibid., file 3-0-6 Pt. I, p. 94.
8 PAC, RG11, Series III, subject 294, Vol. 86, file 53,465, John Page Report, 6 May 1861.
9 Ibid., subject 227, Vol. 82, file 45,797, pp. 20-5, John Page Report, 28 Feb. 1860.
10 Ibid., file 9,342, p. 709, Report, Gourdeau Bros., 1 Feb. 1870.
11 Ibid., file 9,346, Deputy Minister's Report, Ottawa, 2 Feb. 1870.
12 PAC, MG11, Q Series, Vol. Q.180, pp. 16-18.
13 Canada. *Legislative Assembly, Journals, Lower Canada, 1828*, Vol. 38, p. 199.
14 PAC, RG7, G7, Vol. 11, pp. 125-127.
15 Ibid., pp. 138-9.
16 Ibid., pp. 143-4.
17 Canada. *Legislative Assembly Journals, Lower Canada*, Vol. 41-2, App. M. Statement of Monies Appropriated by Legislature for Roads and Other Local Objects from 1828-31 inclusive.
18 Ibid., Vol. 38, pp. 453, 7 Feb. 1829.
19 Ibid., Vol. 36, pp. 98-100.

20 W. A. Callandine, "Lighthouses Along the St. Lawrence." Unpubl. MS., p. 3.
21 Canada. *Legislative Assembly, Journals, Lower Canada.* Vol. 36, p. 101.
22 Ibid.
23 Ibid., Vol. 40, Lower, p. 113.
24 Ibid., Vol. 39, p. 280.
25 Ibid., Vol. 40, pp. 118-119, 18 Jan. 1831 ; Ibid., p. 117, 7 Jan. 1831 ; Ibid., p. 115, 5 Oct. 1830 ; Thomas Corwin, op. cit., p. 100.
26 Thomas Corwin, op. cit., p. 106.
27 Canada. Department of Transport, *List of the Lights, Buoys and Fog Signals, Atlantic Coast . . .* (Ottawa : Queen's Printer, 1970), p. 143.
28 Canada. *Journals of the Legislative Assembly of the Province of Canada,* App. JJJ.
29 Ibid.
30 Ibid.
31 Raoul Lachance to Capt. G. E. Gaudreau. This item is merely a note shown the author by another researcher, found in one of his files, originating with the Department of Transport or its precursor, the Department of Marine. The Department of Transport *List of Lights and Fog Signals* does not record a date earlier than 1859 for the first installation at Father Point, some 10 miles downstream from Rimouski.
32 PAC, RG11, Public Works Records, Series III, subject 285, file 85,289. Additional information beyond burning of the first lighthouse and estimates for its replacement received from the Quebec agency by telephone.
33 PAC, MG11, Q Series, Vol. Q.37, pp. 198-9, 206.
34 PAC, RG1, E1, Book E, Pt. III, fol. 297.
35 PAC, MG8, A18, Vol. 1-1, fol. 204-5, 25 Nov. 1806.
36 Ibid., Vol. 1-2, fol. 532-3, Report I. Painter, Deputy Master, Trinity House, 20 Sept. 1810.
37 Ibid., Vol. 1-1, fol. 270, 18 April 1808.
38 Ibid., Vol. 1-2, fol. 401, 19 Sept. 1809.
39 Ibid., Vol. 2-1, fol. 116, 20 Dec. 1811.
40 Canada. Department of Transport, *List of the Lights, Buoys and Fog Signals, Atlantic Coast,* 1969, pp. 195, 208.
41 Canada. *Legislative Assembly, Journals, Lower Canada.* Vol. 38, pp. 98-9.
42 PAC, MG11, Q Series, Vol. Q.249-2, p. 340.
43 Ibid., Vol. Q.258, pp. 59-60.
44 Ibid., Vol. Q.218, p. 28, Beaufort Report to Admiralty, 29 July 1834.

The Great Lakes Region and the Upper St. Lawrence

1 Ontario. Department of Public Records and Archives, *Sixth Report of the Bureau of Archives for the Provinces of Ontario 1909* (Toronto, 1911), p. 409.
2 Act 3rd, Will. IV, cap. 35 ; PAC, RG1, E3, Vol. 102, pp. 186-7, Report of the Inspector General, Toronto, 31 July 1839.
3 PAC, RG1, E1, State Book C, Upper Canada, fol. 350-1.
4 PAC, RG5, A1, Vol. 3, pp. 1070-1.
5 PAC, RG8, C Series, Vol. C923, pp. 42-3.

6 Material required for the project was the following :

250 feet pine quartering		4 x 4
30 " "		9 x 5
50 " oak		10 x 12 in four equal lengths
40 " "		8 x 8
20 " "		10 x 12 in two equal lengths
30 " "		9 x 4
750 " two inch pine plank		
30 " Oak		14 x 8
one large pair of hook and strap hinges		
50 feet of inch boards		
100 " pine		9 x 3 in four equal lengths
scaffold poles 12		40 feet long
150 feet of rope 1½ inch diameter		
candles 6 pounds		
24 . . . of stone		
304 bushels of lime		
72 panes of glass 12 x 10		
50 days of a team		

(PAC, RG1, E3, Vol. 69, p. 41)
7 PAC, RG5, A1, Vol. 7 pp. 3041-2, Gore to Allan, York, 1 May 1808.
8 John R. Stevens, "Lighthouses on the Great Lakes, National Historic Sites Service, (1965), (hereafter cited as *Report*), pp. 195-6.
9 PAC, RG1, E1, State Book G, Vol. 51, fol. 229-30.
10 PAC, RG5, A1, Vol. 30, p. 14206, Sherbrooke to Gore, Quebec, 31 Dec. 1816.
11 Canada. *Journals of the House of Assembly of Upper Canada, 1832-3,* p. 209, Report of a Select Committee on Lighthouses, Jan. 1833.
12 PAC, RG5, A1, Vol. 89, pp. 48977-8, J. W. Macaulay to G. Gillier, Kingston, 12 May 1828.
13 Ibid., p. 49327.
14 PAC, RG42, Marine Records, file 21754R, pp. 236-7, memorandum of district engineer, Ottawa, 27 May 1924.
15 PAC, RG1, E3, Vol. 102, pp. 182-3, J. W. Macaulay 31 July 1938.
16 John R. Stevens, *Report*, pp. 185-6.
17 Canada. *Journals of the House of Assembly of Upper Canada, 1832-3,* App., p. 215, Report of the Commissioners, Kingston, 16 Nov. 1832.
18 Ibid., App., p. 216, Report of Commissioners for erecting a Light House on Point Peters.
19 John R. Stevens, *Report*, pp. 189-90.
20 Thomas Corwin, op. cit., p. 104.
21 John R. Stevens, *Report*, pp. 199-201.
22 Ibid., p. 205.
23 Ibid., p. 203.
24 PAC, RG7, G2, Vol. 1, enclosure No. 19.
25 J. A. Bannister, *Lighthouses of Long Point* (London : Ont.) : Univ. of Western Ontario, 1944), first printed in *Simcoe Reformer,* 9 July 1942.
26 PAC, RG1, E3, Vol. 102, pp. 188-9.
27 J. A. Bannister, op. cit.
28 Ibid.
29 Thomas Corwin, op. cit., p. 105.
30 PAC, RG1, E3, p. 195.

31 PAC, RG11, Public Works Records, Series II, Vol. 29, file 8836, J. McIntyre, Report on Lighthouses for 1845 to the Board of Works, 21 Nov. 1845.
32 Ibid., pp. 11-13.
33 Ibid., Series III, Vol. 84, subject 265, file 56,151.
34 Canada. Parliament, *Sessional Papers, 1903,* No. 21, Report of the chief engineer, p. 59.
35 John R. Stevens, *Report*, p. 213.
36 Ibid., p. 216.
37 Peter J. Stokes, National Historic Sites Service, Peter J. Stokes Report, pp. 255-6.
38 John R. Stevens, *Report*, pp. 218-9.
39 PAC, MG11, CO 42, Vol. 648, Admiralty List of Lights, 1864.
40 PAC, *Public Works,* Series III, Vol. 87, subject 302, file 560.
41 Canada. Department of Transport, *List of Lights and Fog Signals Inland Waters, 1965* (Ottawa : Queen's Printer, 1965), p. 90.
42 PAC, MG11, CO 42, Vol. 648, p. 83, Admiralty List of Lights 1864.
43 Canada. Department of Transport, *List of Lights and Fog Signals Inland Waters, 1965,* p. 102.
44 PAC, RG7, G14, Vol. 60, "Information upon the various statements called for by the memorandum of His Excellency the Governor General, No. 2, Additional Light Houses since 1 January 1855 completed."
45 John R. Stevens, *Report*, p. 176.
46 Canada. Parliament, *Sessional Papers, 1874,* No. 4, pp. 111.

The Pacific Coast

1 Canada. Parliament, *Sessional Papers, 1873,* No. 8, p. 28.
2 Ibid., *1874,* No. 4, App. No. 9, p. 90.
3 Ibid., *1873,* No. 8, p. 28.
4 Ibid., *1879,* No. 3, App. No. 5, p. 127.
5 Ibid., *1873,* No. 8, App. No. 7, p. 91.
6 Ibid., *1877,* No. 5, Annual Report, Department of Marine, p. xxiv.
7 Ibid., *1877,* No. 5, p. xxiv.
8 Ibid., *1875,* No. 5, p. xxiii.
9 Ibid., *1878,* No. 1, App. No. 6, p. 238.
10 Ibid., *1875,* No 5, App. No. 6, pp. 163-4.
11 Ibid., *1885,* No. 9, p. xxxi.
12 Ibid., *1891,* No. 7, pp. 24-25.
13 Ibid., *1892,* No. 10, p. 42.
14 Ibid., *1900,* No. 11, pp. 63-4.
15 PAC, RG42, Marine Records, file 22317K, Part II, letter at end of file, John H. Walsh to Secretary Civil Service Commission, 30 April 1926.
16 Ibid., file 22316L, pp. 209-16, 5 Nov. 1925.
17 Ibid., file 22316L, pp. 69-70.
18 PAC, RG42, B1, Vol. 6, file 22389C, P.C. 537, 19 March 1913.
19 Ibid., Notice to Mariners, No. 16, 2 Feb. 1914.
20 Ibid., file 22386.2C, Part 3, p. 233, J. H. Hildritch to marine agent, Prince Rupert, 25 Jan. 1921.
21 Ibid.
22 Ibid., p. 194, Notice to Mariners No. 80, 1920.
23 Ibid., file 15796, p. 108, 3 Dec. 1904.

Sub-Arctic Waters: Hudson Strait and Hudson Bay
1 Canada. Parliament, *Sessional Papers, 1916*, No. 21, App. 1, Report of the chief engineer, pp. 37-8.
2 PAC, RG42, Marine Records, file 1-8-0, Pt. I, memorandum 28, Jan. 1928.
3 Ibid., Pt. II, p. 355.
4 Ibid., Pt. II, p. 396, memorandum, chief engineer, 13 Dec. 1929.
5 Ibid., p. 394.
6 Ibid., Pt. III, p. 93, *Notice to Mariners No. 42 of 1932*.
7 Canada. Department of Marine, *Annual Report 1932-3*, p. 80.

Selected Inland Waterways
1 PAC, RG11, Public Works Records, Series III, Vol. 86, subject 287-8, file 45, 652, John G. Sippell to Public Works, Montreal, 2 March 1860.
2 Ibid.
3 Canada. Department of Transport, *List of Lights and Fog Signals Inland Waters, 1970*, pp. 130.
4 Ibid., *1969*, p. 130.
5 PAC, RG42 Marine Records, file 22243K, p. 15, chief engineer to fishery officer, 3 Oct. 1898.
6 Canada. Department of Transport, *Annual Report for year ended 31 March 1957* (Ottawa: Queen's Printer, 1957), p. 14.
7 Canada. Department of Transport, *List of Lights and Fog Signals Inland Waters, 1965*, pp. 149-154.

Primary Sources

Canada. Department of Marine and Fisheries.
Annual Reports, 1867-1936.

Canada. Department of Transport.
Annual Reports, 1936-1969.

Canada. Legislative Assembly.
Journals.

Canada. Parliament.
Sessional Papers, 1867-1930.

Canada. Public Archives.
MG1 B. Lettres envoyées, 1663-1789.
 $C^{11}B$ Correspondance générale, Ile Royale.
 $C^{11}C$, Amérique du Nord, 1661-70.
MG8, A18, Quebec Trinity House Minutes, 1805-10.
MG9, A1, New Brunswick, Executive Council, 1784-1867.
MG11, CO42, Canada, Original Correspondence, 1842-1867.
 Q Series, Canada, Original Correspondence, 1760-1841.
 C0188, New Brunswick, Original Correspondence, 1784-1867.
 C0194, Newfoundland, Original Correspondence, 1700-1909.
 C0217, Nova Scotia and Cape Breton, Original Correspondence, 1603-1867.
 C0220, Nova Scotia and Cape Breton, Original Correspondence, 1767-1869.
 C0226, Prince Edward Island Original, Correspondence, 1769-1873.
 Nova Scotia A, Correspondence, 1603-1840.
RG1, E1, State Records of the Executive Council, Minute Books, 1764-1867.
 E3, Upper Canada, State Papers, 1791-1840.
RG2, 1, Privy Council Office, Minutes and Orders of Council, 1867-99.
 2, Privy Council Office, Records, 1867-1930.
RG4, S (formerly known as "Bound S"), Civil Secretary's Correspondence, Quebec, Lower Canada and Canada East, 1760-1840.
 C1, Provincial Secretary's Numbered Correspondence, 1839-67.
 C2, Provincial Secretary's Correspondence, Letter Books, Quebec, Lower Canada, 1765-71, 1812-19, 1828-65.
RG5, A1, Civil Secretary's Correspondence, Upper Canada, Sundries, 1766-1840.
RG7, G2, Despatches from the Colonial Office, 1794-1909.
 G7, Despatches from Lieutenant Governors to Governors General, 1820-69.
 G14, Miscellaneous Records, 1774-1914.
RG11, Department of Public Works, Records, Series II and III.
RG42, Department of Marine Records.

Lower Canada
Statutes.

Newfoundland. House of Assembly.
Journals.

Upper Canada. House of Assembly.
Journals.

Secondary Sources

AGA News
Aids to Navigation, 1969.

Anderson, William P.
"Modern Types of Danger Warnings on the Sea Coast." Unpubl. MS. N.p., n.d.

Bannister, J. A.
Long Point and Its Lighthouses. Univ. of Western Ontario, London, Ont., 1944.

Bird, Will R.
"Nova Scotia Has Many Lights." *Canadian Geographical Journal*, Vol. 54 (March 1957), pp. 90-103. Ottawa.

Bowen, John Poland
British Lighthouses, Longmans, Green, London, 1947.

Calladine, W. A.
"Lighthouses Along the St. Lawrence." Unpubl. MS. N.p., n.d.

Canada. Department of Marine and Fisheries.
Review of the Improvements in Lighthouse and Coast Service of Canada between 1896 and Year Ending 31 December 1903. King's Printer, Ottawa, 1904.

Canada. Department of Public Works.
Report of the Commissioner of Public Works for the Year Ending 30 June 1867, Hunter Rose, Ottawa, 1868.

Canada. Department of Transport.
List of Lights, Buoys and Fog Signals, Atlantic Coast and the Gulf and River St. Lawrence to Montreal, Pacific Coast and the Rivers and Lakes of British Columbia, Newfoundland including the Coastal Waters of Labrador, and Inland Waters West of Montreal and East of British Columbia. 1965, 1966, 1970 eds. Queen's Printer, Ottawa.

Canadian Economic Journal
1885. Montreal.

Corbin, T. W.
The Romance of Lighthouses. Seeley, London, 1926.

Corwin, Thomas
Report on the Trade and Commerce of the British North American Colonies with the United States and Other Countries. Printers to the Senate, Washington, 1851.

Encyclopaedia Britannica
11th ed., 14th ed. (1929), 1960 ed.

Encyclopaedia Canadiana
1966 ed. Grolier, Toronto.

Findlay, Alexander George
The British Navigator. A Sailing Directory for the Island and Banks of Newfoundland: the Gulf and River St. Lawrence; Cape Breton Island, Nova Scotia; and the Coasts thence to Boston. 4th ed. Richard Holmes Laurie, London, 1872.

Great Britain. Admiralty Hydrographic Office.
Admiralty List of the Lights on the Coasts and Lakes of British North America Corrected to January 1864. Eyre and Spottiswoode, London, 1864.

Hawkins, Alfred
Quebec Directory and Strangers' Guide. W. Gowan and Son, Quebec, 1844.

Johnson, George
Alphabet of First Things in Canada. 3rd ed. Mortimer and Co., Ottawa, 1897.

McLennan, J. S.
Louisbourg, From Its Foundation to Its Fall, 1713-58. Macmillan, London, 1918.

MacMechan, Archibald
"Mary Crowell: The Heroine of Seal Island." Unpubl. MS. N.p., n.d.

Majdelany, Fred
The Red Rocks of Eddystone. Longmans, London, 1959.

North American Lights 1847
W. Clowes and Sons, London, 1847.

Oke, Robert
"Plans of the Several Light Houses in the Colony of Newfoundland." Unpubl. MS. N.p., n.d.

Permanent International Association of Navigational Congresses
Principal Advances Made Recently in Lighting, Beaconing and Signaling of Coasts. Brussels, 1923.

Phillips, Godfrey W.
Lighthouse and Lightship: And the Men Who Man the Trinity House Service. Robert Ross, London, n.d.

Powell, Henry J.
Glass-making in England. University Press, Cambridge, 1923.

Putnam, George R.
Sentinel of the Coasts. The Log of a Lighthouse Engineer. Morton and Co., N.Y., 1937.

Radford, J.
"Modern Lighthouses and Light-Vessels." *Nautical Magazine*, Vol. 169, No. 6 (June 1953), pp. 339-41. Glasgow.

Richardson, E.
We keep a Light. Ryerson Press, Toronto, 1945.

Ryder, Alfred P.
Heads of Inquiry into the State and Condition of Lighthouses. Harrison and Sons, London, 1864.

Santangini, Ernest
Fixed Structures to Replace Lightships. U.S.G.P.O., Washington, 1950.

Scott, George
Scott's New Coast Pilot for the Lakes, Containing a Complete List of all Lights, Lighthouses, Fog Signals and Buoys on American and Canadian Shores. 3d ed. Free Press, Detroit, 1890.

Smeaton, John
A Narrative of the Building and a Description of the Construction of the Eddystone Lighthouse with Stone. H. Hughes, London, 1791.

Stevens, John R.
"Lighthouses on the Great Lakes." Manuscript Report Series No. 94. Parks Canada, Ottawa.

Stevenson, D. Alan
The World's Lighthouses Before 1820. Oxford Univ. Press, London, 1959.

Tait, Thomas R.
Early History of Lighthouses with a Short Account of Lighthouse Legislation in the United Kingdom and Excerpts from Existing Acts Affecting the Commissioners of Northern Lighthouses. J. Hedderwick and Sons, Glasgow, 1902.

United States Coast Guard
Historically Famous Lighthouses. U.S.G.P.O., Washington, 1957.
The Significance of Aids to Marine Navigation. U.S.G.P.O., Washington, 1943.

United States Coast Guard. Civil Engineering Division.
Visual Signalling: Theory and Application to Aids to Navigation. Civil Engineering Report No. 37. U.S.G.P.O., Washington, 1964.

Wilkinson, Roderick
"Odd Lighthouses." *Nautical Magazine*, Vol. 170, No. 1 (July 1953), pp. 30-32. Glasgow.

National Historic Parks and Sites Branch, Ottawa

Index

Table Glass Excavated at Fort Amherst, Prince Edward Island

by Paul McNally

Canadian Historic Sites
No. 9

Abstract

The table glass from Fort Amherst is limited to 16 objects but provides a good representation of English glass in the third quarter of the 18th century. Objects include twist and facet-cut stemware, a cut-glass cruet, a monteith, a stopper finial, firing glasses and tumbler fragments. The dates established for the glass coincide with the 1758 to 1771 period of known occupation of the fort.

The glass is more expensive than is typical of military sites excavated in Canada. The small quantity and relative fineness of the glass appear to indicate selective use and availability of table glass in the limited period during which Fort Amherst was occupied.

Submitted for publication 1972
by Paul McNally,
National Historic Parks and
Sites Branch,
Ottawa

Introduction

Fort Amherst, situated near Charlottetown, Prince Edward Island (Fig. 1), was built by the British in 1758 after the capitulation of the Fortress of Louisbourg, on or near an Acadian settlement which dated from 1720. Between 1758 and 1763 the garrison at the fort varied between 110 and 190 men. The fortification lost its military importance in 1763 with the end of the Seven Years' War, but some two companies (totalling 110 men) remained until the summer of 1768 when the fort was abandoned. Chief Justice John Duport took up residence at the site for an undetermined length of time in 1771 and after 1771 the site was used for agricultural purposes (Hornby 1965 ; Gillis : personal communication).

Partial archaeological investigation of the site was conducted by John H. Rick and Ian C. Rodger of the National Historic Parks and Sites Branch in 1963 (Rick 1970 : 23–5). This paper is a study of the table glass recovered in the course of the excavations.

Identification, Dating and Attribution

No table glass in the Fort Amherst collection can be related to the French occupation prior to 1758. With the exception of only one fragment, the glass is British and, where datable, was manufactured in the second half of the 18th century. There is no table glass from any later period. The collection is very small—only 16 objects—but 15 of them are identifiable and represent a surprising cross-section of the fashionable glass styles available in England in the 1760s. In addition to fragments from three tumblers, two firing glasses and a probably plain monteith, there are a teared ball finial from a decanter stopper, a knopped air-twist stem, five opaque-twist stems; a facet-cut stem and a facet-cut cruet. A sixteenth artifact, a fragment of a handle from a vessel of non-British origin, is not certainly identified.

Plain tumblers of lead glass remain ubiquitous and undiagnostic. They occur on sites of British occupation from early in the 18th century until well into the 19th and as yet there is no way of dating them within these boundaries.

Preliminary evidence from sites so far studied indicates that firing glasses may have been much used on shipboard in the 18th century because of their stability ; that is, their occurrence is high on sites such as Fort Beauséjour and Beaubassin in the maritime provinces, and low on sites otherwise quite similar but inland, such as the fort at Coteau-du-Lac. This can only be tentatively suggested because Fort Beauséjour and Beaubassin date from the 1750s and the fort at Coteau-du-Lac dates from 1779, and therefore the variation in the occurrence of firing

1 Eastern Canada, showing the locations of sites mentioned.

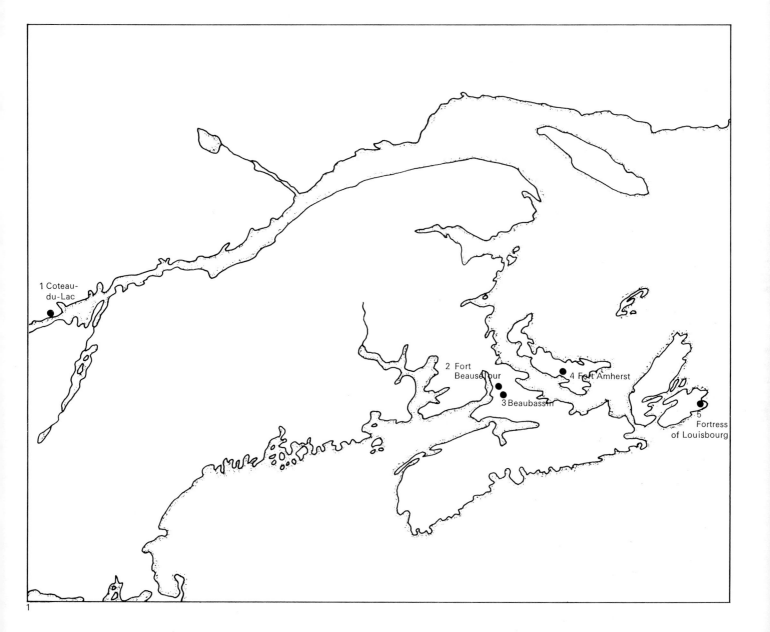

1 Coteau-
du-Lac

2 Fort
Beauséjour

3 Beaubassin

4 Fort Amherst

5
Fortress
of Louisbourg

1

2 Typical English firing glass, lead metal; popular about 1750-1800. The example shown is from Fort Beauséjour.

3 English teared ball-stopper finial, horizontal diameter: 36 mm., lead metal; made from the early 18th century until at least 1760. The example is from Fort Beauséjour.

4 Knopped fragment from an English air-twist stem, single-series multiple-spiral twist, lead metal; popular 1740-70.

glasses at these sites may reflect decreasing popularity of the glasses.

The popular connotation of firing glasses is as toasting glasses, the heavy feet sounding loud approval on table tops. They are primarily British and occur from 1730 until well into the 19th century (Ash 1962 : 84–6). Although firing glasses are a long-lasting form, their period of popularity may be limited to the second half of the 18th century (Hughes 1956 : 229). The Fort Amherst examples are typical of the form (Fig. 2).

A fragment of a foot is from either a jelly glass or a monteith, the distinction being based largely on bowl form. This particular artifact has very little bowl extant, but corresponds closely to a monteith (or salt) illustrated by Haynes (1964 : Plate 96e) and dated to the third quarter of the 18th century. Whichever it may be, it probably dates after 1750 and not much later than 1800 (Haynes 1964 :291) since this period encompasses all specimens found to date on Canadian historic sites.

Teared ball-stopper finials have been considered, for want of other evidence, to have been too heavy to have lasted very long into the Excise Period of English glass (after 1745) when glass was taxed by weight. They appeared about 1710 (Hughes 1956 : 254) and were associated with a type of decanter, the shaft and globe, which did not last long after the middle of the century (Ash 1962 : 123). However, archaeological evidence has emerged to indicate that the finials were popular into the Seven Years' War. An ex-

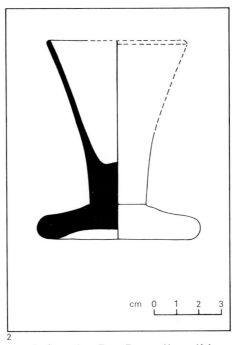

2

ample found at Fort Beauséjour (McNally 1971 : 89–90) probably was deposited after 1755 ; another at Beaubassin (Harris 1972 : 35), not until 1760 ; and now this specimen, 1758 or later. The similarity in manufacture and decoration between teared finials and air-twist stems may be considered to indicate that they enjoyed concurrent popularity at least until 1760. The air enclosures in the finial from Fort Amherst form a circuit of rather irregular bubbles around the horizontal circumference : a better preserved example from Fort Beauséjour is illustrated in Figure 3.

The fragments of glass which represent the leading styles of the English Excise Period are mostly stemware. In this period the demands of rococo decoration, particularly the emphasis upon delicacy, curvature and ornament, merged with a need to make ves-

3

4

sels light enough to offset the economic effects of taxation by weight. The two types of twist stem and the sparkling refractive effect of light faceting may thus be viewed in terms of "compensation by ornament" (Thorpe 1969 : 201).

Earliest of the three stem types is the air-twist stem with which glassmakers had experimented well before the Excise Period. They became very popular when that ill-advised regulation was implemented, and were

5 English opaque-twist stem, single-series corkscrew twist, with foot, lead metal; popular 1750–80.

cm 0   1   2   3

5

eclipsed through the late 1760s by opaque-twist and facet-cut stems. Thus 1740 to 1770 is a safe dating range (Elville 1961 : 13; Thorpe 1969 : 213). The example from Fort Amherst is a single-series multiple spiral with a swelling knop (Fig. 4).

Opaque-twist stems, probably inspired by the example of the air-twist and Venetian filigree precedents, commenced by 1750 and lasted until 1780 (Thorpe 1969 : 213–4). Four of the examples from Fort Amherst are double-series twists, and the fifth, shown in Figure 5, is a single-series corkscrew twist with a plain conical foot.

The facet-cut stem has a longer history than either of the twist stems, being made as early as 1745 and lasting as late as 1810. Several considerations narrow the dating somewhat in this instance. They did not become very popular until about 1760 (Haynes 1964 : 284) and the facets evolved into flutes late in the period. Bridge-fluting (carrying the facets onto the bowl) apparently did not commence until 1760 (Ash 1962 : 104–5) and the style became less popular after 1780 or 1790 (Ash 1962 : 106). The Fort Amherst specimen has hexagonal facets and bridge-fluting (Fig. 6) and 1760 to 1790 is probably a reasonable date to assign to it.

Not dissimilar in conception is the facet-cut cruet. The fragment in question has diamond cutting on the body and scale cutting on the neck. Thorpe's illustration of various mid-century cruet types (1969 : Plate 151) shows two very similar examples, dated 1750 and 1770. A designation of third quarter 18th-century English is reliable for the Fort Amherst fragment since shapes changed markedly after that time.

The final specimen from Fort Amherst is a puzzle. It is the top part of a wide flat handle, attached to a thin-walled vessel of which little is left. It is of non-lead glass while all other table glass found is of lead crystal and this makes an English attribution questionable. The form of the handle tells us little, although it may be dated before 1830 because the handle was apparently attached initially at the higher of the two weld points (Wilkinson 1968 : 21). Small as the fragment is, it bears close comparison with a Bohemian export decanter found at the Fortress of Louisbourg. The decanter dates to the second half of the 18th century (Charleston : pers. com.) and was found in a 1760s archaeological context (McNally 1973: Fig. 8).

Interpretation

Ivor Noël Hume has pointed out (1969 : 27) that glass on American domestic-colonial sites tends to lag markedly behind the dates commonly given to styles by collectors and analysts of English glass, but this argument has never seemed to hold true for 18th-century military sites in Canada. Table 1 demonstrates the periods of popularity for each identified style of table glass found at Fort Amherst, with dates based largely on standard authorities of English glass. The limits of occupation at Fort Amherst are indicated by

vertical dotted lines. Clearly, glass styles were in use at Fort Amherst in the period of their vogue in England.

In addition, the glass found at Fort Amherst must be considered nothing less than fancy. During the 1760s, English glassmakers were making undecorated or plain glass, and glass of the sort which has been discussed was necessarily more expensive. For example, an air-twist glass cost about 25 per cent more than its plain counterpart, an opaque-twist glass 40 per cent more than an air-twist, and a facet-cut glass still more by a quarter than the opaque-twist (Hughes 1956 : 99, 111 ; Elville 1951 : 104). The occurrence of such glass is not in itself surprising since there are precedents on other sites such as Fort Beauséjour (McNally 1971) ; however, the table glass from Fort Amherst seems to present a different view of the use of table glass during this period than does that from Fort Beauséjour.

The Fort Amherst collection is remarkable, in contrast to the Fort Beauséjour collection, for the relative frequency of fine tablewares. Using decorative features, either intrinsic or extrinsic, to make a categorical distinction between plain and fine wares, it is evident that at least nine of 16 table glass artifacts represent fine wares—English filigree and cut glass of some fashionability and high cost. Without asserting this ratio to be statistically reliable in so small a sample, it is reasonable to acknowledge a tendency in the collection toward elegant rather than simple functional wares. In studying a much larger collection from Fort Beauséjour and applying a similar distinction between elegant and utili-

tarian wares on the basis of decorative attributes, it was found that 77 per cent of the Fort Beauséjour collection was plain or utilitarian (McNally 1971 : 137).

Coupled with the apparently close parallel between deposition dates of artifacts and dating of styles in England, the elegance of the Fort Amherst table glass appears to profile a site population who had close metropolitan ties and who are readily divided into those possessing little glass and those possessing fine glass ; that is, the small collection suggests that not very much glass was used and, given the expensiveness of the glass recovered, one is led to the not-revolutionary conclusion that officers alone used table glass. It is also possible that some of the table glass was deposited during Duport's short stay at the site.

Checking these observations with the ceramics found at Fort Amherst reveals a similar profile of ceramic wares in use — a high proportion of decorated and expensive pieces including creamware with over-glaze transfer prints or with low-fired enamel decoration, and high quality oriental porcelain. Once more, there is considerable contrast with Fort Beauséjour in terms of the fineness of wares, especially when the fine wares are represented as a portion of the total ceramics collection from each site.

The extremity of this contrast is mitigated when the Fortress of Louisbourg collections of table glass and ceramics are considered. Both the quality of the fine pieces from Fort Amherst and their relative quantity approximately duplicate the quality and relative quantity of fine table glass and ceramics recovered from the Fortress of Louisbourg, of which the

Prince Edward Island fort was an outpost. Fort Beauséjour, during its first period of British occupation (1755 to 1768), was no less an outpost of the fortress, but Fort Beauséjour was considerably less bucolic than Fort Amherst. While the early history of Fort Beauséjour under British control is characterized by the animosity of Acadian subjects in the Chignecto region and operations against the French and Indians, Fort Amherst's history is characterized by nothing so much as dull routine, broken only by the arrival of provisions in the fall and a relief garrison in the spring, and by a brief mutiny in 1762 (Hornby 1965). Fort Amherst may also have been easier to supply because there was a direct sea link between the Fortress of Louisbourg and Fort Amherst.

It is difficult to conceive that such historical differentiation of the two forts fully accounts for a rather dramatic contrast between their table furnishings. Even if Fort Amherst afforded a relatively more retiring existence than did Fort Beauséjour, it is doubtful that it afforded greater opportunities for conviviality — there were only five officers at the fort and they had little contact, social or otherwise, with other forts. Therefore, a marked difference between lifestyles at the two forts is not supportable as an explanation for difference in table glass collections.

As mentioned above, Ivor Noël Hume's observation of anachronisms in glass styles in use in the colonies does not apply to sites such as those which have been mentioned in this report. Glass styles on these sites quite accurately reflect styles in England in the mid-18th century. They are enlightening, moreover, in that they help to reconstruct the economic availability and social use of table furnishings through the period. The contrast drawn between table glass at Fort Amherst and at Fort Beauséjour, for instance, points up much more widespread use of glass for utilitarian purposes at the latter site than at the former, a disparity for which lifestyles at the two forts in the 1760s can hardly account. The contrast devolves especially from the occurrence of tumblers at Fort Beauséjour in immense quantities along with very ordinary stemware. Since plain tumblers, on the basis of style, must be taken as nearly ubiquitous in time and space through the second half of the 18th century, it is impossible to establish from external evidence that they were more used at one time than at another. But since Fort Beauséjour was re-occupied by the British in 1776 and again in 1809, while Fort Amherst and the Fortress of Louisbourg remained essentially unoccupied after 1768, it is possible to conclude, from the contrast in proportionate representation of fine and utilitarian wares on the sites, that the availability and use of glass had expanded greatly by the fourth quarter of the century and had probably extended much lower on the social scale. Such a conclusion suggests that the burgeoning of common table glass wares was a relatively sudden and comprehensive phenomenon during the 1770s and 1780s.

It is argued, then, that the table glass (and, presumably, ceramics) in use at Fort Beauséjour and Fort Amherst in their concurrent occupations — up until 1768 — may have been rough-

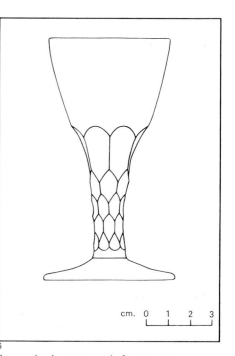

cm. 0 1 2 3

6

ly equivalent at each fort: not numerous and tending toward decorative and elegant pieces. At Fort Beauséjour the occurrence of plain wares, which are difficult to date out of archaeological context, apparently sharply increases during subsequent occupation periods, presenting a misrepresentative picture of table glass in use during the 1760s. The Fort Amherst collection, much more discrete in time, may reveal more truly the nature and quantity of table glass to be found on relatively unimportant British forts in North America during the Seven Years' War and immediately after.

Table 1.
Periods of Popularity for the Identified Styles of Table Glass

	1730	1740	1750	1760	1770	1780	1790	1800
Plain tumbler	■	■	■	■	■	■	■	
Firing glass			■	■	■	■	■	
Monteith			■	■	■	■		
Teared ball finial	■	■	■		■			
Air-twist stem		■	■	■				
Opaque-twist stem			■	■	■			
Facet-cut stem				■	■	■	■	
Facet-cut cruet				■	■			

Conclusions

Although archaeological investigation of the site is incomplete, the history of Fort Amherst is outlined by the artifacts recovered during the excavations there: the dates established for the table glass recovered from the site coincide with the 1758 to 1771 period during which the fort is known to have been occupied. It is impossible to make positive conclusions on the basis of the presence or absence of certain types of table glass when a site has been only partially examined and , when only a small collection of glass has been recovered, yet a clear image of juxtaposed life styles can be discovered in the table glass collection from Fort Amherst, an image which is reinforced by the ceramics collections and by archaeological and historical evidence. Glass was not extensively used at the fort, and that which was used belonged to a privileged segment of its population or to the subsequent tenant of the site, Chief Justice Duport, in 1771.

Wider conclusions reflecting trade and military supply patterns in the maritime colonies are necessarily dependent upon the above hypothesis and are therefore still more tenuous ; however, table glass styles at Fort Amherst, as at the Fortress of Louisbourg in its English periods, were certainly in step with English metropolitan fashion as it is recorded in collectors' histories.

References Cited

Ash, Douglas
1962
How to Identify English Drinking Glasses and Decanters 1680-1830. G. Bell and Sons, London.

Elville, E. M.
1951
English Tableglass. Country Life, London.
1961
The Collector's Dictionary of Glass. Country Life, London.

Harris, Jane E.
1972
Glassware Excavated at Beaubassin, N.S. Manuscript Report Series No. 65, National Historic Parks and Sites Branch, Ottawa.

Haynes, E. Barrington
1964
Glass Through the Ages. Penguin Books, London.

Hornby, Brock
1965
"Fort Amherst." Manuscript on file, National Historic Parks and Sites Branch, Ottawa.

Hughes, G. Bernard
1956
English, Scottish and Irish Table Glass from the Sixteenth Century to 1820. Bramhall House, New York.

McNally, Paul
1971
Table Glass at Fort Beauséjour, New Brunswick. Manuscript Report Series No. 21, National Historic Parks and Sites Branch, Ottawa.
1973
"Table Glass in the Collections of the National Historic Parks and Sites Branch, 1710-1850." Manuscript in preparation.

Noël Hume, Ivor
1969
"Glass in Colonial Williamsburg's Archaeological Collections." *Colonial Williamsburg Archaeological Series,* No. 1. Colonial Williamsburg, Williamsburg, Va.

Rick, John H.
1970
"Archaeological Investigations of the National Historic Sites Service, 1962-1966." *Canadian Historic Sites: Occasional Papers in Archaeology and History,* No. 1, pp. 10-44. Ottawa.

Thorpe, W. A.
1969
A History of English and Irish Glass. Holland Press, London. Facs. of 1924 edition.

Wilkinson, R.
1968
The Hallmarks of Antique Glass. Richard Madley, London.

Halifax Waterfront Buildings: An Historical Report,

by Susan Buggey

Canadian Historic Sites
No. 9.

Abstract
The study attempts to explain and doc-
ument the historical role and associations of a complex of 19th-century
Halifax waterfront buildings. It under-
takes as well to distinguish their
architectural features and structural
alterations.

Submitted for publication 1973
by Susan Buggey,

National Historic Parks and
Sites Branch,
Ottawa

*Figures 3-21 will be found
in back pocket.*

Acknowledgements

I wish to thank the many people of Halifax and Ottawa who have given me such willing assistance in the preparation of the historical report. I am particularly grateful to Mr. R. J. Fisher of Pickford & Black, Mr. Louis Collins and Mr. Gilbert Hutton of the Halifax Landmarks Commission, Miss Phyllis Blakeley, Mrs. Lois Kernaghan and Mrs. Virginia Clark of the Public Archives of Nova Scotia, and Dr. Charles Armour of the Dalhousie University Archives for their help and suggestions. I am also indebted to the Restoration Services Division, Technical Services Branch, especially Mr. Martin Weil and Miss Gouhar Shemdin, for architectural information and useful criticism.

I wish to acknowledge as well permission to publish various extracts from copyright manuscripts and books granted by the Controller of H. M. Stationery Office, London, the Canadian Imperial Bank of Commerce and the Regents of the University of Wisconsin.

Introduction

The 19th-century waterfront buildings here examined occupy two wharfs extending east from Water Street into Halifax Harbour (Fig. 1). They lie between Duke and Buckingham streets immediately north of the County Court House and south of the old Ordnance Yard. At the head of the south wharf stand the Pickford & Black Building and Collins' Bank and Warehouse ; east of them are situated the Carpenters' Shop and the Red Store respectively. On the north wharf, running east from Water Street, are the Simon's Building, the Privateer's Warehouse and, at the water's edge, the Wooden Storehouse (Fig. 2). Three blocks uphill from the site towers the shopping and office complex of Scotia Square.

Controversy surrounding the future use of the central portion of the waterfront, including the site of these buildings, prevailed in the city through the 1960s. Plans for a sewerage outlet and a southward extension of a harbourside freeway through the district were designed to meet urgent urban problems. Citizens who valued the historical and architectural character of the downtown area, however, opposed the sacrifice of the old warehouses. By 1969, both the civic and federal governments were committed to retaining and restoring the buildings which had been declared of national historic importance. The seven structures discussed in this paper are presently being restored to 19th-century exteriors in an historic landscape for late 20th-century use. This study was prepared in partial fulfillment of a legal agreement between the Department of Indian and Northern Affairs and the City of Halifax regarding this restoration.

From the founding of Halifax in 1749 until at least World War I, the portion of the Halifax waterfront designated for restoration was associated with men and events prominent in the commercial and civic life of the city. Aldermen and mayors, legislators and councillors, consuls and a member of Parliament all had business offices on the wharfs. Merchants and shipping men with international connections and reputations located there. The mid-19th-century owner of the south wharf was such a man. Reputedly by influence of the lieutenant-governor of the day and in the interest of the province, Enos Collins was appointed a member of the conservative but influential council board and married to the daughter of the future chief justice and niece of the bishop of Nova Scotia during the 1820s. With one of the several Nova Scotian fortunes acquired from patriotic privateering during the Napoleonic Wars, he invested in commercial enterprises and transacted in property for more than half a century until, when he died in 1872, he was believed to be the wealthiest man in British North America.[1]

Activities on the wharfs have likewise been connected with many aspects of the city's development. The auctioning on Collins' Wharf of the stores and provisions of the American frigate *Chesapeake* denoted the town's

1 The Halifax peninsula, showing the location of the
  waterfront buildings.

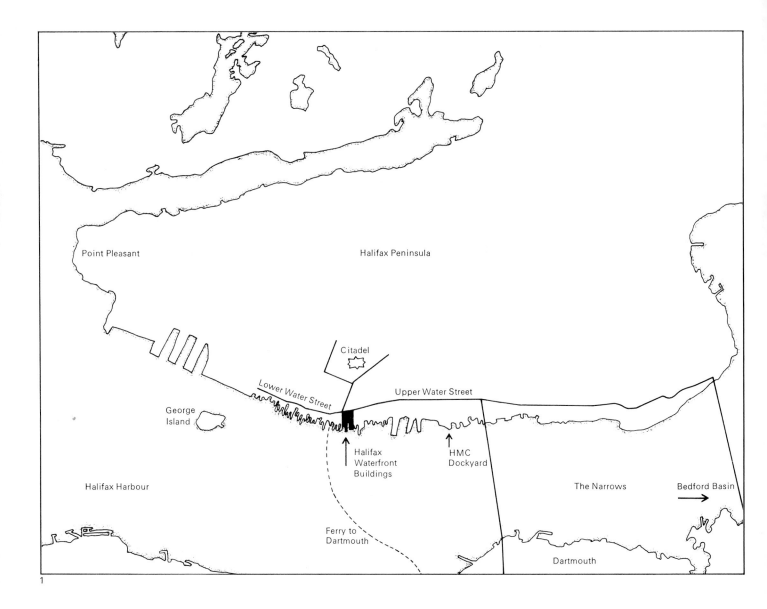

Point Pleasant

Halifax Peninsula

Citadel

Lower Water Street

Upper Water Street

George
Island

Halifax
Waterfront
Buildings

HMC
Dockyard

The Narrows

Bedford Basin

Halifax Harbour

Ferry to
Dartmouth

Dartmouth

1

rise to prominence during the late Napoleonic Wars.[2] The sailing of the first Nova Scotian ship to India from Clark's wharf in 1825 signalized expansion of the province's shipping to the seven seas, the basis of its mid-19th-century prosperity.[3] The Nova Scotian built *Dayspring*, moored at Collins' wharf in 1863 before departing for missionary service in the New Hebrides, symbolized the province's strong religious heritage.[4] Legendary attributions of the wharfs include both privateering and rum-running.

Fancifully considered to have been constructed of stone brought from the French fortress at Louisbourg, the seven historic waterfront buildings discussed in this study remain a tribute to the foresight, wealth, and influence of their 19th-century creators. Built between 1815 and 1875, they too have been closely affiliated with the evolution of the city. On the north wharf, the two stone edifices were erected for a father and a son, one with profits made during the Napoleonic War years, the other during the halcyon mid-1850s. One of these structures appeared when stone buildings, despite the local prevalence of ironstone, were still a rarity in the town. The other, with its coursed granite façade, signified the greater elegance to which inhabitants of the mid-century city aspired. The two massive ironstone structures at the head of the south wharf were built for Collins. Their expensive slate roofs

were both a fire preventive in the largely wooden town and a symbol of their owner's prosperity. One housed the Halifax Banking Company, an eight-member firm composed of the economic, social and political elite of the community. Founded in 1825, it was the first formally organized banking institution in the province. A number of firmly established and far-trading mercantile houses tenanted the other structure until, in the 1870s, Pickford & Black made it headquarters for its international steamship line. Then carts and wagons lined Water Street daily carrying goods to and from the pioneering steamers to the West Indies (Fig. 44). The buildings nearer the harbour were wooden. Here were situated such marine-oriented services as coopering and sail-making, the more transient businesses of auctioneers and small-scale commission merchants, and public or private storage facilities. From shipbuilding to lobster packing, from the lumber trade to the voluminous dry goods and grocery businesses which flourished or failed according to economic fluctuations, the buildings have known the many long- and sometimes short-term interests of the Halifax commercial community.

By the late 19th century, more extensive local operations centring upon regional distribution of products gathered in worldwide shipping were replacing the multi-interest entrepreneur whose highway was the sea. The accompanying separation of wholesale and retail houses coincided with the first shift away from the harbour toward a more city-centred orientation. The coursed, smooth facade of the north edifice and the Clas-

sical Revival alteration of the south building, both fronting Water Street, were signs of this trend. The subdivision of warehouses to accommodate the offices of specialized businesses or agencies marked the functional decline of the south wharf in the 20th century. The amalgamation of the Halifax Banking Company with a national chartered bank, relocated in new uptown offices, reflected the expansion of large corporate interests into the region. The tendency in the modern urban community to displace the supplying of goods with the provision of services contributed to the subsequent by-passing and deterioration of the buildings and site in the mid-20th century.

2 The waterfront buildings in relation to the downtown area of Halifax.

Spring Garden Road

Brunswick St.

Barrington St.

Granville St.

Hollis St.

Lower Water St.

Duke St.

George St.

Buckingham St.

Upper Water St.

HMC
Dockyard

Cunard's Wharf

Central Wharf
(Halifax Waterfront Buildings)

Court
House

Pickford &
Black Wharf

Ferry to
Dartmouth

1 Citadel
2 St. Paul's Church
3 Province House
4 Scotia Square

1

2

3

4

2

The Restoration Site

The Site

For more than two centuries, the restoration site has reflected the physical, commercial, and urban development of Halifax. In its history may be seen the extension of waterfront properties to meet the demands of a busy shipping centre in the ages of sail and steam. The contraction of the wharfs in the mid-20th century also records the transition from sea to air travel.

When Halifax was founded in 1749, the present wharf property was part of the harbour. On the site to the north which was later the Ordnance Yard, a nine-gun battery was soon erected as part of the town's defences.[1] The area along the shore south of the battery, however, remained unfilled as far as Ephraim Cooke's wharf at the foot of Duke Street (Fig. 3). In 1753 Cooke sold to John Creighton the southern portion of his extensive waterfront lot, 210 ft. by 96 ft. east of Hollis and between Duke and Buckingham streets.[2] In the same year Cooke returned to England where he turned over all his remaining property in Halifax to his creditor, Stephen T. Janson. Three years later the remaining waterfront portion of his lands returned to Haligonian ownership in the hands of Governor Charles Lawrence who, in turn, sold it three years later to Thomas Saul, one of his ardent political supporters as well as the prosperous army provisioner and navy victualler at Halifax. The property, 134 ft. x 81 ft., was north of Creighton's and apparently extended from Hollis Street to the water's edge.[3] In front of it, Saul obtained permission of the governor's council in 1759 "to erect or build a Wharf or breast work . . . to begin from the Battery and to extend Southward before [the] said Saul's House One hundred and sixty nine feet."[4] In 1779, having been resident in England nearly 20 years, Saul transferred his property in Halifax, including the waterfront lot and the breastwork in front of it, to Alexander Brymer, one of the principal merchants of the town.[5] Although the wharf then standing between the battery and Cooke's wharf appears to have been south of Brymer's acquisition (Fig. 4), by the mid-1780s, the new owner had erected two wharfs on his property as well as a number of stores (Fig. 5). These two wharfs constituted the basic form of the wharfs which stand today, although they have been both broadened and extended in the succeeding two centuries.

In 1790 Brymer, not only an eminent merchant but also son-in-law of Lieutenant-Governor John Parr, obtained the grant of a wharf lot opposite the property which he had purchased from Saul. This extension of his lands measured

on Water Street . . . north fourteen degrees, west one hundred and sixty two feet, then at right Angles nine feet, three inches, then northerly ten feet ten inches, thence north, sixty degrees, east three hundred feet into the Harbour of Halifax which makes the northern bound line, and bounded southerly by Creighton's wharf, course north, seventy six degrees east three hundred feet into the Harbour, and bounded on the east by a line drawn from the respective ends of the North and South line.[6]

The grant represented the first transfer of ownership of this property from the crown to a private citizen. As well, it superseded the restrictive clause of Saul's authority of 1759 which had not granted ownership and which had made the wharf subject to stringent regulations of the governor and council.[7] The definition therefore encompassed the wharfs which Brymer had already erected and extended his property 300 ft. east of Water Street into the harbour. A decade later Brymer sold the lot he had purchased from Saul and the wharf lot granted him in 1790 to the influential Haligonian merchants Thomas, James, and William Cochran.[8] Shortly after the death of their senior partner, James and William Cochran transferred the property, in settlement of their debts, to William Smith of Smith, Forsyth & Company who sold it immediately to Robert Lester and Robert Morrogh, merchants of Quebec and part of the Phyn, Ellice & Inglis mercantile network of London, with which Smith, Forsyth & Company was also connected. The property transferred in 1803 to Lester and Morrogh did not, however, include the 134 ft. by 81 ft. block west of Water Street; it encompassed only the wharf lot east of the thoroughfare. It is this land which was sold in 1806 to Charles Prescott and William Lawson in common and later divided between John Clark and Enos

Collins.[9] The wharf property granted to Brymer in 1790, and not the earlier land belonging to Cooke, Lawrence and Saul, therefore constitutes the western portion of the present wharfs.

The eastern portion of the wharfs falls within four later water-lot grants — one to Prescott and Lawson in 1809, two to Pickford & Black in the late 19th century, and one to Margaret E. Wood by the early 20th century (Fig. 21).[10] By 1803 the wharf later known as Collins' — that is, the southerly portion of Brymer's Wharf — had already been extended beyond the eastern property boundary, and in 1809 it was partially filled on the north side to enable Prescott and Lawson to construct the stone foundation of the building which was only 17 ft. south of the property line drawn the following year.[11] At the same time Prescott and Lawson had the bar of the ell-shaped wharf of 1803 removed and the wharf lengthened an additional 50 ft. (Fig. 7). From 1810 until Confederation, the wharf remained at this length, about 400 ft., from the east side of Water Street (Figs. 10, 11, 13, 14). Shortly thereafter the Seetons, owners since 1865, increased it about 225 ft. further, at which length it remained until nearly the mid-20th century (Fig. 15).[12] In the early 1950s when Pickford & Black quitted the steamship business, they had the wharf cut back to its present size. At that time they estimated that its annual upkeep was costing the firm $10,000.[13]

The wharf later known as Clark's — that is, the northerly portion of Brymer's Wharf — had many more, though shorter, extensions than had Collins' Wharf. By 1803 it had already been considerably extended beyond its length of 20 years earlier to about 300 ft., and in 1809 a further extension was intended. If erected, it had been cut back to its length of 1803 before 1830, and in the following 30 years it was increased only about 50 ft. (Figs. 5, 6, 7, 10, 11, 13). In the mid-1860s, however, it was lengthened to reach about 340 ft. from the east side of Water Street, and before 1878 a further approximate 80 ft. into the harbour. Two later additions of about 80 ft. each extended it to about 500 ft. by 1895 and about 580 ft. by 1914 (Figs. 14, 15, 16, 17, 18), which appears to have been its greatest length. By 1939 it had been cut back to about 375 ft. from Water Street.[14]

Streets and Sidewalks
Initially a mere path along the beach which must either have traversed Cooke's property or run along the beach at the water's edge, Water Street by 1779 ran east of the town blocks including that owned by Saul and Creighton southwest of the Ordnance Yard (Figs. 3, 4). Its route remained unchanged until 1811-12 when the way through the yard was blocked and the street rerouted to its present location. No alteration appears, however, to have occurred to the road in front of Clark's, Prescott's, Collins', and Creighton's wharfs at this time.[15] In the years following the rerouting, citizens frequently complained about the impassable state of the thoroughfare which was laden with mud and sometimes under water. As a result, in 1816-17, the street was regraded and apparently raised. A decade later, however, the improvements had been worn away by heavy traffic, and in 1830 Water Street was again repaired and the surface lines permanently fixed. At this time the street commissioners reported that they had required all obstacles such as steps, porches and cellar doors to be removed from within the bounds of the road.[16]

By 1830 Captain William Moorsom stated that the roads in Halifax were generally macadamized. As early as 1810, 200 tons of paving stones had been demanded for the repair of the streets, and 15 years later 1,000 tons of stones as well as sand and gravel were needed. In 1839 Hugh Murray kindly described the roads as "now generally spacious, the principal one well paved, and the others macadamized," although in the mid-1850s the disgruntled F. S. Cozzens considered that "the middle street was in its original and aboriginal clay." In the early 1840s J. S. Buckingham found the streets dusty and remarked upon them being mostly unpaved. Isabella Lucy Bird, an Englishwoman, discovered them at mid-century to be not only littered but sometimes in an "almost impassable state," as when she "waded through them ankle-deep in mud."[17] Making allowances for poetic licence in the travellers' journals, it is evident that Halifax had attempted, if not very successfully, to put a more or less permanent covering upon most of the streets in the central portion of the town. In 1850 some streets, however, still did not have sidewalks, and those which existed were mostly made of wood, as was common in Canadian towns. Buckingham complained that many of them were in "a most dilapidated and neglected state," while Cozzens observed that they were neither bricked nor paved with flags as they would have been in an American seaboard city.[18] An experiment with flagstones reputedly imported from Scotland was made, but disintegration of the stones under heavy frost apparently caused it to be abandoned.[19]

During the latter half of the 19th century, both road building and sidewalk construction were controversial subjects in Halifax.[20] New legislation of 1861 provided both a structure and a mode of financing to replace the former road taxes and nearly independent street commissioners. The new appointees, for the first time fully responsible to city council and financed from city revenues, initiated the use of broken stone for road building in place of the "worse than useless material" employed in the past. They also put into effect for the first time legislation providing for the construction of brick sidewalks. Although it is not clear that brick sidewalks were in fact laid in Water Street, the importance and the heavy traffic of the thoroughfare suggest that during the long period of their continuance such walks were installed along the waterfront road. Because of the frequent and costly repairs required for the bricks, however, gravel sidewalks were also introduced in the town, and by the mid-1880s some experiments, under the direction of City Engineer

E. H. Keating, were performed with asphalt and other materials. In the early 1890s when the street was paved, new tar and concrete sidewalks with granite curbs were laid on both sides of Water Street. These again proved short-lived and expensive to maintain, and by the early 1900s the city engineer recommended cement concrete in their place. By 1907 this building material was extensively used, and by 1915 a cement concrete sidewalk 5 to 6 ft. wide extended at least to the southern edge of the Pickford & Black property.

Road building presents a similar story of debate and experiment, although fewer changes were actually put into operation. After more than 18,500 bu. of broken stone were used in the repair of Water Street in 1861-62, macadamizing with stone broken by city and prison labour remained the principal mode of road building in Halifax for the next 30 years. Keeping the streets in good repair required constant and expensive upkeep within a limited budget. To this end, Water Street was watered daily, cleaned weekly, and thoroughly macadamized in 1875-78 and again in 1883-85. Yet the roads were still, depending on the weather, either muddy or dusty. In 1880, pointing out that the maintenance of Water Street alone required thousands of loads of hand-broken stone every year, the city engineer recommended that it be paved with blocks of wood or stone, preferably with granite. During the next decade, however, Water Street was ordered not paved but gravelled. The experiment proved a failure, as the city engineer advised the mayor and

council late in 1889 : "It would be cheaper and better to remove the so-called gravel that is now being landed for that street, at once from the wharf to the dumping ground, rather than to spread it over the roadway to form the intolerable nuisance it does on the first wet day."[21] In the early 1890s two experiments were performed in paving with granite blocks, and in 1895 the more satisfactory mode was applied to Water Street between the Ordnance Yard and Morris Street. Porphyry was laid upon a concrete foundation and topped with granite paving blocks (setts) brought from the Shelburne quarry. At this time the whole street was brought to proper grade and the curbs were straightened. This surface remained well into the 20th century until the present road surface was laid, mainly over the granite blocks. A 6-in. granite step in front of the Simon's Building is said to have been covered over at this time.[22]

The Wharf
No early descriptions of either Collins' or Clark's wharfs have been found. Some picture of them can, however, be derived from newspaper advertisements offering their stores to let and from descriptions of other wharfs advertised for rent or sale.[23] In the early 19th century and until Collins began erecting the ranges of stone stores near Water Street in the mid-1820s, the south wharf was headed on either side

by a house and shop or office, while east of these structures there were stores. Elsewhere there were a cooperage, a blacksmith shop, a store with "an excellent fish screw," and, perhaps housing one of them, a red store.[24] From 1825 the Halifax Bank stood at the north head of the wharf, while opposite and beyond it were stone and wooden stores. Firms of importance, like Fairbanks & Allison and Pickford & Black, usually occupied the south head, and commission merchants, auctioneers and sailmakers regularly leased the more easterly premises. A variety of tradesmen probably also rented portions of the wharf stores. By 1812 Clark's Wharf to the north had a small ell-shaped building at the south head and by 1831 a large enclosed yard extending around the Privateer's Warehouse from about the centre of the wharf to the harbour. On the north side were two wooden stores (Fig. 11).

Isabella Lucy Bird, landing from a Cunard steamer in the 1850s, has provided a vivid if jaundiced glimpse of the physical form of a wharf and its bustling activity.

The wharf was dirty, unlighted, and under repair, covered with heaps and full of holes. . . . A large gateway, lighted by one feeble oil-lamp at the head of the wharf, was then opened, and the crowd pent up behind it came pouring down the sloping road. There was a simultaneous rush of trucks, hand-carts, waggons, and cars . . . it must have been fully half an hour before we had extricated ourselves from this chaos of mismanagement and disorder, by scrambling over gravel-heaps and piles of timber.[25]

Gates at the heads of wharfs do not appear to have been uncommon. In 1855, for instance, James Forman's Wharf could be "completely closed in . . . when required from the Street side."[26] Ten years later Collins' Wharf had a gate which ran from near the east end of the Pickford & Black Building to the southeastern corner of the Collins' Warehouse. It may, however, have been removed before 1876,[27] and its appearance is unknown. A type of gate in use along Water Street is illustrated in a late 19th-century photograph of Dwyer's Wharf (Fig. 45).

Like the Cunard Wharf, the Pickford & Black Wharf sloped toward the harbour (Fig. 39). By the late 19th century, the surface between the Pickford & Black Building and Collins' Bank and Warehouse, running east from Water Street, appears to have been packed earth or gravel (Figs. 25, 30, 39). Beyond the two buildings, however, the wharf was planked (Figs. 30, 33, 36). Planks 10 in. wide running east and west overlaid 18 in. by 18 in. timbers, which were laid in earth and ran north and south. The timbers were waterlogged so did not rot, but the planked deck required annual repair. This surface remained until the mid-1940s when earth was laid on top and the wharf paved east from Water Street.[28] The earth surface of the Central Wharf, on the other hand, dated from at least the early 20th century (Fig. 43).[29] The levels of the wharfs have been altered during the past 150 years to accommodate the recorded rise of mean sea level at Halifax by about one foot per century.[30]

Although there was no sidewalk north of the Simon's Building (Fig. 43), by the 1890s wooden sidewalks ran along the Pickford & Black Building, the Bank, and the Red Store. By the turn of the century they had been extended in front of Collins' Warehouse. The entrances to the bank and warehouse and the Red Store were two steps above the level of the wharf, although those of the Pickford & Black Building were level with it. Posts for tethering horses stood on either side of the wharf near Water Street, where about 1890 an old lamp standard remained. Farther down the wharf, the head of a cannon protruded from the decking at the southwest corner of the Red Store to protect it from the heavy wagon traffic. The wharf appears normally to have been kept clear of obstacles except for an occasional barrel (Figs. 25, 30, 39), although in the early 20th century lumber merchants who occupied premises in the stores left their lumber stacked outside.[31] By the 1850s both Collins' and Clark's wharfs had private fire plugs, and during the many waterfront fires of the early 20th century a fire engine was regularly stationed on Pickford & Black's wharf.[32]

Pickford & Black Building

Historical Information

The stone warehouse fronting Water Street on the south side of the wharf has stood solidly for nearly a century and a half. Its appendage to the south, less than half a century old, has already settled four inches. Such is the permanence of the four-storey building erected in 1830.

This structure was not the first on the site. In the mid-1780s three of the stores erected on the wharf by Alexander Brymer stood in this significant location (Fig. 5). In the loft of one of them the prominent navy victualler at Halifax, John Grant, stored biscuit, peas and flour.[1] By 1803, when Quebec merchant Robert Lester attempted unsuccessfully to sell the property to the British Ordnance department, there was "a neat and compact Dwelling House and good Stores"[2] on the spot (Fig. 6). Part of this establishment was apparently occupied until 1809 by the glass and crockery warehouse in which Michael Forrestall featured a variety of tumblers and "a few neat and elegantly cut oval Dishes and Pickle Urns" imported from London. Mrs. Ann Bell then fitted up the dwelling "in a genteel manner" as "a *House of Entertainment* (italics in original)."[3] From 1819 to 1823 William Skinner rented the house and premises, while in 1827 G. P. Lawson carried on his trade with the southern states in pitch, tar, staves and shingles from the office at the head of the wharf and the store on the south side.[4] By 1830 the house and stores were occupied by the firm of Pringle & Downie. These, as well as

"the next building . . . occupied as a Sail Loft, and Cooperage," were demolished that year, and the materials, except bricks and foundations, sold.[5] In their place Enos Collins, owner of the south side of the wharf since 1811, immediately erected the present stone edifice.

Toler's map of Halifax, published in 1830, provides the first evidence of the new "immense ranges of stone stores" that appeared on the wharf (Fig. 10). In July of the following year they were lauded as among the most conspicuous of recent improvements to the town which afforded "undeniable evidence of the extension of [its] commerce."[6] By the spring of 1831 the warehouse was the scene of auctions and private sales. E. Collins & Company probably occupied the building from shortly after its completion until the dissolution of the firm, by Collins' retirement, in 1833. Thereafter, the wharf experienced the economic depression which enveloped the Halifax business community during the mid-1830s, and in 1836 the building apparently stood vacant.[7] William Fairbanks and Jonathan C. Allison, the continuing partners of Collins' firm, united in 1840 with David Allison, the surviving partner of Joseph Allison & Company; as Fairbanks & Allisons, they rented the premises until 1855. They pursued the trade of their predecessors, sending ships regularly not only to North American ports and Britain but also to the West Indies and occasionally to South America, Iberia, India and Russia. In 1839, for example, Fairbanks & Allison's imports from Russia included 2,500 bushels of prime red wheat, 100 pieces of Russian sail cloth, two bales of black grain skins,

and one case of furs consisting of cloaks, gloves and cloak linings; the pièce de résistance was a case of reindeers' tongues.[8] In 1855 S. A. White & Company moved from the head of Clark's Wharf and continued their commission trade at the head of Collins' Wharf until 1863,[9] when Collins sold the property. From 1863 to 1876 it was both owned and occupied by Joseph and Robert Seeton, commission merchants and agents for the Inman Steamship Company.[10] In the latter year, Pickford & Black, a recently established and aggressive firm of shipchandlers, purchased the property. Taking advantage of the transition from sail to steam, they transformed the office facing Water Street into a busy shipping agency where a variety of international lines as well as their own passenger, freight and mail steamers were booked. With the former Cunarders *Alpha* and *Beta*, Pickford & Black established a regular steamship service between Halifax and the West Indies. They also ran ships to Jamaica, Demerara and Turk's Island, bringing to Nova Scotia tropical fruits and sugar products in exchange for North American lumber, fish and flour. Nearer home they operated lines to Prince Edward Island, Cape Breton and Newfoundland. By the early 20th century they were believed to be the second largest owners of tonnage in the Maritime Provinces, and in their office the prestigious Lloyd's agency was located.[11] The partners of the firm also held other influential positions and significant reputations. For instance, in addition to being the consul for Panama, William A. Black was a Conservative member of the Nova Scotia legislature from 1894 to 1897, the representative for Halifax in the House of Commons from 1923 until his death in 1934, and a federal cabinet minister in the Meighen administration.[12]

A series of commission merchants, including the former owners, rented the adjoining stone warehouses.[13] Swelling of grain stored damp by one of these tenants during the late 19th century is said to have caused some of the beams to split.[14] The principal occupants of the warehouse during the 20th century were Messrs Bryant & McDonald, tea merchants, whose premises could accommodate their product to an estimated value of $100,000 in 1909.[15] Subsequently, this firm amalgamated with Morse's Teas, which also owned the fine early Victorian stone building opposite the head of the wharf (Figs. 34, 48).[16]

Architectural Information

The Pickford & Black Building reflects the practical-mindedness and foresight of its original owner, Enos Collins. Set upon a six-foot stone foundation, the thick outer walls were constructed of "iron-stone of Acadia," popular and prevalent in early 19th-century Halifax.[17] The roof was pitched "to keep the snow off" and made of slate. Within, heavy timber beams measured 18 in. square, and gabled brick fire walls

subdivided the 132 ft. length into three essentially separate warehouses (Figs. 16, 17, 18).[18] The structure was designed, therefore, to withstand not only weathering but also the most destructive urban enemy of the age, fire.

As late as the 1890s, much of the principal style of the original building remained ; the north view revealed its balanced proportions (Fig. 25). Three sets of wooden loading doors marked the main divisions. Each was topped by a dormer containing a hoist, and each ground floor door afforded access to the building. The only interruption of this neatly executed pattern occurred where the most westerly door was exchanged with the window west of it. Forty windows, which allowed light to reach the interior, otherwise symmetrically flanked the loading doors in horizontal and vertical rows. The double-hung sashes contained six panes per sash, except on the upper storey where the topmost sash had only three. The quoins of both the doors and the windows were made of sandstone. Four pipes capped with ornate cornices drained the narrow eavestrough (Figs. 24, 25).

By the 1880s, several alterations had updated the appearance of the building. Mastic[19] covered the west front and the north wall as far as the first loading doors, that is, the exterior walls of Pickford & Black's office (Figs. 24, 25). The pillars flanking the glass-topped west door suggest that the renovations belonged to the Classical Revival of the previous decade. The

windows north and south of the door each contained a single sash of nine large panes, while the three older, smaller windows to the north each had six similar panes ; the windows of the upper storey remained unchanged. Unornamented drain pipes carried off the accumulations of the overhanging eavestrough (Figs. 24, 25, 26, 27). A hipped truncated roof connected the Pickford & Black Building with the Black Brothers' brick edifice which abutted the structure to the south by 1862 (Figs. 16, 17, 23, 24).[20] The sides of the roof were slated and its false top wooden (Figs. 16, 17) or tarred. A skylight of wood covered with zinc and situated "in the front on top" gave access to the roof,[21] above which towered two huge stone chimneys (Fig. 25). Within, old ironclad doors, with the metal partly off, blocked the apertures in the fire walls, and by the mid-1890s openings 30 in. by 30 in. had been cut in several portions of the brick walls. A hot-water heating system and a hoist in the easterly warehouse had also been installed (Figs. 16, 17).

The greatest alteration to the structure occurred as the aftermath of a devastating fire which "gutted" the edifice in 1904 ; only the "strong, well built walls" of the "fine stone building" were left standing (Fig. 34) when the seven-hour conflagration was finally extinguished. Renewal began immediately on what the owners modestly described as "more convenient premises than even those occupied before the fire."[22] The original one-storey office facing Water Street was opened to double-storey height, lending grandeur to a successful firm nearing the zenith of its power. Three broad, full-length windows along the west wall brightened the office, while similar desk-to-ceiling level windows supplanted the small apertures in the north wall. The door remained in its northerly location, though its small lobby may have been added at this time. Extensive changes were also made to the interior decor. A delicately ornamented ceiling replaced the previous heavy wooden beams, while pressed tin, popular at the turn of the century, covered the walls in place of plaster (Figs. 27, 28, 29). Through the enlarged window in the central section of the warehouse, spectators might watch the employees of Bryant & McDonald blending and tasting teas.[23] A motorized hoist was also installed on the east side of this warehouse (Fig. 18). A flat composition roof topped the modernized structure (Fig. 52) on which the mastic or stucco covering was renewed.

A transfer of the ownership of Pickford & Black in 1936 was followed two years later by further alterations to the century-old building. The south wall of the office was opened and an archway constructed to give entrance to a double-storey appendage to the south. At the same time not only the entrance to the office but the casing of the door itself was removed from the wharf passageway to the southwest front. Executive offices along the north side were subdivided off the main room, and a mezzanine in the addition replaced a spiral staircase in the southeast corner. The new president, Ralph P. Bell, successfully obtained a sufficient further supply of the existing tin wall covering from the manufacturer to sheathe the expanded interior.[24]

The Pickford & Black Building remained in possession of the firm whose name it bears until expropriated by the City of Halifax in 1968.[25]

Carpenters' Shop
Historical Information
The buildings on the south front of the Pickford & Black Wharf appear always to have been of a secondary, though not insubstantial, nature. Lying outside the "brick district,"[1] they were consistently constructed of wood during the 19th century.

When Quebec merchant Robert Lester attempted to sell his property east of Water Street to the British Ordnance department in 1803, there appears to have been an enclosed dock rather than a building at the southeastern end of the wharf (Fig. 6). By 1810, approximately 100 ft. of this dock had apparently been filled (Fig. 7). Either upon it or opposite it was probably erected the following year Edward Foster's new blacksmith shop where he and his sons offered services as "SHIP-SMITH, Mill Smith, House-Smith, Anchor-Smith, Axe, Edge Tool, and Screw Maker."[2] The south front of the wharf seems again to have been partially cut back toward its length of 1803, for its eastern end measured only 200 ft. from Water Street in 1830 (Fig. 10). The building then on the site, occupied as a sail loft and cooperage, was demolished that year[3] when Collins had the south side of his wharf cleared to make way for the range of stores he erected at its head.

The structure which stood on the site by 1831 reached from the water's edge on the east to adjoin the Pickford & Black stone warehouse on the west (Fig. 11). This building overlooking the harbour was one of the King's Warehouses which served local merchants during the years when Halifax was a free-warehousing port. From the early 1830s Drillio and Longard used its upper floor for their sail-making, while from time to time the lower floor was occupied by one of the several auctioneers situated on the wharf. In 1836 the assessable value of the building was £800.[4]

By the early 1860s, when commission merchants Joseph and Robert Seeton bought the east and southwest sections of the wharf from Enos Collins, the building on the site housed George Drillio's sail loft and probably contained William Ackhurst's auction rooms on the lower floor.[5] The wooden store of the 1860s does not, however, appear to have been the same structure that stood on the spot 30 years earlier. It was slightly longer than the previous building, and a partial wing on the southeast extended over filled land which reached several feet beyond the end of the building. Unlike its predecessor, it did not reach to the water's edge. Nevertheless, like the building shown in 1831, the wooden structure of the 1860s was narrower than the stone warehouse to the west

(Fig. 13). The west end of the front structure measured approximately 38½ ft. and apparently adjoined the Pickford & Black warehouse rather than, like its successors, using the wall of the stone edifice as a common wall.[6] The building appears to have remained as late as 1876 when Robert Pickford and William A. Black purchased the property.[7]

Within two years, a much longer structure extended from Pickford & Black's stone warehouse to the water's edge, where the east end of the building was in line with that of the Red Store opposite (Fig. 15). Two distinct buildings were apparently contained within this elongated frame. The west one adjoining the Pickford & Black stone warehouse was three storeys high and had a composition gable roof. Windows along its north wall overlooked the wharf (Figs. 16, 23). By the mid-1890s the building had been remodelled, and numerous double-hung sash windows, spasmodically interrupted by larger windows and loading doors, replaced the earlier, sparser lighting. The exterior of the structure was clapboarded (Figs. 25, 30, 34). The larger east building, although approximately the same height as its companion, contained initially only two storeys beneath its composition gable roof. Three windows were shown on the upper floor, and a single loading door in the centre of the east

end afforded access to the water (Figs. 16, 23). When remodelled during the early 1890s, the main room was divided into three floors, and the small eastern section, which had originally been a coal shed, was split into four levels (Fig. 17). The 108-ft. length was topped by a shed-style composition roof, and the words SAIL LOFT painted in large letters across the harbour end.[8] A double-hung sash window was the only aperture in the east end (Fig. 31). Along the north side a plain trimmed, double-hung sash and a taller, narrower, shuttered window opened onto the top floor. On the ground and second levels there were no apertures in the eastern end of the north wall (Fig. 32).

About 1870 Thomas Forhan succeeded to Drillio's sail-making quarters on the southeast side of the Pickford & Black Wharf, and by the late 1880s tenanted the "commodious premises" on the top floors of both structures. The west section constituted his "spacious sail loft, 30 x 60 feet in size" where he employed 12 hands in "the leading firm in making the sails for yachts in Canada." The eastern one served for storage of the ships' wares in which he also dealt — canvas, corkwood, ships' blocks and running gear.[9] In the lower floors Pickford & Black warehoused their ship-chandlery goods. By the mid-1890s, when Pickford & Black had established themselves as a shipping agency, the premises were occupied as a customs warehouse to store goods destined for transhipment in bond or for delivery to city merchants upon payment of the duty due

upon them. When a devastating fire reduced the whole structure to "huge piles of smouldering debris" in 1904, the warehoused goods were valued at $30,000.[10]

Architectural Information
The building presently on the front of the wharf dates from 1905[11] when it replaced the mutilated timber frame and clapboarded west end which survived the fire (Fig. 34). The new two-storey structure was constructed principally of wood. The western portion of the south wall was, however, composed of concrete and the west wall formed by the 3-ft.-thick extremity of the Pickford & Black stone warehouse. Elsewhere the walls measured 2¼ in. (Fig. 18). The exterior covering of the building had a blocked appearance suggestive of the pressed tin sheathing which remains, but it appears to have been unpatterned. A nearly flat shed roof topped the structure. The eaves were trimmed with a boxed and decorated cornice as were the two projecting pediments which contained hoists above the loading doors on the north side. The vertically boarded loading doors had long metal hinges, and the lower door, which did not reach the ground, was fitted with a large lock. Equally spaced wooden buffers separated the two doors. Two plain-trimmed doors led from a railed landing east of the loading doors to the second-storey interior. Midway between the two sets of loading doors was a plain-trimmed, lugsilled eight-over-eight window on each floor (Figs. 35, 36). Doors and windows also patterned the western portion of the north wall (Figs. 51, 53). A drain pipe between the two small eastern

doors reached from the roof to the ground; its main floor section appears to have been encased. A second drain pipe hung about the same distance east of the more westerly loading doors (Figs. 35, 36). Two windows on the upper storey and one on the north side of the lower storey overlooked the harbour during the late 1920s, but a decade later the latter had been closed up (Figs. 50, 54). The ground floor served a variety of merchants for warehousing their groceries, dry goods and lumber, and was sometime, like its predecessor, a bonded warehouse.[12] About 1915 the carpenters' shop from which the building has derived its title occupied the second storey (Fig. 18).

Collins' Bank and Warehouse
Historical Information
Collins' Bank is undoubtedly the most renowned of the historic structures in the complex area. Home of the Halifax Banking Company for more than 75 years, its connections with the commercial development of Halifax were rich and intimate.

By the mid-1780s Alexander Brymer already had a structure in this convenient location (Fig. 5). It does not, however, appear to have been the same building which stood on the site in 1803 when Robert Lester offered "a neat and compact Dwelling House with good Stores" to the British Ordnance department (Fig. 6).[1] Archibald M'Coll's "Wholesale Store," which stocked a large assortment of English and Scottish merchandise, probably occupied these premises between 1801 and 1805. From 1806, when

Charles Prescott and William Lawson purchased the wharf, until 1812, when Prescott, Lawson & Company was dissolved, the building apparently housed their "stores opposite the Jerusalem Coffee House." During these war years they traded actively with London, Madeira and the West Indies as well as with American and Canadian ports.[2] In 1813 Joseph Allison, the continuing partner of Prescott, Lawson & Company, and Enos Collins, owner of the south side of the wharf, united in a prosperous partnership which lasted 12 years. In addition to their profitable transactions during the late Napoleonic War years in prize vessels condemned by the Vice-Admiralty Court, Collins & Allison regularly imported groceries and dry goods from the United States, the West Indies and Great Britain. The firm was also busily engaged as shipping agents, while the partners were apparently active as well in insurance, exchange and real estate transactions. In 1822 both men were elected to the Committee of Trade and selected members of the newly formed Chamber of Commerce; three years later they were among the eight original partners of the Halifax Banking Company. Subsequently both were seated at the oligarchic 12-member Council Board.[3]

By 1825, the year in which the firm of Collins & Allison was dissolved and in which the Halifax Banking Company was formed, the stone edifice known as "Collins' Bank" was already standing at the head of the

wharf. A number of factors enable the historian to date the building with considerable accuracy. First, no evidence has been found to support the contentions that the structure was erected by 1806 or by 1812.[4] Collins apparently did not own the property on which the building stands until 1821 or 1822;[5] yet, the similarity in architectural style between the bank and the Pickford & Black Building erected in 1830 suggests that they were the work of the same designer for the same owner. T. B. Akins dated the structure to 1823, and a legal agreement drawn in mid-1854 stated that the building had been standing for 30 years. The small number of tenants assessed on the wharf in both 1823 and 1824 implies that building on the north side of the wharf may have been in progress in both years.[6] The edifice first appeared on Toler's plan of the north and south suburbs in 1830 and then on a more detailed map of the area in 1831 (Figs. 10, 11).

Collins' Bank
When the Halifax Banking Company announced its opening in September 1825 "in the new stone building owned by Mr. Collins,"[7] it was not the chartered corporation it had hoped to be but a partnership of eight men whose personal wealth assured the business community of the institution's integrity. A monopoly until the establishment of the Bank of Nova Scotia in 1832, the Halifax Banking Company soon acquired significant London agents and British West Indies connections with which it dealt exten-

sively in exchange. The partners also had other influence nearer home, however, as "Omicron" pointed out in *The Novascotian.*

[The] *Bank has controul over nearly half a million of property, or they hold securities to that amount. Now, taking into consideration the influence the members of the establishment possess in the Council, will it be denied by any man that the proprietors of the old Bank possess the majority of power in the town and Province, and are capable by their weight, to carry almost any political question.*[8] Although the bank's political power was reduced during the movement toward responsible government in the 1840s, it nevertheless remained a private company for a further 40 years. Its periodically redrawn partnership agreements reflected the transition from the older generation to the younger, but did not otherwise substantially alter the operations of the "Halifax Bank," as it was then known. Expansion into branches throughout the province followed incorporation in 1872, and by the late 1870s the second generation partners had also withdrawn. From then until 1903, when the Halifax Banking Company amalgamated with the Canadian Bank of Commerce,[9] its assets increased nearly tenfold, although its capital remained comparatively small and its banking practices conservative.[10]

From at least the mid-19th century, the Halifax Bank building housed not only the bank but also private offices. These may have existed from 1825 or the early 1830s, for Enos Collins is reputed to have kept an office on the wharf from the time of his public retirement until his death 40 years later in 1872. From the mid-1860s, offices, apparently on the ground floor, were also occupied primarily by partners of the bank who were at the same time Collins' immediate family. For at least 20 years, for example, Collins' son-in-law P. C. Hill, while mayor of Halifax and a Liberal member of the provincial legislature, maintained an office there; he had, however, removed before he became premier of Nova Scotia in 1874. Likewise, Collins' eldest son, Brenton, a lawyer like Hill, kept an office in the bank building from 1863 until he retired to England in the late 1870s. Two members of the Allison family, insurance agents, also occupied an office during the 1870s.[11] After a three-year vacancy the Halifax Banking Company expanded into the premises, and the bank retained them until 1908 when the Bank of Commerce moved to its present edifice on George Street. During the next seven years the bank building appears to have been occupied only in 1912, by the Merchants' Bank of Canada. Thereafter it was rented by Gunn's Pork and Beef Packing Company and before 1920 by Roue's Mineral Water Factory.[12] W. J. Roue's first interest always appeared to his companions on the wharf to be ships rather than bottling, and in this building he is believed to have designed the racing schooner *Bluenose.*[13]

Collins' Warehouse
The stone warehouse on the north side of Collins' Wharf was never only the home of the Halifax Banking Company. The eastern half of the building was occupied from 1825, as the whole edifice apparently had been since its erection, as a store and warehouse. E. Collins & Company, in which Enos Collins was the senior partner and William B. Fairbanks and Jonathan C. Allison the juniors, occupied the premises from the spring of 1825. Their busy trade included goods brought by the brig *Indus* from St. Petersburg, France and Gibraltar, but the firm is more infamously known by its petition for a drawback on imported liquors which provoked the "Brandy Dispute" of 1830.[14] During the 1830s the warehouse appears to have been occupied principally by Joseph Allison & Company, a partnership of Joseph Allison with his brother David, which traded extensively in Iberian wines but also dealt in Canadian and West Indian products.[15] Cochran & Company offered a wide variety of groceries, construction materials and ships' wares for sale at the warehouse in the 1840s and 1850s, while after 1857 the local manager, William H. Creighton, carried on in his own name until the late 1870s. He apparently occupied the same store where he imported "Charente, Brandies, Rotterdam Gin" and later acted more generally as a commission merchant and an official assignee.[16] This warehouse appears also to have been the stone store which the British War Department rented for £150 per annum in 1862-63.[17]

One or more of the commission merchants located on the wharf continued apparently to occupy the building during the late 19th century. J. P. Cox & Company, for example, leased a part of the premises for a quarter-century from the late 1880s to house their milling and flour agency, while in the early 20th century Charles Harvey carried on his wholesale grocery and fruit trade there (Fig. 17); like Cox, he had developed an extensive provincial business. From 1906 until the late 1920s part of the building was used as a bonded warehouse, of which the carved CUSTOM WAREHOUSE on the lintel remains a sign. C. E. Choat & Company, grocery brokers, occupied the other portion from 1910 until the property was transferred in the 1940s.[18]

The Property

When the property was sold in 1943 to Halifax real estate broker Melvin S. Clarke, the bank and warehouse had been owned by successive generations of the Collins family for more than 120 years. For half that time, the lands had been administered, for instance by the Eastern Trust Company,[19] in the absence of the owner. That the registered deed of 1811, transferring the south side of Charles Prescott's wharf to Enos Collins, was then applied to the property on the north side of the wharf, which Collins also owned, is therefore understandable. A careful reading of several deeds makes evident, however, the confusion be-tween the two properties that occurred when the northwest side of the wharf was sold in 1943. First, the south boundary of the water lot granted to Prescott and Lawson in 1809 was the same south boundary as that described, in reverse directions, in the deed of transfer from Prescott to Collins in 1811. Therefore, the north division line described in the deed of 1811 as running north 76 degrees east 450 ft. from Water Street into the harbour fell near the centre of Prescott's, later Collins', wharf. Moreover, this north division line was clearly not the south boundary of the wharf sold by Prescott and Lawson to John Clark in 1810, which ran north 74 degrees east (Fig. 20) and was confirmed as the division line between the two properties in 1822.[20] The property on which the bank and warehouse stand was not then the land sold to Collins in 1811 but rather that transferred from Prescott to Collins by a presumably unregistered deed of 1821 or 1822.

Melvin S. Clarke immediately transferred the property through Darcy Sullivan to Sullivan Storage Company, which owned the warehouse until expropriated by the City of Halifax in 1968.[21] In 1947, however, Sullivan Storage Company sold the western half of the edifice to the Bluenose Bottling Company, successor to Roue's earlier Mineral Water Factory. Two years later the building was again transferred, to the Cleveland Realty Corporation, from which Donald C. Keddy first leased and then purchased it. Keddy's electrical supply firm owned the western portion of the building until it was expropriated in 1968.[22]

Architectural Information

Erected of local ironstone in 1823 or 1824, the three-storey building bore a hipped slate roof with a cornice, spouts and conductors extending under and beyond the eaves.[23] The walls — 25 in. thick on the first floor, 21 in. on the second floor and 17 in. on the third (Fig. 18) — were formed of two layers of stone filled with rubble in mortar.[24] Sandstone belts marked the floor levels, while the second- and third-storey windows of the warehouse and the three small parallel windows on the south side beside the westerly loading doors indicate the original pattern of openings along the south and west sides of the edifice. The ironstone-filled aperture on the west wall, which resembles a loading door (Fig. 39), suggests that the western as well as the eastern portion of the structure may originally have been intended as a warehouse and store. A brick fire wall divided the interior into two almost equal sections (Fig. 17).

Alteration to the building may have occurred very early in its history. After a robbery in "Messrs. Collins & Co.'s Counting House" in 1829,[25] security was probably increased. Perhaps the upstairs safe, whose door matches that of the vault in the Pickford & Black office, was then added. The old main door of the building, possibly in the casing headed BANK, may also have been installed at this time. The door was of

wood sheathed inside with iron, the outside being studded with large iron bolts which went through the door and clamped the large cross-bars of iron on the outside of the door to the inner sheathing, the length of the key representing nearly the thickness of the door. . . . when the iron hinges got rusty it was with great difficulty that the door could be moved.[26]

Although in 1905 the cashier of the Halifax Banking Company believed the old door to have been original, so early an alteration was then beyond living memory. The large key to the door was "of English manufacture" and was "believed to have been in use from the founding of the bank in 1825 until about 1881, when more modern methods were adopted."[27] Moreover, a safe-makers firm of Toronto, when consulted in the 1910s, dated the keys, either Barron's or Bramah's, from 1800 to 1834 ; they considered the locks to which they belonged to have been constructed by "the foremost manufacturers" and to have been "recognized as the very best of their time."[28] If, as reported, however, the £1,200 burglary in 1849 was effected with skeleton keys,[29] the locks in use in 1880 may not have been installed so early in this building.

Significant alteration to the building did occur about mid-century. According to an agreement of 1854 between Enos Collins, owner of the bank and warehouse, and William Clark, owner of the property adjoining to the north, a crowning roof, intended to be zinc, was to be constructed over the buildings ; it was to unite the ridge of the existing roof of the bank and warehouse with that of a similar hipped slate roof to be erected on Clark's stone structure then under construction (Fig. 41). At the same time, the skylights on the north side of the roof of the bank and warehouse, which would be covered by the crowning roof, were to be replaced in "the same number and kinds" on the south side overlooking Collins' Wharf.[30] The roof, built apparently with a composition crown, gave the appearance of being a single hipped truncated roof above the two stone edifices (Figs. 23, 39, 43). A photograph taken about the turn of the century showed it with three shingled hoistway dormers, but no skylights, on its south side (Fig. 39). There was also a fourth dormer on the east hip. Three brick chimneys topped the structure, one above each of the fireplaces at opposite ends of the warehouse and one in the western section of the building (Figs. 39, 51).

The alteration of the western portion of the building from a three-storey structure with parallel rows of small windows into a double-storey banking hall with two-storey windows on the lower floors has not been positively dated. While the transformation may have been carried out for the second generation partners in the 1850s or

1860s, the changes may instead have followed the incorporation, appointment of new directors, and expansionist mood of the 1870s. As no architectural evidence has been found to suggest that the double-storey windows were shuttered, the iron shutters which were "closed from the outside and then fastened inside by an iron bar" appear to have belonged to the older, smaller windows before their removal.[31]

By the turn of the century, the small third-floor windows appeared with sandstone quoins, lugsills, and three-over-six sashes. The five long windows were topped by transoms beneath plain heavy lintels ; they also had sandstone quoins, lugsills and three panes of glass (Fig. 39). The door labelled BANK at the southern edge of the front probably contained the new locking arrangements to which the cashier of the Halifax Banking Company referred.[32]

The eastern warehouse portion of the building had also been altered by the 1890s. The westerly loading doors on the first and second floors had been filled by cement and had two different types of windows in their centres. That on the second floor appears to have followed the pattern of the other second-storey windows of the warehouse and have been a two-over-two double-hung sash, while that on the main floor had a double window set into the door opening. In place of the ground-floor loading doors beneath the middle and eastern dormers, there were respectively a plate-glass window and a doorway. The other main-floor apertures had also been elongated. Two window wells were evident at the basement level of the warehouse (Fig. 30). The fact that the belt course stopped beneath the north window on the west front suggests that there was once a window well there (Fig. 39) ; at least one other on the southwest side of the building is also reported.[33]

Two major alterations to the structure have occurred in the 20th century. On Christmas Day 1934, a fire, which caused an estimated $30,000 damage to the building and its contents, swept through wooden partitions on the upper floor, feeding upon empty boxes and straw stored there. The fire began in the western section of the building, but spread north and east to the Simon's Building and Collins' Warehouse respectively, destroying the hipped truncated roof.[34] A flat roof with cornices subsequently replaced it. At the same time a fourth storey of brick was added to the warehouse, and the windows on the east end were bricked up (Fig. 55).[35] No other major structural alterations have been made to the warehouse since the mid-1940s.[36]

The western section of the building, on the other hand, has been extensively changed to suit the needs of tenants and recent owners. By the early 1860s, in addition to the bank on the ground floor, there had been an office "over [the] Halifax Bank" and another advertised as being in the "Halifax Bank Building." In the renumbering of the streets in 1861, however, the building was assigned two street numbers[37] which, a quarter-century later, were clearly applied to the two portions of the main floor—the bank on the south and an office on the north—which were separated by a wooden partition. Division of the main

floor seems therefore to have occurred by, at latest, the 1860s. A brick partition parallel to the fire wall also set off the easterly section of the bank building from the bank and office fronting Water Street (Fig. 16). The wooden partition had apparently been removed before the end of the century, and the brick one by 1914 (Figs. 17, 18). A mezzanine floor fronted by glass overlooked the banking hall,[38] but its date of construction is unknown. By 1914 the old iron-clad doors on all floors of the fire wall had been replaced by a solid wall ; it was not, however, until later that elevators were placed in both sections of the building (Fig. 18). Substantial changes do not appear to have been made within the building until the late 1940s. Then, Cleveland Realty Corporation, under a lease to Donald C. Keddy, agreed to renovate the premises for use as a general warehouse and office, as well as to electrify the elevator and install two space heaters of the pot oil burning type.[39] Either in these renovations or in changes made by Keddy after he purchased the property later the same year, the bank door on the west front was closed up and a loading door opened on the south side. At the same time, the mezzanine was replaced by a full second floor, the west stairway put in and the upstairs offices redivided. Later Keddy had the basement filled with rubble and concrete ; at that time he removed the main floor vault which was discovered to have been bolted with cannon balls.[40] The intricate system of locks upon this vault contributed substantially to the reputed impregnability of the old bank.[41]

Red Store
Historical Information
The three-storey wooden building near the north front of the wharf has a very old foundation, three discernible main floor levels, and evidence of extensive repairs throughout the structure.

As late as 1803 part of the site of this building was still open water, although a long wharf just south of it extended into the harbour (Fig. 6). Within the next few years Charles Prescott and William Lawson, owners of the property from 1806, filled in the site and erected the first building to occupy the situation. The structure had a stone foundation and was already standing in 1810 when they sold the northern portion of their wharf to John Clark.[1] At a "red store," which was probably upon this foundation if it was not this building, Charles Hill & Company auctioned the rich prize goods of successful Nova Scotian privateering in American water during the War of 1812. This "red store" was apparently one of the "three large and convenient Stores" which were still owned by Prescott in 1821 but which were advertised to let by his tenants, Collins & Allison, in the spring of that year.[2] The buildings did not rent easily, and within the next two years Collins purchased the property, including the "large Red Store."[3] As its northeast corner measured only about 218 ft. from Water Street,[4] this building occupied at most the western 50 ft. of the present structure. By 1831, however, an edifice of the present dimensions stood upon the site (Fig. 11).

The 35-ft. width of the present Red Store[5] suggests that this structure on the wharf may have been the one for which Enos Collins was pressing delivery of timber from the Liverpool (N.S.) firm of Seely & Gough in midsummer 1830. The members of the lower frame, accumulated from a variety of Queen's County entrepreneurs, were ready for shipping by July, although the "long pieces" for the second storey were apparently not sent until September. The other materials included "five long Sticks of 36 feet by 14 Inches square." These were probably of red pine, as it could be squared from 12 to 13½ in., whereas a 36-ft. stick of white pine, apparently the material requested, squared 18 or 20 in. By August, "70 pieces of Joists with a quantity of other pieces" were also loading and were to be shipped with "a deck load of 14 Inch Timber by 17½ feet long ;" if the whipsaw was run twice through the latter, Seely & Gough instructed, it would answer the dimensions of the joists. William Foster supplied some "refuse Timber" at the same time. The whole of the merchantable scantling cost £250.[5]

The new building does not appear to have been occupied by any of the important firms situated on the wharf, but rather to have been rented as advantageously as possible by its owner, Enos Collins. During the early 1830s it may have been occupied by auctioneer Edward Lawson or commission merchant Edward Shortis, who dealt in such groceries as Quebec beef and pork, Genesee flour and Digby herring.[7] By the time of the *Trent* crisis of the early 1860s, the British War Department already rented a part of this store, and after 1863 they probably rented all of it. During the shortage of military storehouses they appear to have continued their lease until at least 1870.[8] The "long wooden salt and fish store" which Enos Collins withheld from his sale of the eastern portion of the wharf to Joseph and Robert Seeton in 1865 had practically the same dimensions as the present Red Store. Despite the unlikelihood of a store of such description being rented by the War Department, so prominent a tenant paying a reliable and no doubt substantial rent goes far to explain the reservation by a man himself no longer active in shipping. The sale of the building to the Seetons in 1872, after Collins had died and the War Department had apparently vacated the premises, confirms the probability of this reserved building having been the Red Store.[9] Moreover, no other structure on the wharf in the mid-1860s fits the description given (Fig. 13).

Uninterrupted by the transfer of the wharf from the Seetons to Robert Pickford and William Black in 1876,[10] a succession of commission merchants occupied the wooden warehouse from the early 1870s. William Kandick's wholesale groceries, tobacco and imported spirits appear to have been sold there for nearly 15 years, while by the early 1880s William Ackhurst— auctioneer, commission merchant, provision dealer, city alderman, and long-term tenant on the wharf—had apparently moved over from the south side of the property.[11] From 1878 until the mid 1880s the upper floor of the warehouse was used for the uncommercial purpose of holding Sunday services for seamen. Although the promoters of the St. Andrew's Waterside Mission failed to convince shipping men of the practical benefits of this evangelical enterprise, Pickford & Black apparently granted the premises rent free. Sir E. C. Inglefield, the admiral on the North American station, acted as lay reader and his ship's crew as choir for the struggling mission.[12]

In the late 1870s two long-term occupants established their ground-floor offices in the building. Isaac H. Mathers initiated a more than 40-year tenancy for his firm in 1876. Beginning as a commission merchant, he dealt principally in forest products. By the turn of the century, however, he had acquired not only important English timber connections but also several steamship agencies, a large chartering business, and three Scandinavian consulships. Regarded as one of the best-known business men in Halifax, he retired in 1906 in favour of his son and was subsequently appointed as Canadian member of an imperial commission to inquire into the existence of an alleged shipping combine.[13] In 1879

R. B. Seeton, in a reorganized firm, returned to the wharf he had sold three years earlier. He continued as a shipping agent and, within 20 years, had developed his commission trade into a prosperous wholesale grocery business. Sugar, molasses, flour, fish, beans and dried fruit were among the many products the firm imported and distributed through the province. In 1916 the company occupied nearly half the building and had stored there almost $20,000 worth of groceries.[14] For 25 years from the mid-1880s, the ship builder David McPherson maintained an office on the wharf, apparently in this building. During that time, he was a city alderman, mayor of Halifax, a member of the legislative assembly, and a provincial cabinet minister. William Chisholm, a lumber and commission merchant, also had premises in the Red Store for about 20 years (Fig. 30).[15]

After 1880 the building was increasingly divided among numerous tenants. Through the 1880s, they continued to be principally commission merchants who required substantial warehousing space rather than formal offices (Fig. 16). By the mid-1890s, however, offices clearly supplemented the warehousing facility (Fig. 17), and later in the decade the number of tenants increased by about 50 per cent. Thereafter, the number of lessees remained fairly stable, although a more formal arrangement of offices apparently took place during the 1930s.[16] Such a transformation of the warehouse reflected the expansion of services and the pressures upon space concomitant with the development of a large urban community.

Pickford & Black continued to own the building and to rent its premises to a variety of short and long term tenants until the property was expropriated by the City of Halifax in 1968.[17]

Architectural Information
Although a building of the dimensions of the present one was already standing on the site in 1831 (Fig. 11), no information has been discovered as to the style, construction or alteration of the structure until nearly half a century later. By then the building was three storeys high and bore a hipped roof. At the east end four windows lighted the third storey, while the two on each of the lower floors flanked a central loading door. A single dormer appears on the north side of the roof above a loading door; elsewhere the north wall is shown as containing numerous though irregularly positioned windows (Fig. 23).

By the 1890s substantial alterations had apparently been made to the building.[18] It remained a three-storey structure which was believed to have been "constructed completely of southern hard pine"[19] and which bore a hipped roof. The exterior was clapboarded and coated with fireproof paint (Fig. 17). The roofing material is unknown, but shingles, such as those used on the three-storey office and warehouse of H. H. Fuller & Company at 45 Upper Water Street, would have been the usual covering for such

a structure (Fig. 17). On the south side of the roof were three dormers, and on the north side two. In addition, there were at least three skylights on the north side and one on the west. The corners of the roof were covered with a wood or metal overlap. A hot-water heating system had been installed in the building (Fig. 17), but four evenly spaced chimneys still remained. The windows along the north wall reveal a fairly symmetrical pattern which hints at an earlier façade of the building. The shuttered casements in three parallel rows along the east section were continued beyond the eastern loading door on the top floor of the middle section; beneath them, however, the size and arrangement of the windows had been altered to larger, double-hung sashes (Fig. 32). Likewise, along the south side, numerous openings are discernible, but their pattern cannot be identified (Fig. 30). The windows on the ends of the building were of the most motley types and positions. On the east façade, three six-over-six sash windows lighted the third storey; however the fourth aperture near the north side of the front appears to have been a smaller single sash with only three panes. The window below it on the second floor was again of a different size and may, like the large centre window, have been a casement. There seems also to have been a single window on the ground floor very near the south edge and therefore not aligned with the most southerly opening on the third storey (Fig. 32). At the west end were four windows, all apparently plain-trimmed and slipsilled, single-sash, flat openings. The two windows on the second storey had two-over-two sashes which differed from both the small casement on the third floor and the large storefront window on the ground floor. Two steps up from the wharf and near the south edge of the façade was a plain-trimmed door opening with a flush transom (Fig. 30).

By 1914 the south wall had two distinct characters (Fig. 40). The eastern section retained much evidence of the original warehousing function of the building. Beneath a hoist-way dormer were loading doors on the second and third storeys. Buffers separated them, and small single windows flanked them on either side. On the ground floor the four long windows east of the doorway to H. I. Mathers' office may still have been shuttered. Beyond a similar window west of the door hung a leader connected to the gutter at the edge of the roof. In the central section three unevenly spaced and sized doors were followed on the ground floor by five double-hung windows with two-over-two sashes. Above, but not aligned with these windows and doors, were seven slipsilled windows which extended to beneath a loading door at the eastern end of the third floor of the section. A window similar to those flanking the loading doors nearer the

harbour stood west of the loading door and above the third and fourth windows of the second storey. In the westerly portion of the building, after a wider space than separated the previous apertures, two parallel windows on the first and second storeys continued the pattern of the central section. One more, similar window appears on the ground floor near the west end, but the photograph does not show the upper portion of the western half of the building. Tenants' nameplates flat against the façade and above their respective entrances had discreetly replaced the earlier signs protruding from the south wall. A very small one-storey appendage abutted on the west side (Fig. 18).

The present flat tar and gravel roof dates from the aftermath of a serious fire which swept the upper storeys of the store in early December of 1916. Beginning at the southwestern end of the structure, the fire worked through the interior partitions, gained stronger hold in the centre of the building, and broke out through the roof. At one stage the building was "practically a mass of flames from end to end." "The whole upper portion of the structure" was destroyed, but the ground and second storeys appear to have suffered only scorching and smoke and water damage.[20] There was talk of replacing the building with a concrete structure in the spring, but within two months of the fire tenants were already returning to their former premises.[21] The several alterations evident in the south wall by 1929 may or may not have been performed as part of the repairs following the fire. In the eastern section four windows replaced the loading door and flanking windows on the second storey, while on

the first floor the door was closed up and the row of windows, now eight in number, extended westward into the central section. Above them three windows had been added on the second storey, and the third-floor loading door had been removed (Fig. 49).

The much divided interior of the Red Store reflects the change in its function which occurred during the late 19th century. Some subdivision of the main floor at least, had evidently taken place by the late 1880s, and extensive breaking up into offices followed shortly thereafter (Fig. 17), as both the interior decor and the increased number of tenants reveal. The double-hung sashes of the central portion of the north wall and the long two-over-two sash windows of the south façade were probably installed during this period for the principal tenant of the building, R. B. Seeton and Company. In 1904 this firm's redecorated premises in the southwestern portion of the main floor, "resplendent in white paint with a surface of enamel," were rated "one of the smartest looking offices in the city."[22]

Simon's Building
Historical Information
The granite-faced walls and the slate roofing of the building at the head of the Central Wharf reflected the heady prosperity of mid-19th-century Halifax. The structure was built in an era of the wartime riches of Crimea and the looming American Civil War, of the wealth of the West Indies trade and approaching reciprocity with the United States.

The site was by no means a new one. By the mid-1780s the Honourable Alexander Brymer, merchant, gentleman and councillor, had already erected buildings on his wharf which extended southward from the Ordnance Yard at the foot of Buckingham Street (Fig. 5). In 1805, however, the only noteworthy structure on the wharf was "A LARGE substantial building" which was "commonly used as a stable, coach-house, &c."[1] After 1810, when Haligonian merchants Charles Prescott and William Lawson sold the north side of their wharf to John Clark, he rented the two buildings along the north side to the Ordnance department whose yard adjoined them. As he had already established himself in the rich American wartime trade,[2] he probably occupied the ell-shaped building at the south head of the wharf himself, at least until the middle of the decade when he apparently erected the Privateer's Warehouse fronting the harbour.[3] When James N. Shannon Jr. opened his "New Store" with "New GOODS" from London at the "head of Clark's wharf" in 1819, his shop may have been the ell-shaped structure vacated by Clark. Shannon and his successors —the prominent dry-goods firm of James Lyon & Company and the successful auctioneers and commission merchants David and Edward Starr, who later erected the building now known as Morse's Teas—more likely, however, occupied the extensive store at the north head of the wharf which

the Ordnance department had surrendered in mid-1818.[4] No identifiable tenant occupied the ell-shaped building through the 1820s, and Clark may have continued to use it himself.

How long this structure remained cannot be determined. The substantial increase in the assessable value of Clark's Wharf during the early 1830s suggests that a new store had been erected; it may have replaced this old and small building. The latter may, however, have been the low wooden building which adjoined Collins' stone store to the north in 1854. In that year William, son and heir of John Clark, took down the wooden structure and in its place erected the edifice which stands today.[5]

The subsequent history of the building reflects the ups and downs of Halifax as a commercial community. William Clark apparently had not his father's business acumen and, like many others during the 1850s, overreached himself in undertaking to erect his new stone store. Within the succeeding four years he found it necessary to mortgage his wharf to his wealthy neighbour Enos Collins; heavily mortgaged, Clark died intestate in 1859, leaving debts well in excess of his liquid assets. His widow, under licence of the Court of Probate, subsequently had the wharf sold at auction to relieve the financial stringencies of the estate.[6] R. W. Fraser, an established commission merchant, bought the premises for £8,500, cleared the mortgage, and immediately sold all of the property except the Simon's Building to two separate mercantile firms.[7] Fraser himself occupied the building he

retained for warehousing and retailing the groceries he imported from Baltimore, Philadelphia and Richmond. He continued to occupy premises on the wharf until 1874, and he may have used the eastern half of the building for his concerns until then.[8]

About 1865 Fraser let the impressive stone store facing Water Street to Esson & Company, a recently reorganized and prosperous grocery business which surrendered its retail activities on Barrington Street and confined its Haligonian enterprise during the next 20 years to wholesaling from its new office and warehouse. An old and respected firm, it imported West Indies produce, American groceries, Asian teas, and British liquors which it traded throughout the Maritime Provinces and Newfoundland; by the early 1880s its business was valued at nearly half a million dollars a year. After Fraser sold the edifice in 1880, Esson & Company owned as well as occupied the premises at the south head of the wharf.[9] In 1888, nevertheless, hard times, overextension and long unsettled financial affairs drove the firm into receivership. Its premises were rated as "convenient, centrally situated, and in every way a desirable business stand" when advertised for subsequent sale at auction.[10]

James A. Chipman, the new owner, occupied the western half of the "large and commodious . . . Granite Warehouse," while Miner T. Foster, tea merchant, later insurance and mining agent, appears to have rented the eastern portion.[11] Chipman's flour and feed business apparently flourished, but within ten years he sold the property and probably the interest of the firm to his junior since 1881, Ingraham B. Shaffner, and his new partner James Adams.[12] Shaffner was an enterprising merchant who, through effective advertising and reliable service, expanded the flour, feed and grain trade into a prominent and prosperous business. By 1909 the firm was dealing extensively in its own brands of flour as well as in "all grades of Manitoba flour, Western feed in large quantities, grain, etc." and was regarded as "among the leading houses in [Nova Scotia] identified with the business."[13] In 1917, however, Shaffner sold the Upper Water Street premises to George H. Hooper.[14]

In 1919 the property was again transferred, from Hooper to J. B. Mitchell. C. E. Creighton and Son housed their wholesale grocery business there from 1920 to 1923, while the Franco Canadian Import Company thereafter rented the store until the early 1930s.[15] The building was owned by Joseph Simon, a successful junk dealer, from 1937 until the City of Halifax expropriated the property in 1968[16] to make way for its intended Harbour Drive and an improved sewerage system.

Architectural Information

The two-walled structure built in 1854 stands equal in height with Enos Collins' stone store adjoining it to the south. The three-and-one-half storey building used 129 ft. of the north wall of the latter in common, and on the east it utilized the 38 ft. 3 in. gable end of the Privateer's Warehouse. Its own north wall ran 69 ft. 6 in. parallel to the Collins' property line, then angled 61 ft. southwest toward Water Street where its west front measured only 26 ft. 6 in.[17] Dressed granite blocks backed up by rubble stone constituted the north and west walls; the regularly coursed west wall was surface dressed as befitted a commercial office of importance, but the north wall, randomly coursed, remained rough (Fig. 43). The building was originally intended to have a crowning roof of zinc which would connect the ridge of a hipped slate roof with the older, similar roof of the adjoining store.[18]

No early pictures of the building have been located to indicate its appearance before the apparently extensive remodelling of its west end. Architectural evidence reveals alteration in the first-floor windows and doors on the north and west walls, but no documentary evidence as to the nature of these changes has been found. Esson & Company, who rented the building from 1865 and purchased it in 1880, appear most likely to have remodelled it during the early 1880s.[19]

Detailed views of the edifice in the late 19th and early 20th century reveal little change in the exterior appearance of the building during that period.[20] The hipped truncated roof facing Water Street, which united the Simon's and Collins' buildings, gave the outward appearance of topping a single structure. Its crown appears to have been composition rather than the intended zinc. The east end was also hipped, and a projection from its north edge protected the joint between the Simon's Building and the adjoining Privateer's Warehouse from leakage (Figs. 23, 51). Three hoistway dormers ranged along the north side of the roof; goods were thus lifted through the parallel loading doors beneath into the upper storage areas of the warehouse. On the north side of the west hip was a single skylight. Projecting eaves trimmed the roof edge, but no rafters protruded beneath them. The drain pipe at the northwest corner of the building, dilapidated by the early 20th century, still hung in place; its less wasted companion at the southwest edge may have been of later date or may only have fared better from its more protected situation. A single stack stone chimney topped the structure.[21]

The location of the doors and windows along the west front continues unchanged since the 1880s; slight alterations had, however, already taken place in their details by the early 20th century. The basic form was a flat lugsilled aperture. This style remained, although the plain lintels sketched above the second- and third-floor windows were not confirmed by photograph, and one awning on the street level had been removed. On the ground floor the double windows were set inside a cast-iron frame. Although the 1887 engraving indicates two-over-two sashes on the west wall, the 1909 photograph shows that earlier style six-over-six sashes were then still in place; presumably the artist who created the engraving attempted to upgrade the building by depicting the more fashionable two-over-two sashes. By the early 20th century, the single-leaf, three-panel door of the 1880s had been replaced by a double door with a circular-headed, glazed panel in each leaf.

The north wall is likewise largely unaltered. Five rows of parallel windows on each of the three floors reached from the northwest corner to the first set of loading doors, the bottom one of which was one column offset to the east. Two additional ranks of windows completed the angled wall of the structure. All the windows were shown in 1887 as topped with plain lintels, but the photograph of 1909 again failed to confirm this decoration. All contained double-hung sashes; the paning is, however, impossible to determine. As along the west front, the ground-floor windows were noticeably taller than those on the second and third floors. Moreover, by 1909 the fifth window from the west on the ground level appears to have been broader than the preceding four. A drain pipe extended between the third and fourth rows of windows in both views (Figs. 42, 43).

No major alteration to the exterior appearance of the building occurred until 1935. After an extensive fire spread through the upper storey of the building on Christmas Day 1934,[22] a flat roof replaced the damaged hipped truncated roof (Fig. 54). Subsequently, at the east end of the north wall, an enlarged door topped with a steel beam was opened to allow trucked goods to enter the interior directly. The symmetrical pattern of the wall was thus interrupted. Less elegant window panes also replaced the large arched glass panels in the north wall, and a more functional door superseded the circular-headed, glazed panels.[23]

Almost no information has been found about the interesting interior of this building. A wooden partition, beginning at the point of angle in the north wall and extending in line with the fire wall of the adjoining stone warehouse, apparently at one time divided the structure (Fig. 16). By 1895, a gas engine had been installed in the premises (Fig. 17), and by 1914 a wooden partition, parallel with and somewhat north of the party wall, had been added in the attic (Fig. 18). The most recent owner covered the boarded ceiling of the main office with acoustic tiles and the upstairs walls with beaverboard.[24] The uneven floor levels, the herringbone brick paving in the rear portion, and the plaster in the basement survive from an unrecorded past.[25]

Privateer's Warehouse
Historical Information
A local tradition claims that this fortress-like warehouse dates from about 1800 and that its title derives from Enos Collins having stored there the rich prize goods he gained in privateering during the Napoleonic Wars. As is common in legend, there is some basis in fact and a good deal of romanticizing in both the dating of the building and Collins' particular association with it.

By the mid-1780s the influential Alexander Brymer had already erected structures from Water Street to near the harbour along his wharf which extended southward from the new Ordnance Yard (Fig. 5). Here at the turn of the century, Charles Hill regularly auctioned a variety of Canadian and other goods. By 1803, when Quebec merchant Robert Lester attempted to sell the property to the British military establishment as an extension of the Ordnance Yard, "a large Building" stood on the wharf. In 1805 "a very extensive Lumber-Yard" adjoined the building which was "commonly used as a stable, coach-house, &c," but which was considered "suitable for various useful purposes."[1] It was not shown on the plan accompanying Lester's proposal, although two other structures, apparently of wood, were precisely indicated (Fig. 6). A stone edifice on the property would not, however, have escaped Lester's attention; nor would it have passed unnoticed by the Commanding Royal Engineer who based his opposition to purchasing the site in part upon the prevalence of wooden buildings in the area. In a town where he felt it necessary to justify requesting the appointment of a successor to the master builder and mason employed in his department, such premises as the Privateer's Warehouse would have been a sufficient rarity to attract his and others' notice.[2] It must therefore be concluded that no such major stone structure stood upon the wharf by 1805.

Subsequent plans of 1812 to 1819 (Figs. 8, 9) likewise fail to indicate the erection of Clark's "noble Warehouse."[3] By 1812 three buildings stood on the wharf. Two were on its north side against the wall of the Ordnance Yard. The British military establishment rented the eastern one as a carpenters' shop from 1811 until at least 1819 and the larger one at the head of the wharf from 1813 until mid-1818.[4] The third, at the head of the wharf on its south side, was an ell-shaped structure which still stood in 1831 (Fig. 11). By 1814 a rectangular building running north and south had been added about half-way down the south side of the wharf, somewhat east of the ell-shaped structure and west of the site of the present stone warehouse (Fig. 9).

Although the Ordnance department continued to use this plan of 1814 through 1819, it cannot, however, be claimed to represent accurately the structures on the wharf to that date for the plan failed to make alteration for "the new store of Mr. John Clarke" occupied in the late fall of 1816 by George Grassie and Company while their own premises, destroyed by fire, were being rebuilt.[5] As a building of the dimensions and location of the present structure is the only addition to the wharf shown by a very detailed map of 1831 (Fig. 11), this new store appears, in fact, to have been the present stone warehouse. The edifice likewise appears on Toler's plan of 1830 in which only the three early stone buildings of the complex area are shown (Fig. 10).

Such a dating of the Privateer's Warehouse in itself substantially discounts the legendary associations of the structure. There is, however, further evidence. It will be acknowledged that Enos Collins, still resident in Liverpool (N.S.), was already associated with the partnership of Prescott and Lawson in ownership of the brig *Liverpool* before they purchased Lester's wharf in 1806.[6] He may well thereafter have made their wharf his Haligonian headquarters, perhaps staying at Mrs. Ann Bell's house of entertainment at its head when he visited the town, or renting a store nearer the water when he had goods to sell. In January 1809, nevertheless, when Prescott and Lawson expanded their firm, it was not Collins but his later associate Joseph Allison who was taken into the partnership. Moreover, only in 1811 did Collins begin to advertise his situation in the commercial columns of the Halifax newspapers. He had by then, on the eve of the dissolution of Prescott, Lawson & Company, purchased from Charles Prescott the south side of the wharf which later bore Collins' name for half a century.[7] At about the same time he bought in Vice Admiralty sales a dilapidated slaver *The Black Joke*, which he repaired and renamed the *Liverpool Packet*. While awaiting the outbreak of war with the United States when the schooner might be licensed as a privateering vessel, he ran it regularly between Halifax and Liverpool (N.S.). It was this ship's infamous record that established Collins' reputation as a privateer operator and reaped his most substantial shipping profits.[8] By then the land on which the Privateer's Warehouse stands was already owned by John Clark who must have occupied the only building not rented to the Ordnance Department for the business he presumably transferred from Fairbanks' Wharf at the time of his purchase in 1810.[9] While Collins' association with the site of the complex of historical buildings may therefore have begun as early as 1806, documentary evidence has not been found to support the legend that Collins' privateering activities were centred in the old stone warehouse which now stands on the Central Wharf.

On the other hand, by the early 1820s, John Clark had established himself as an important figure in the Haligonian merchant community. He not only styled himself "merchant" in 1822 rather than "carpenter" as in 1810, but was Halifax agent for the Boston packet and a partner in the exclusive Halifax Banking Company. The

Privateer's Warehouse was commensurate with the position, and he very likely occupied the stone building himself with the variety of foodstuffs and construction materials he regularly received from American ports.[10] By the late 1830s his wharf had, however, been rented and apparently continued subsequently to be leased, for instance in the 1850s to George H. Starr. Starr himself probably filled the stone warehouse with the American and Canadian foodstuffs which were frequently auctioned on the wharf on his behalf.[11]

The Clarks, father John and sons Charles and William, owned the wharf from 1810 to 1859 when it was sold by William's widow to Robert Fraser, who immediately disposed of the eastern half of the property to William Tarr and William Chisholm, commission merchants like himself. Three years later, Enos Collins foreclosed their unpaid mortgage, owned the land and buildings briefly himself, and then sold them in 1864 to George C. Harvey, a commission merchant and insurance agent.[12] Harvey's long occupation terminated in the early 1880s when he removed to the United States.[13] In 1886 Joseph Wood, a shipping agent, rented the premises, and he probably managed the property until 1904 when he purchased it from Harvey's executors (Fig. 17). From the mid-1890s Wood apparently rented the stone warehouse to a variety of tenants, including a dealer in junk and marine stores and a wholesale sugar and flour merchant.[14] More recently, during the 20-year ownership of C. J. Burke & Company, the building was occupied as a fish warehouse. The City of Halifax purchased the property from Burke's widow in 1962.[15]

Architectural Information

Heavy ironstone walls, symmetrical freestone-quoined apertures along the the exposed north wall, and a pitched roof are the most immediately discernible features of the 150-year-old building. Apparently built adjoining a long wooden structure which once stood to the south (Fig. 6), the south wall was constructed without windows and has remained unopened. The north wall, by contrast, contains five windows on each of the second and third storeys,[16] while on the ground floor loading doors stand in place of the second and fourth windows. All are headed by large plain lintels and surrounded by quoins; the windows are based by sills. The east and west walls constitute gable ends to the structure, and both appear to have been originally freestanding. The east end fronted on the water, and the west end on an enclosed yard which began about halfway down the wharf and continued, north of the building and parallel to the wall of the Ordnance Yard, to the water's edge (Fig. 11).

On the first and second storeys of the east end were loading doors near the north side and windows near the south side; in line above them on the third floor were two smaller windows. In the attic stood an arched window, trimmed with quoins like the openings on the north wall. At a later date the windows near the south side, the lower loading door and the arched upper aperture were filled in; the second-floor loading door and the third-storey window above it allowed access between the Privateer's Warehouse and the adjoining wooden store. Likewise, at the west end, the windows — one near the north side on the first floor, two on each of the second and third floors, and one in the attic — have been bricked up. As the floor levels of the Simon's Building coincide with the closed windows, it is apparent that the work was done in 1854 when the structure was erected.[17] During the late 19th and early 20th centuries the three-and-one-half storey structure bore a pitched slate roof (Figs. 16, 17, 18, 23). No early historic photographs of this building have been found, but aerial views of the 1920s to 1940s show two skylights on each side of the roof (Figs. 51, 55).

Wooden Storehouse

Historical Information

A structure of some architectural interest, the wooden store at the eastern end of the Central Wharf is the most recent of the historical buildings in the complex. The building has been styled a "wooden loft," but there is no evidence to suggest that it was ever used for sail-making as such nomenclature implies.

By 1830, a small building stood on filled land east of the Privateer's Warehouse. Its north wall was flush with that of the adjoining stone store and its width that of the present structure (Figs. 10, 11). Architectural examination suggests that the east wall of the Privateer's Warehouse has never been exposed to weathering and that this easterly building was therefore erected about 1815. Why such a structure was built can only be speculated upon, but part of its function may have been to protect the adjoining stone wall from the driving salty spray of winter storms. The building still stood in 1859 when Clark's Wharf was sold to R. W. Fraser and immediately to William Tarr and

William Chisholm (Fig. 12). They occupied the building, presumably as a warehouse, until 1862 when Enos Collins foreclosed their unpaid mortgage.[1] Two years later George C. Harvey, a West Indies and commission merchant, bought the property[2] including the building which stood until at least 1866 (Figs. 13, 14).[3] Within the following decade, he replaced it by the present structure (Fig. 15).

Harvey himself probably used the building until the early 1880s, while from 1886 until about 1940 it was occupied as a general warehouse, seemingly by Joseph Wood & Company, shipping agents.[4] Subsequently, C. J. Burke & Company owned the property[5] and appear from the apparatus remaining in the building to have let it most recently as a fish-packing plant. The structure was purchased by the City of Halifax in 1962.[6]

Architectural Information

The most immediately noticeable characteristic of the three-and-one-half storey building (Figs. 16, 17) is its north-south orientation, in contrast with the east-west alignment of the other structures of the complex. It has, however, further distinctions. Constructed primarily of spruce, it symbolizes the region's long and prosperous connections with the forest and the sea. Its heavy beams are mounted upon hardwood corbels of birch and are braced by the strong roots of the tamarack known as ship's knees. Its mortise and tenon framing is comple-

mented by offset scarfes.[7] The east wall of the stone Privateer's Warehouse serves as the west wall of this otherwise wooden store.[8]

Outside, the gable ends of the building lead to a pitched roof. Architectural investigation failed to confirm the representation in a panoramic view of 1879 of two ground-floor accesses on the north side of the building and the rows of four and three windows lighting the second and third floors respectively. The single attic window was accurately depicted (Fig. 23).[9] On the east side, two gable dormers, fitted by the 1890s with double-hung sashes, protruded from the roof. Beneath, plain-trimmed windows on the second and third storeys stood in two parallel rows of three apertures each (Figs. 23, 32). This symmetrical pattern appears, however, to have been broken by the last decade of the century by a larger opening, perhaps a loading door, situated below and slightly to the south of the central window (Fig. 32). By the early 1930s, further alterations had introduced the present window pattern along the east front (Fig. 53). On the narrow west wall was a row of windows opposite the northern row on the second and third storeys of the east side and extended to the ground level. By the early 20th century, the middle window appears to have been a double-hung sash, while the upper one may have been a casement; the number of panes cannot be distinguished (Fig. 43). The brick chimney, evident in photographs of the 1930s, was probably knocked down to its present attic level in the mid-1940s, when the dormers were also removed[10] and the necessary roof repairs effected (Fig. 55).

22 Aerial view of the Halifax waterfront, about 1965.
(*Halifax Photo Service Ltd.*)

22

23 A section of the "Panoramic View of the City of
Halifax Nova Scotia 1879." Pickford & Black's
wharf is the long one above the steamer in the foreground. (*Public Archives of Nova Scotia.*)

24 Letterhead of the firm of Pickford & Black, 188—.
(*Pickford & Black Co. Ltd., Halifax.*)

23

24

25 The Pickford & Black Building as it appeared about
   1890. (*Nova Scotia Museum, Halifax.*)
26 A sketch of Pickford & Black's office, about 1900.
   (*Plan of the City of Halifax*, comp. F. W. W. Doane
   [Halifax: McAlpine Publishing Co., n.d.].)

25

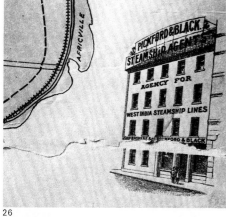

26

27 The interior of Pickford & Black's office before renovation, about 1902. (*Pickford & Black Co. Ltd., Halifax*)

27 The interior of Pickford & Black's office before renovation, about 1902. (*Pickford & Black Co. Ltd., Halifax*)

28 The interior of Pickford & Black's office after renovation, about 1910. (*Pickford & Black Co. Ltd., Halifax.*)

27

28

29 The interior of Pickford & Black's office, 1930. (*Pickford & Black Co. Ltd., Halifax.*)
30 The Pickford & Black Wharf, about 1895. In the foreground are Collins' Warehouse and Pickford & Black's stone warehouse; nearer the harbour are the Red Store, with William Chisholm's sign, and the wooden warehouse which burned in 1904. Beyond is the western end of a long freight shed.

31 Black Brothers' Wharf adjoining the Pickford & Black Wharf to the south, about 1900. The Red Store appears on the right. (Pickford & Black papers, Fire Investigation before Stipendiary Magistrate George H. Fielding, 1904. *Public Archives of Nova Scotia.*)

29

30

31

32 William A. Black, of Pickford & Black, owned the controlling interest in the *Fastnet* after 1892. The north and east sides of the Red Store appear near the centre; on the right is the Wooden Store and on the left a long freight shed. In the background the wooden warehouse with sail loft is visible on the south side of the wharf. (*Pickford & Black Co. Ltd., Halifax.*)

32

33 This view illustrates the bustling activity of the
Pickford & Black Wharf, about 1900. (*Nova Scotia
Museum, Halifax.*)

34 View of the Pickford & Black Wharf from the east
after the fire in September 1904. (*Pickford & Black
Co. Ltd., Halifax.*)

35 Harry I. Mathers, of I. H. Mathers & Son, in front of
the Carpenters' Shop, 1911. (*I. H. Mathers & Son
Ltd., Halifax.*)

33

35

34

36 Burned cotton unloaded from the SS *Sowwell*, 1913. The upper portion of the Carpenters' Shop shown here stands directly above the section which appears in Fig. 35. (*I. H. Mathers & Son Ltd., Halifax.*)

37 The eastern extremity of the Pickford & Black Wharf. The view shows the typical wharf construction of piles, timbers and joists. (*I. H. Mathers & Son Ltd., Halifax.*)

38 The eastern section of the Pickford & Black Wharf at its greatest length. (*I. H. Mathers & Son Ltd., Halifax.*)

39 Collins' Bank and Warehouse as it appeared about 1900. (Victor Ross, *Bank of Commerce*, Vol. 1, opp. p. 52.)

40 The Red Store as it appeared in February 1914, after an unusually heavy snowstorm. (*I. H. Mathers & Son Ltd., Halifax.*)

36

37

38

39

40

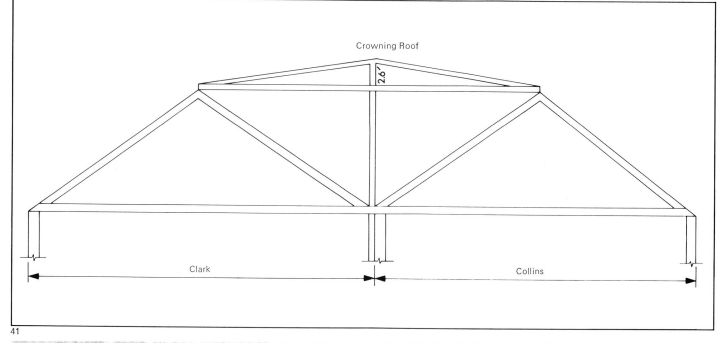

41

42

43

44 View of Water Street at the north end of Bedford
   Row (from a postcard), about 1885. (Louis W.
   Collins, Halifax.)

44

45 Dwyer's Wharf, Upper Wharf Street, late 19th century. (*Nova Scotia Museum, Halifax.*)
46 Samuel Cunard's office and warehouse, Upper
   Water Street, before 1917. (*Nova Scotia Museum,
   Halifax.*)

47 Cronan's Wharf: *top*, late 19th century; *centre*, early
   20th century; *bottom*, 1966.

45

46

47

48 Morse's Teas, opposite the head of the Pickford &
Black Wharf, 1925. (*Nova Scotia Museum, Halifax.*)

49 Aerial view of Halifax waterfront, 1929. The arrow
indicates the Pickford & Black and Central wharfs.
(*National Air Photo Library, Ottawa, A1953/17.*)

50 Aerial view of Halifax waterfront, 1929. The arrow
indicates the Pickford & Black and Central wharfs.
(*National Air Photo Library, Ottawa, A1953/49.*)

51 Aerial view of Halifax waterfront, 1929. The arrow
indicates the Pickford & Black and Central wharfs.
(*National Air Photo Library, Ottawa, A1238/26.*)

52 Aerial view of Halifax waterfront, about 1930. The
Pickford & Black and Central wharfs lie on the extreme right side of the photograph. (*Public Archives
of Nova Scotia.*)

48

50

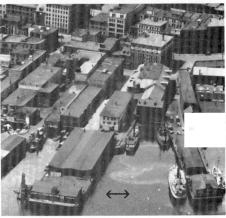
51

52

49

53 Aerial view of Halifax waterfront, 1931. The arrow indicates the Pickford & Black and Central wharfs. (*National Air Photo Library, Ottawa, A3766/49.*)

54 Aerial view of Halifax waterfront, after 1938. The arrow indicates the Pickford & Black and Central wharfs. (*Nova Scotia Communications and Information, Halifax.*)

55 Aerial view of Halifax waterfront, 1947. The arrow indicates the Pickford & Black and Central wharfs. (*National Air Photo Library, Ottawa, A12676/301.*)

53

54

55

Introduction

1 *Dictionary of Canadian Biography* (Toronto: Univ. of Toronto Press, 1972) (hereafter cited as *DCB*), Vol. 10, pp. 188-90, "Enos Collins."
2 Auction notice, *Acadian Recorder*, 3 July 1813.
3 Editorial notice, *Acadian Recorder*, 25 June 1825.
4 "The Mission Vessel," *The Presbyterian Witness and Evangelical Advocate*, 7 November 1863.

The Restoration Site

1 Harry Piers, *The Evolution of the Halifax Fortress, 1749-1928*, ed., G. M. Self and Phyllis Blakeley. Public Archives of Nova Scotia, Publication No. 7 (Halifax: 1947), p. 7.
2 Halifax County Court House, register copy (hereafter cited as HCCH), bk. 2, fol. 331, deed of transfer, Ephraim Cooke to John Creighton, 1753.
3 HCCH, bk. 3, fols. 50-53, deeds of transfer, Stephen Theodore Janson et al., creditors of Ephraim Cooke, to Charles Lawrence, 1756; bk. 5, fols. 8-9, Charles Lawrence to Thomas Saul, 1759; T. B. Akins, "History of Halifax City," *Collections of the Nova Scotia Historical Society*, Vol. 8 (1892) (hereafter cited as "Halifax City"), p. 33; John Bartlett Brebner, *New England's Outpost: Acadia Before the Conquest* (New York: Columbia Univ. Press, 1927), p. 257.
4 Nova Scotia. Public Archives (hereafter cited as PANS), Halifax Allotment Book, 1749-86, p. 124.
5 HCCH, bk. 16, fols. 203-7, deed of transfer, Thomas Saul to Alexander Brymer, 1779; T. B. Akins, "Halifax City," p. 72; *The Royal Gazette*, 1769 et seq.
6 Nova Scotia. Department of Lands and Forests, Description Book 5, No. 757, pp. 84-85, "A Grant for Brymer's Wharf."
7 Canada. Public Archives (hereafter cited as PAC), MG9, B3(4), pp. 30-32, "An Act relating to the Building Wharves upon the Beach before the Town of Halifax, made and passed in Council at Halifax the 24th Feb'y 1749/50."
8 HCCH, bk. 35, fols. 12-14, deed of transfer, Brymer to T., J., and W. Cochran, 1800.
9 HCCH, bk. 35, fols. 432-5 and bk. 36, fols. 6-8, deeds of transfer, J. & W. Cochran to William Smith, Smith to Robert Lester and Robert Morrogh, 1803; PANS, MG3, No. 150, William Forsyth & Co. Letter Book, 30 August 1796 to 3 October 1798, passim; HCCH, bk. 37, fol. 261, deeds of transfer, Lester and Morrogh to Charles R. Prescott and William Lawson, 1806; bk. 39, fols. 14-16, Prescott and Lawson to John Clarke, 1810; bk. 39, fols. 345-6, Prescott to Enos Collins, 1811.
10 Nova Scotia. Department of Lands and Forests, Grant Book A, No. 357; Grant Book 51, No. 12504; Grant Book 56, No. 14744.
11 HCCH, bk. 39, fols. 16-18, legal agreement, Prescott and Lawson with John Clarke, 1810.
12 PAC, Map Division, E. H. Keating, comp., *Map of the City of Halifax*. Drawn expressly for *McAlpine's Directory 1872-73*.
13 Interview: R. J. Fisher of Pickford & Black Co., 9 May 1972.
14 Insurance Plan 1939-51, block 12, in possession of the Nova Scotia Board of Insurance Underwriters.
15 PAC, WO55/859, fols. 402 and 412.

16 "Water Street," *Acadian Recorder*, 27 February 1813; *The Nova-Scotia Royal Gazette* (hereafter cited as *NSRG*), 1 May 1816; "Halifax Streets. Report of Commissioners," *The Novascotian*, 16 December 1830.
17 Capt. W. Moorsom, *Letters from Nova Scotia; comprising Sketches of a Young Country* (London: Henry Colburn and Richard Bentley, 1830), p. 11; Contracts offered, *The Weekly Chronicle*, 13 April 1810 and *Acadian Recorder*, 23 April 1825; Hugh Murray, *An Historical and Descriptive Account of BRITISH AMERICA; comprehending Canada Upper and Lower, Nova Scotia, New Brunswick, Newfoundland, Prince Edward Island, The Bermudas, and the Fur Countries: ... to which is added, a Full Detail of the Principles and Best Modes of EMIGRATION* (Edinburgh: Oliver & Boyd, 1839), Vol. 2, p. 157; James S. Buckingham, *Canada, Nova Scotia, New Brunswick, and the other British Provinces in North America, with a plan of National Colonization* (London: Fisher, Son, & Co., [1843]), pp. 320, 333; Frederic S. Cozzens, *Acadia; or, A Month with the Blue Noses* (New York: Derby & Jackson, 1859), p. 19; Isabella Lucy Bird, *The Englishwoman in America*, ed., Andrew Hill Clark (Toronto: Univ. of Toronto Press, 1965), p. 16, copyright 1966 by the Regents of the University of Wisconsin.
18 Isabella Lucy Bird, op. cit., pp. 16, 21; James S. Buckingham, op. cit., p. 333; Frederic S. Cozzens, op. cit., p. 19.
19 Robert Malcolm advertisement, *The British Colonist*, 3 September 1863; Halifax, N.S., *Annual Report of the Several Departments of the City Government of Halifax, Nova Scotia for the Municipal Year 1879/80* (Halifax: various publishers, 1858-1915) (hereafter cited as Halifax, *Annual Report*), p. 60.
20 The analysis in this section is based upon Halifax, *Annual Report*, 1858-1915. Most of the information has been drawn from reports by the city engineer and the Board of Works.
21 Halifax, *Annual Report*, 1888-89, p. 283, E. H. Keating to the mayor and council, city engineer's office, 12 November 1889.
22 Conversation with Mr. Joseph Simon, May 1972.
23 Descriptions in some detail of Haligonian wharfs occur, for instance, in *Acadian Recorder*, 24 April 1819, 2 November 1822, 22 March 1823, 22 January and 30 April 1825; *The Free Press*, 28 March and 2 November 1820, 28 May, 11 June and 23 July 1822; *The Novascotian*, 13 October 1830, 28 June, 4 October 1838; *The Daily Sun*, 3 February 1855.
24 Robert Lester advertisement, *NSRG*, 9 February 1804; Prescott, Lawson & Co. advertisements, *The Weekly Chronicle*, 4 August 1809 and *The Novator, and Nova Scotia Literary Gazette*, 11 June 1810; Edward Foster advertisement, *NSRG*, 24 July 1811; Collins & Allison advertisements, *Acadian Recorder*, 30 January and 3 April 1813, 24 March 1821, 5 October 1822.
25 Isabella Lucy Bird, op. cit., pp. 15-16, and *see* Fig. 45.
26 "Valuable Wharf Property to Let at Auction," *The Daily Sun*, 3 February 1855.
27 HCCH, bk. 205, fols. 450-3, deed of transfer, J. and R. B. Seeton to Robert Pickford and William A. Black, 1876.
28 Interview: R. J. Fisher of Pickford & Black, 9 May 1972. The wharf was repaved in the 1950s.

29 Conversation with Mr. Joseph Simon, May 1972.
30 Architectural investigation; G. C. Dohler and L. F. Ku, "Presentation and assessment of tides and water level records for geophysical investigations," *Canadian Journal of Earth Sciences*, Vol. 7, No. 2 (1970), p. 613.
31 *McAlpine's Halifax City Directory for 1893-94 to 1924* (Halifax: v.p., v.d.); "Two Conflagrations," *The Acadian Recorder*, 4 December 1916, p. 3.
32 Halifax, *Annual Report*, 1857-58, p. 8; on the engines *see*, for instance, "Fifty Thousand Dollar Fire on the Waterfront," *The Morning Chronicle*, 27 September 1912, p. 1.

Pickford & Black

1 PAC, MG23, C8, Letterbook 1786-89, [J. Grant] to Robert Grant, Halifax, 4 August 1787.
2 PAC, WO55/857, pp. 150-4, "Plan of the Wharfs and Buildings in the front and near the centre of the Town of Halifax, late the property of the Honble Alex'. Brymer and by him sold to Messrs. Cochrans of Halifax Merchants, now in the possession of R. Lester and R. Morrogh Esqrs." [by] Charles Morris, Survr Genl, copy, enclosed W. Fenwick to Captain Rowley, Halifax, 24 December 1803 (hereafter cited as "Plan of the Wharfs and Buildings now in the possession of R. Lester and R. Morrogh").
3 M. Forrestall advertisements, *NSRG*, 11 July 1809; *The Weekly Chronicle*, 4 August 1809; Mrs. Ann Bell advertisement, *NSRG*, 20 February 1810.
4 PANS, RG35-A, assessment books, Vol. 1 (1819, 1821, 1822), Vol. 2 (1823); Collins & Allison advertisement, *Acadian Recorder*, 23 August 1823; G. P. Lawson advertisement, *The Novascotian*, 28 February and 31 March 1828.
5 PANS, RG35-A, assessment books, Vol. 2 (1830); auction notice, *Acadian Recorder*, 24 April 1830.
6 Editorial, *The Novascotian*, 6 July 1831.
7 Henry L. Billings and William Allan advertisements, *The Novascotian*, 21 April and 19 May 1831; notice, *The Halifax Journal*, 7 January 1834; PANS, RG35-A, assessment books, Vol. 3 (1833, 1836).
8 Partnership notice, *The Novascotian*, 9 January 1840; Fairbanks & Allisons, like many mercantile firms, advertised regularly in the Halifax newspapers; *see*, for instance, *The Novascotian*, 17 September 1840 and *British Colonist*, 1 September and 20 December 1849; HCCH, bk. 140, fols. 487-8, deed of transfer, Collins to J. and R. B. Seeton, 1863; Fairbanks & Allison advertisement, *The Halifax Journal*, 14 January 1839.
9 S. A. White & Co. advertisements, *The British Colonist*, 22 October 1851; *The Halifax Morning Sun*, 16 January, 24 April 1863; *Nugent's Business Directory of the City of Halifax for 1858-9* (Halifax, 1858) (hereafter cited as *Nugent's Directory*, 1858-9); *The Halifax, Nova Scotia Business Directory for 1863*, comp. Luke Hutchinson Halifax, 1863) (hereafter cited as *Halifax Directory*, 1863).
10 Messrs. Seeton paid £6,000 to purchase the building and the property on which it stood. Deed of transfer, Enos Collins to Joseph and Robert B. Seeton, 1863, in possession of R. J. Fisher of Pickford & Black Co.; J. and R. B. Seeton advertisement, *The Presbyterian Witness and Evangelical Advocate*, 14 November 1863; *Hutchinson's Nova Scotia Directory for 1866-67* (Halifax: D. McAlpine

& Co., 1866) (hereafter cited as *Hutchinson's Directory*, 1866-67) ; *McAlpine's Halifax City Directory for 1869-70 to 1875-76* (Halifax : D. McAlpine, v.d.) (hereafter cited as *City Directory*) ; "The Inman Line" and "Royal Mail Steamships," *The Morning Chronicle*, 1 January 1868.

11 HCCH, bk 205, fols. 450-3, deed of transfer, J. and R. B. Seeton to Robert Pickford and William A. Black, 1876 ; Dalhousie University Archives, Pickford & Black Papers, microfilm copies, passim ; I. J. Isaacs, comp., *The City of Halifax. The Capital of Nova Scotia, Canada. Its Advantages and Facilities. Compiled under approval of the Board of Trade. Also a series of comprehensive sketches of some of its representative business enterprises* (Halifax, 1909) (hereafter cited as *The City of Halifax*), pp. 48-49 ; John F. Kennedy, ed., *Who's Who and Why in Canada (and Newfoundland). A Biographical Dictionary of Eminent Living Canadians and Notable Men of Newfoundland* (Ottawa : Canada Press Association, 1912), Vol. 1 (hereafter cited as *Who's Who in Canada*). Pickford and Black advertised very widely ; *see*, for instance, their shipping notices in the *Halifax Herald*, 1898, passim, and *The Morning Chronicle*, 1910, passim.

12 Canada. *Sessional Paper* 29a (1914), App. A, Alphabetical List of Foreign Consuls, Vice-Consuls, Consular Agents, and Commercial Agents in the Dominion, according to the latest information supplied to the Department of External Affairs ; Charles B. Fergusson, ed., *A Directory of the Members of the Legislative Assembly of Nova Scotia 1758-1958* (Halifax : PANS, 1958) (hereafter cited as *MLAs of N.S.*) ; J. K. Johnston, ed., *The Canadian Directory of Parliament 1867-1967* (Ottawa : PAC, 1968).

13 *City Directory*, 1879-80 to 1903-04 ; "Another Big Fire," *Acadian Recorder*, 19 September 1904.

14 Interview : R. J. Fisher, Pickford & Black Co., 29 February 1972.

15 *City Directory*, 1903-04 ; "Yesterday's Fire Laid Fine Business Block in Ruins," *The Morning Chronicle*, 20 September 1904 ; *The City of Halifax*, p. 118.

16 On Morse's Teas, *see* J. E. Morse & Co. papers, Dalhousie University Archives. On the building, *see* Lynne Redden and Don MacKinnon, "Jerusalem Warehouse," and Don MacKinnon, "Morse's Tea Building, A Brief History," in PANS, History 199/C, Essays.

17 Interview : R. J. Fisher, 29 February 1972 ; "New Building," *Acadian Recorder*, 4 June 1825 ; John Trider advertisement, *Acadian Recorder*, 30 January 1819.

18 PANS, Fire Investigation before Stipendiary Magistrate George H. Fielding, 1904 (hereafter cited as Investigation), testimony of Joseph R. Bennett of Pickford & Black, p. 7 ; Interview : R. J. Fisher, 29 February 1972 ; PANS, RG35-A, assessment books, Vol. 3 (1836).

19 PANS, Investigation, testimony of Joseph R. Bennett, p. 7.

20 PANS, Investigation, testimony of Joseph R. Bennett ; John Calder of Black Brothers ; Dominick Healey, District Chief of Fire Department ; pp. 7, 10, 17, 116-7 ; *The British Colonist*, 28 February 1861 ; PANS, RG35-A, assessment books, Vol. 4 (1862).

21 PANS, Investigation, testimony of George Hensley, partner of Pickford & Black, p. 51.

22 "The Fire Fiend Again Scourges Water Front," *The Evening Mail*, 19 September 1904 ; "Yesterday's Fire Laid Fine Business Block in Ruins," *The Morning Chronicle*, 20 September 1904 ; "Plans of the Firms Burned Out," *The Maritime Merchant and Commercial Review* (hereafter cited as *The Maritime Merchant*), 6 October 1904, p. 25.

23 Interview : G. D. Webb, I. H. Mathers & Son, 1 May 1972.

24 "Halifax Waterfront Firm Changes Hands ; Under New Control," *Halifax Daily Star*, 20 July 1936, p. 14 ; Engineering Department, Halifax City Hall (hereafter cited as EDHCH), Vol. 3, 10 August 1938, permit issued to architect C. St. J. Wilson to remodel Pickford & Black property on Upper Water Street ; Interview : R. J. Fisher, 9 May 1972.

25 HCCH, expropriations, No. 1937, Pickford & Black, July 1968.

Carpenters' Shop

1 The so-called "brick district" encompassed a central area of Halifax in which no new wooden buildings could legally be erected. Preliminary legislation on the subject was in effect from 1822 to 1831, but the act of 1857 "to limit the erection of Wooden Buildings within the City of Halifax" provided the basic form. The law was ambiguous and frequently evaded. Moreover, in 1904 the restricted district extended only 50 ft. east of Water Street. Nova Scotia, *Statutes*, 3 Geo. 4 c. 29, 1 Will. 4 c. 18, 20 Vict. c. 35, 36 et seq. ; Halifax, *Annual Report*, 1872-73, pp. 12-13 ; "Brick and Wood District Is Defined By Law," *The Morning Chronicle*, 23 September 1904.

2 Edward Foster advertisements, *NSRG*, 24 July 1811, 7 January 1824. Although Foster's principal store was in Dartmouth, he maintained a blacksmith shop and iron store on Collins' Wharf until 1823.

3 Auction notice, *Acadian Recorder*, 24 April 1830.

4 PANS, RG35-A, assessment books, Vol. 3 (1833, 1834, 1836).

5 HCCH, bk. 140, fols. 487-8 and bk. 148, fols. 560-1, deeds of transfer, Enos Collins to Joseph & R. B. Seeton, 1863 and 1865 ; PANS, RG35-A, assessment books, Vol. 4 (1862) ; *Nugent's Directory*, 1858-59 ; *Halifax Directory*, 1863 ; *Hutchinson's Directory*, 1866-67.

6 HCCH, bk. 140, fols. 487-8 and bk. 148, fols. 560-1, deeds of transfer, Collins to J. and R. B. Seeton, 1863 and 1865. The west wall is specified in the deed of 1863 to measure 38 ft. 7 in. "more or less" and in the deed of 1865, 38 ft. 4 in. "more or less."

7 HCCH, bk. 205, fols. 450-3, deed of transfer, J. and R. B. Seeton to Robert Pickford and William A. Black, 1876.

8 PANS, Investigation, testimony of Joseph Bennett, pp. 5-6 ; testimony of Thomas Forhan, p. 3.

9 *Our Dominion. Mercantile and Manufacturing Interests. Historical and Commercial Sketches of Halifax and Environs* (Toronto : The Historical Publishing Co. of Canada, 1887) (hereafter cited as *Our Dominion*), p. 71 ; *City Directory*, 1871-72 to 1904 ; PANS, Investigation, testimony of Thomas Forhan, pp. 2-3. Forhan seems to have been associated with the wharf during the previous 15 years when he was perhaps an employee of Drillio. I. H. Mathers & Son, Daily Journal, 30 January 1897.

10 *City Directory*, 1878-79 to 1906-07 ; "Origin of the Conflagrations Will Probably Be Investigated" and "Yesterday's Fire Laid Fine Business Block in Ruins," *The Morning Chronicle*, 20 September 1904, pp. 1 and 8 ; PANS, Investigation, testimony of Joseph Bennett and Thomas Ryan, pp. 6-7 and 86.

11 EDHCH, Building Permit Registers, Vol. 1, 10 July 1905, permit issued to George B. Low for Pickford & Black to "erect a wood and cement building," No. 377.

12 *City Directory*, 1905-06 to 1924.

Collins Bank and Warehouse

1 PAC, WO55/857, fol. 150, "Plan of the Wharfs and Buildings now in the possession of R. Lester and R. Morrogh."

2 Archibald M'Coll advertisement, *NSRG*, 21 May 1801 ; Forsyth, Smith & Co. advertisement, *NSRG*, 3 January 1805 ; HCCH, bk. 37, fols. 261-2, deed of transfer, Robert Lester and Robert Morrogh to Charles Prescott and William Lawson, 1806 ; notice, *NSRG*, 15 January 1812 ; Prescott & Lawson advertisements, *NSRG*, 1 September 1807, 5 January, 30 August 1808 ; 6 and 27 June 1809 ; 13 February 1810 ; 20 February, 24 April 1811.

3 Notices, *Acadian Recorder*, 17 April 1813 and 9 October 1824. On the career of Enos Collins, *see* C. B. Fergusson, ed., *Letters and Papers of Hon. Enos Collins*, Bulletin of the Public Archives of Nova Scotia, No. 13 (Halifax : 1959) (hereafter cited as *Collins*), and *DCB*, Vol. 10, pp. 188-90, "Enos Collins ;" prize sales, *Acadian Recorder*, 24 April 1813 ; Collins & Allison advertisements, *The Weekly Chronicle*, 11 March, 14 December 1814 ; *Acadian Recorder*, 8 February, 28 June 1817 ; 26 June, 28 August 1819 ; 13 December 1823 ; *The Free Press*, 23 November 1820 ; HCCH, index to deeds, 1749-1836 ; Reports of meetings, *Acadian Recorder*, 2 February, 9 March 1822 ; "Bank!" *Acadian Recorder*, 3 September 1825 ; PAC, MG24, D9, Halifax Banking Company ; PANS, Vol. 113½, pp. 25-26 ; notice, *Acadian Recorder*, 27 August 1831.

4 "Upper Water Street Building Is Damaged By Fire," *The Halifax Chronicle*, 26 December 1934, p. 12 ; Victor Ross, *A History of the Canadian Bank of Commerce with an Account of the Other Banks which now form Part of its Organization* (Toronto : Oxford Univ. Press, 1920) (hereafter cited as *Bank of Commerce*), Vol. 1, opp. p. 52.

5 The deed of transfer from Prescott to Collins does not appear to have been registered, but documents drawn in November 1822 state that the property was then owned by Collins. See "Red Store," n. 3.

6 T. B. Akins, "Halifax City," p. 157 n. ; HCCH, bk. 109, fols. 146-8, legal agreement, Enos Collins to William Clark, 1854 ; PANS, RG35-A, assessment books, Vol. 2 (1823, 1824).

7 "Bank!" *Acadian Recorder*, 3 September 1825.

8 "Omicron," *The Novascotian*, 5 February 1834.

9 The union was viewed as "one of the most important transactions in the history of Halifax financial institutions," and five of the seven columns on the front page of *The Morning Chronicle* (4 March 1903) were devoted to the news.

10 A history of the Halifax Banking Company will be found in Victor Ross, *Bank of Commerce*, Vol. 1, pp. 22-124. The original partnership agreement of 1825 is transcribed in App. III, pp. 432-7; it and the later agreements are summarized in App. III, pp. 430-2. Ross apparently saw at least some of the minute books of the Halifax Banking Company, but inquiries of the archivist of the Canadian Imperial Bank of Commerce and of Haligonian repositories have failed to locate them. A messenger book, a cash book, and three account books are filed at PANS, MG3, Nos. 361-5. For an evaluation of the role of the Halifax Banking Company in Canadian banking, *see* Bray Hammond, "Banking in Canada before Confederation, 1792-1867," *Approaches to Canadian Economic History*, eds., W. T. Easterbrook and M. H. Watkins (Toronto: McClelland and Stewart, 1967), pp. 154-7.

11 Notice, *The Halifax Journal*, 7 January 1834; *City Directory*, 1871-72; P. C. Hill advertisement, *British Colonist and North American Railway Journal*, 14 October 1851; *MLAs of N.S.*; *Nugent's Directory*, 1858-59; *Halifax Directory*, 1863; *Hutchinson's Directory*, 1866-67; *City Directory*, 1869-70 to 1871-72.

12 *City Directory*, 1882-83 to 1919.

13 Interview: R. J. Fisher of Pickford & Black, 9 May 1972; Marion F. Moore, "A Case for Preservation," *The Atlantis Advocate*, January 1965 (hereafter cited as "Preservation"), p. 64.

14 Partnership notice, *Acadian Recorder*, 30 April 1825; auction notices, *The Novascotian*, 1 November 1827, 3 December 1829; E. Collins & Co. advertisements, *The Novascotian*, 23 April 1829; 18 August 1830, 2 October 1833; *Acadian Recorder*, 11 August 1832; *The Novascotian*, 7 April 1830 ff.

15 Notice, *The Novascotian*, 1 January 1840; Joseph Allison and Co. advertisements, *The Novascotian*, 21 May, 10 December 1829; 21 July 1830; *Acadian Recorder*, 25 June, 21 July 1831; 14 July 1832; PANS, RG35-A, assessment books, Vol. 2 (1830), Vol. 3 (1834, 1836).

16 *See*, for instance, their advertisements in the *British Colonist*, 1 September, 1 October, 20 December 1849; 28 March, 23 May 1850; *The Daily Sun*, 3 January 1855; PANS, RG35-A, assessment books, Vol. 4 (1862); *City Directory*, 1869-70 to 1881-82.

17 PAC, RG8, C1366, p. 94, Pengelly to AQMG, military store office, Halifax, 3 August 1863, copy.

18 *City Directory*, 1887-88 to 1911; *Our Dominion*, p. 86; *The City of Halifax*, pp. 75-76; *City Directory*, 1906-07 to 1924; ibid, 1910-35 including C. E. Choat & Co. advertisements 1910, 1914, 1915.

19 "Waterfront Fire Brings Property Loss of $20,000," *The Halifax Mail*, 26 December 1934, p. 3.

20 The water lot granted in 1809 is described in detail in HCCH, bk. 39, fols. 62-5, deed of transfer, William Lawson to Charles R. Prescott, 1810. *See also* HCCH, bk. 39, fols. 345-6, deeds of transfer, Prescott to Collins, 1811, and bk. 39, fols. 14-18, Prescott and Lawson to John Clark, 1810; bk. 47, fols. 303-6, release, Clark to Collins, and deed of transfer, Collins to Clark, 1822.

21 The difficulties in applying the deed of 1811 were apparent at the time that R. L. H. Collins transferred the property through brokers to the Sullivan Storage Company. The land was therefore described not only in relation to the deed of 1811 but additionally in relation to the Ordnance Yard, and it was also specifically identified as 53-55 Upper Water Street (HCCH, bk. 848, fols. 382-5, deed of transfer, Brenton Robie Collins to Richard Leslie Halliburton Collins, 1942; bk. 843, fols. 1253-6, R. L. H. Collins to Melvin S. Clarke, 1943). A plan accompanied the first transfer of the property (HCCH, bk. 857, fols. 337-44, deeds of transfer, Clarke to Darcy Sullivan and Sullivan to Sullivan Storage Company, 1943); a copy of the plan (Fig. 19) is filed in bk. 1027, fol. 537. To ensure that no future question as to ownership could arise, R. L. H. Collins granted a confirming deed to Sullivan Storage Company in 1944 (bk. 887, fols. 217-20). Expropriations, No. 1934, Sullivan Storage Company, July 1968.

22 HCCH, bk. 963, fols. 481-4, deeds of transfer, Sullivan Storage Company to Lawrence H. MacKenzie and Lawrence D. MacKenzie, 1947; bk. 1024, fols. 793-6, L. H. MacKenzie to L. D. MacKenzie, 1947; bk. 1027, fols. 537-40, L. D. MacKenzie to Cleveland Realty Corporation, 1949; bk. 1006, fols. 353-7, lease, Cleveland Realty Corporation to Donald C. Keddy, March 1949; bk. 1037, fols. 261-4, deed of transfer, same, July 1949; expropriations, No. 1933, Donald C. Keddy Ltd., July 1968.

23 HCCH, bk. 109, fols. 146-8, legal agreement, Enos Collins to William Clark, 1854. "Whereas . . . William Clark is in progress of erecting a new store against the north side of a stone store and building of the said Enos Collins which has been standing for thirty years on the line between there respective properties and the water shed the Northern side of which is towards the property of the said William Clark, "And

Whereas a Cornice with spouts and conductors secured by Iron clamps or fastenings on the north side of said stone store . . . and along the whole extent thereof have been erected and maintained under and beyond [*sic*] the eaves of the roof thereof on that side ever since the erection of the said store reaching (?) beyond the northern side of the said Store and over and beyond the line of division between the said properties and over the property of the said William Clark and the said Enos Collins claims the right by user prescription and long occupation forever hereafter for himself and his heirs and assigns to maintain the said cornice spouts and conductors and others in their place with the necessary fastenings and to carry off the water from the northern roof or side of his said stone store or of any other building standing on the side [*sic*] thereof by cornice spouts and conductors projecting to the Northward of the line of division between the said properties.

"Now

these Presents Witness that . . . the said William Clark shall be permited to remove the said cornices spouts and conductors . . . from the eaves of the North roof of the said Enos Collins said building if it shall be necessary and only so far as may be necessary to do so for enabling the said William Clark to carry up the southern side of his said new building under the said proposed roof . . . . and also that the same number and kinds of Skylights now in the north side of the roof of the said stone store . . . of the said Enos Collins and which will be covered in by the proposed roof aforesaid shall be made and put in on the south side of the roof of the said stone store . . . and that the costs of the whole work herein mentioned and whatever further may be necessary to carry into effect the said objects shall be done exclusively by the said William Clark." Agreement was also made to ensure that if any future roof between the two buildings did not satisfy the needs of both structures, Collins' claimed rights should be recognized.

24 Interview: D. C. Keddy, 28 April 1972. Mr. Keddy observed the wall construction when the window on the southwest side of the building was changed to a loading door.

25 This was probably the warehouse portion of the building. Supreme Court, *The Novascotian*, 21 January 1830; Halifax police office notice, *The Novascotian*, 26 November 1829.

26 Letter written in 1905 by cashier of the Halifax Banking Company, quoted in Victor Ross, *Bank of Commerce*, p. 440.

27 Ibid.

28 Report of J. and J. Taylor Limited of Toronto, quoted in Victor Ross, *Bank of Commerce*, p. 439.

29 *British Colonist*, 1 September 1849.

30 HCCH, bk. 109, fols. 146-8, legal agreement, Collins to Clark, 1854.

31 Letter written in 1905 by cashier of the Halifax Banking Company, quoted in Victor Ross, *Bank of Commerce*, pp. 440-1.

32 Ibid.

33 Interview: D. C. Keddy, 28 April 1972.

34 "Upper Water Street Building is Damaged by Fire," *The Halifax Chronicle*, 26 December 1934, p. 12; "Home of Nova Scotia's First Bank Destroyed," *Halifax Herald*, 26 December 1934, p. 1; "Waterfront Fire Damage Fixed at $30,000," *Halifax Daily Star*, 26 December 1934, p. 5; "Waterfront Fire Brings Property Loss of $20,000," *The Halifax Mail*, 26 December 1934, p. 3.

35 Insurance Plan 1939-51, block 112, in possession of the Nova Scotia Board of Insurance Underwriters.

36 Conversation: Mr. Sullivan, C. E. Choat & Co., 24 April 1972.

37 William H. Hill advertisement, *The British Colonist*, 1 November 1862; P. C. Hill advertisement, *British Colonist and North American Railway Journal*, 14 October 1851; Halifax, *Annual Report*, 1861-62, p. 16; *Halifax Directory*, 1863; *Hutchinson's Directory*, 1866-67; *City Directory*, 1869-70 to 1884-85.

38 Interview: D. C. Keddy, 28 April 1972; Conversation: Mr. Creighton of Creightons Ltd., May 1972.

39 HCCH, bk. 1006, fols. 353-7, lease, Cleveland Realty Corporation to Donald C. Keddy, 1949.

40 Interview: D. C. Keddy, 28 April 1972. The demolition of the vault is described in Marion F. Moore, "Preservation," p. 64. Three or four cannon balls, lodged in hemispherical pockets cut into the granite slabs of which the vault was constructed, rendered it immoveable.

41 Letter written in 1905 by cashier of the Halifax Banking Company quoted in Victor Ross, *Bank of Commerce*, p. 441.

Red Store

1 HCCH, bk. 39, 14-19, deed of transfer and legal agreement, Charles R. Prescott and William Lawson to John Clark, 1810.
2 Notice of sales at auction by Charles Hill & Co., *Acadian Recorder*, 30 January, 3 April 1813; Collins & Allison advertisement, *Acadian Recorder*, 24 March 1821.
3 Collins & Allison advertisement, *Acadian Recorder*, 24 March–30 June, 1 September–3 November 1821; HCCH, release, Clark to Enos Collins, and deed of transfer, Collins to Clark, 1822. The deed of transfer from Prescott to Collins does not appear to have been registered, but the release and deed exchanged between Collins and Clark have been, probably in error instead, registered twice—in 1823 (bk. 47, fols. 303-6) and again in 1829 (bk. 51, fols. 369-73). The documents, drawn in November 1822, state that the property was then owned by Collins.
4 HCCH, bk. 47, fols. 303-6, release, Clark to Collins, and deed of transfer, Collins to Clark, 1822.
5 Although the title "Red Store" described a building at one time on part of this site, no evidence has been found to suggest that either the name or the colour to which it refers ever applied to the present building. Mr. Fisher of Pickford & Black Co. had not heard of such a title being attached to the structure. Interview: 9 May 1972.
6 PANS, Liverpool Business Records: Business Letterbook of the firm of Seely & Gough, 1827-33: Seely & Gough to Enos Collins, Liverpool, 3 and 22 July, 2 and 21 August 1830; 5 May 1831; 28 April 1832. There is architectural evidence to suggest that this structure may originally have had only two storeys.
7 PANS, RG35-A, assessment books, Vol. 3 (1833, 1834); Edward Lawson advertisement, *The Novascotian*, 2 April 1834; E. Shortis advertisement, *Acadian Recorder*, 21 January 1832.
8 PAC, RG8, C1363, pp. 456-7 and 461, Mervyn Nugent AQMG to Deputy Commissary General, Halifax, 13 January 1862 and R. R. Pringle to Nugent, military store office, Halifax, 13 January 1862; ibid., C1366, p. 98, E. Pengelly to Nugent, 5 August 1863; p. 288, Nugent to Routh, 15 January 1864; ibid., C1369, p. 421, Collins to Pengelly, 13 August 1866, copies. PANS, RG35-A, assessment books, Vol. 4, (1862); *City Directory*, 1869-70; "Two Conflagrations," *Acadian Recorder*, 4 December 1916, p. 3.
9 The measurements of the long wooden salt and fish store were given as "about" 130 ft. 4 in. by 35 ft. 4 in., HCCH, bk. 148, fols. 560-1, deeds of transfer, Enos Collins to J. and R. B. Seeton, 1865; bk. 180, fols. 39-41, B. H. Collins to J. and R. B. Seeton, 1872.
10 HCCH, bk. 205, fols. 450-3, deed of transfer, J. and R. B. Seeton to Robert Pickford and William A. Black, 1876.
11 *City Directory*, 1871-72 to 1879-80, 1882-83 to 1884-85, including Kandick advertisement, 1871-72; ibid., 1869-70 to 1885-86, including Ackhurst advertisement, 1869-70; Halifax, *Annual Report*, 1861-62, 1867-68, 1871-72, 1872-73.

12 *City Directory*, 1879-80 to 1884-85; "St. Andrew's Waterside Church Mission," *The Church Guardian*, 27 July 1879, 8 April 1880.
13 *City Directory*, 1877-78 to 1920; I. H. Mathers & Son, Daily Journals, passim. For a synopsis of Mathers' interests, *see* "Isaac A. [*sic*] Mathers, Esq.," *The Syren and Shipping* (London, England), 17 September 1902, p. 94, and *Supplement to The Paper-Maker and British Paper Trade Journal*, 1 November 1902.
14 *City Directory*, 1880-81 to 1935; *The Maritime Merchant*, 1904-05, passim; "Two Conflagrations," *The Acadian Recorder*, 4 December 1916, p. 3.
15 *City Directory*, 1885-86 to 1910; *MLAs of N.S.*
16 *City Directory*, 1880-81 to 1935.
17 HCCH, expropriations, No. 1937, Pickford & Black, July 1968.
18 Except where otherwise noted, the analysis in this paragraph is based upon three photographs of the building in the late 19th or very early 20th century. None has been precisely dated, but all precede 1904 when the sail loft on the south side of the wharf was burned. *See* Figs. 30, 31 and 32.
19 "Destructive Fire in Office Building and Warehouse on Pickford and Black's Wharf Last Night," *The Halifax Herald*, 4 December 1916, p. 4.
20 "Two Conflagrations," *The Acadian Recorder*, 4 December 1916, p. 3; "Destructive Fire in Office Building and Warehouse on Pickford and Black's Wharf Last Night," *The Halifax Herald*, 4 December 1916, p. 4.
21 Ibid.; I. H. Mathers & Son, Daily Journal, 1 February 1917.
22 *The Maritime Merchant*, 28 July 1904, p. 102.

The Simon's Building

1 PAC, WO55/857, fol. 150, "Plan of the Wharfs and Buildings . . . now in the possession of R. Lester and R. Morrogh;" P. Ryan advertisement dated 11 October 1804, *NSRG*, 3 January 1805.
2 HCCH, bk. 39, fols. 14-16, deed of transfer, Charles Prescott and William Lawson to John Clark, 1810; John Clark advertisements, *NSRG*, 23 May, 20 June 1809.
3 For discussion of the early development of Clark's wharf, *see* "Privateer's Warehouse," paragraphs 2, 3 and 4.
4 James N. Shannon Jr. advertisements, *Acadian Recorder*, 24 April 1819, and *The Free Press*, 4 June 1822; J. Lyons & Co. advertisements, *The Novascotian*, 8, 15 November 1827; 7 July 1828; 18 April, 27 August, 11 November 1829; 22 April 1830. HCCH, bk. 77, fols. 115-20, assignment of mortgage of David and John Edward Starr (1 June 1840), E. F. Clark et al., executors of John Clark, to Enos Collins, 1844.
5 HCCH, bk. 109, fols. 146-8, legal agreement, Enos Collins to William Clark, 1854.
6 HCCH, bk. 119, fols. 525-27, mortgages, Clark to Collins, 1857, and bk. 118, fols. 638-40, 1858. The mortgages were £3,000 and £6,000 respectively; notice, *The Royal Gazette*, 7 September 1859, p. 284.
7 HCCH, bk. 127, fols. 246-7, deed of transfer, Louisa Sophia Clark to Robert W. Fraser, 1859, bk. 127, fol. 248, release of mortgage, Collins to Fraser, 1859; bk. 127, fols. 248-50, deed of transfer, Fraser to William Tarr and William Chisholm, 1859; bk. 127, fols. 255-7, deed of transfer, Fraser to Jonathan C. and Charles Allison, 1859.

8 *Halifax Directory*, 1863; *Hutchinson's Directory*, 1866-67; *City Directory*, 1869-70 to 1873-74; for instance, *see* Edward Lawson's sales at auction for R. W. Fraser & Co., *Acadian Recorder*, 20 April 1861.
9 *Halifax and Its Business: Containing Historical Sketch, and Description of the City and its Institutions. Also Description of Different Lines of Business, with Account of the Leading Houses in Each Line* (Halifax: Nova Scotia Publishing Co., 1876) (hereafter cited as *Halifax and Its Business*), pp. 137-8, states that Esson & Co. removed to Upper Water Street in 1868, but *Hutchinson's Directory*, 1866-67, already lists the firm in that location. The firm was established about 1830. Esson & Co. advertisement, *City Directory*, 1869-70 to 1875-76; *Halifax and Its Business*, pp. 137-8; *Our Dominion*, p. 102; "Esson & Co. Suspend," *The Novascotian*, 18 August 1888, p. 3; HCCH, bk. 224, fols. 477-80, deed of transfer, Fraser to William Esson, 1880.
10 HCCH, bk. 266, fols. 145-50, deed of assignment, William Esson and Alexander Anderson (Esson & Co.) to Isaac H. Mathers and Brook W. Chipman, 1888. Mathers' office was situated in the Red Store on the adjoining wharf. Advertisement of assignees' sale, *Halifax Acadian Recorder*, 7 September 1888.
11 Advertisement of assignees' sale, *Halifax Acadian Recorder*, 7 September 1888. William Robertson purchased the building for $16,450 which was $6,050 less than Esson had paid for it in 1880. Robertson apparently acted as agent for Chipman in the transaction. Notice of sale, *The Novascotian*, 15 September 1888; HCCH, bk. 224, fols. 477-80, deeds of transfer, Fraser to Esson, 1880; bk. 268, fols. 778-80, Mathers and Chipman, assignees of Esson & Co., to James A. Chipman, 1888; *City Directory*, 1889-90 to 1902-03.
12 HCCH, bk. 323, fols. 27-29, deed of transfer, Chipman to James Adams and Ingraham B. Shaffner, 1897; *Who's Who in Canada*, 1917-18; *The City of Halifax*, pp. 85-6.
13 *City of Halifax*, pp. 85-6; I. B. Shaffner & Company advertisements, *The Maritime Merchant*, 1904-05. Shaffner was a sufficiently important figure to rank entry in *Who's Who in Canada*, 1917-18 to 1921.
14 HCCH, bk. 404, fols. 77-80, deed of transfer, Shaffner to George H. Hooper, 1917.
15 HCCH, bk. 482, fols. 789-91, deed of transfer, Hooper to J. B. Mitchell, 1919; *City Directory*, 1919-24, 1931; "Upper Water Street Building is Damaged by Fire," *The Halifax Chronicle*, 26 December 1934, p. 12.
16 HCCH, bk. 759, fols. 409-12, deed of transfer, Rose Mitchell to Joseph Simon, 1937; expropriations, No. 1936, Joseph Simon, 1968.
17 HCCH, bk. 224, fols. 477-80, deed of transfer, Fraser to Esson, 1880.

18 HCCH, bk. 109, fols. 146-8, legal agreement, Enos Collins to William Clark, 1854. "Whereas . . . William Clark is in progress of erecting a new store against the north side of a stone store and building of the said Enos Collins. . . .

"Now these Presents Witness that the said William Clark has proposed and it is hereby agreed by and between the said parties that the North side of the roof of the said New Building of the said William Clark now in progress and the south side of the roof of the said Stone Building or store of the said Enos Collins shall be united by a crowning roof thrown from the ridge of the one to the ridge of the other whereby the only water sheds required will be from the roof on the North side of the said William Clarks said buildings upon his own property and from the roof on the south side of the said Enos Collins said building upon his own property according to the plan hereunto annexed . . . and it is agreed as aforesaid that the hip roof on the western side of the stone Store be well and sufficiently united with a corresponding high roof to be made by the said William Clark on the west side of his said New Building and brought over to connect with the hip roof on the said store of the said Enos Collins and that the roofs of the eastern side be also securely united and that the roofs of the said William Clark be covered with slate except that the crowning roof be well and securely covered with zinc and that every thing be done necessary to secure and make tight the roofs of the said buildings of the said Enos Collins." See Fig. 41.

19 Unfortunately, Esson & Co.'s papers appear to have been destroyed in Halifax a number of years ago. Nevertheless, because of the firm's probable remodelling of the building and because of its long and prominent association with it as well as with business development in Halifax, the name of Esson & Co. should be more prominently associated with the building than has been the case in the past. Alternatively, the structure might be styled after its builder, Clark, or after its important early 20th-century owner, Shaffner. Such an alteration in titling would be more consistent with the 19th-century nomenclature common to the other historic buildings of the complex than its present 20th-century identification.

20 Unless otherwise indicated, the analysis in the following three paragraphs is based upon a sketch of the building ca. 1887 (Fig. 42) and a photograph of the same ca. 1909 (Fig. 43).

21 "Upper Water Street Building Damaged by Fire," The Halifax Chronicle, 26 December 1934, p. 12.

22 Ibid.; "Home of Nova Scotia's First Bank Destroyed," Halifax Herald, 26 December 1934, p. 1; cf. "Waterfront Fire Damage Fixed at $30,000," Halifax Daily Star, 26 December 1934, p. 5; "Waterfront Fire Brings Property Loss of $20,000," The Halifax Mail, 26 December 1934, p. 3.

23 Conversation with Mr. Joseph Simon, May 1972. Mr. Simon described the window panels removed as ca. 15 in. wide, beginning ca. 4 ft. from the floor and extending to ca. 10 in. from the ceiling. These alterations appear to have been done in 1942. EDHCH, Building Permit Registers, Vol. 3, 4 November 1942, permit issued to Joseph Simon for "repairs," No. 28026.

24 Conversation with Mr. Simon, May 1972.

25 "Waterfront Buildings of Halifax, Nova Scotia," Peter John Stokes, Consulting Restoration Architect, Historic Sites and Monuments Board of Canada, Agenda Paper 1963-18, p. 128; conversation with Mr. Simon, May 1972.

Privateer's Warehouse

1 Charles Hill advertisements, NSRG, 14 May, 17 September, 3 December 1801; PAC WO55/857, fol. 150, "Plan of the Wharfs and Buildings . . . now in the possession of R. Lester and R. Morrogh;" P. Ryan advertisement dated 11 October 1804, NSRG, 3 January 1805.

2 PAC, WO55/857, fols. 151-5, 303-4, 363-4, 83, 84. Fenwick to Rowley, Halifax, 24 December 1803, enclosing Fenwick to R. Lester, engineer's office, Halifax, 13 December 1803, copy; Fenwick to Lt. Gen. Morse, inspector general of works and fortifications, Halifax, 30 January 1805; R. H. Crew, secretary to the Board of Ordnance, to Morse, Office of Ordnance (London), 3 September 1805; Fenwick to Morse, Halifax, 19 September 1805; Fenwick to Rowley, Halifax, 19 September 1803.

3 Fig. 9 is repeated in WO44/88, fol. 343 (1817), WO55/861, fol. 278 (1817), WO44/91, fol. 361 (1819), and WO55/861, fol. 52 (1819). Thereafter the Ordnance department at Halifax seems to have given up the practice of showing adjoining property on their plans of the Ordnance Yard. "Editorial," The Novascotian, 6 July 1831.

4 PAC, WO44/88, fol. 343, Plan of the Ordnance Yard, 9 October 1817, signed W. Gregory, Lt. CRE; WO44/86, fols. 74-5, agreement between Philip Roberts, ordnance storekeeper, and John Clarke, carpenter, 31 October 1811; WO44/82, fol. 43, John Mudge, clerk of the cheque, to The Principal Officers of HM's Ordnance, Pall Mall, London, Office of Ordnance, Halifax, 5 May 1813; WO44/89, fol. 137, George Barron, ordnance storekeeper, to R. H. Crew, Office of Ordnance, Halifax, 23 April 1818.

5 T. B. Akins, "Halifax City," p. 177; George Grassie & Co. advertisement, Acadian Recorder, 11 January 1817.

6 PAC, MG23, C1, Diary of Simeon Perkins of Liverpool, 10 October 1805, typescript, Vol. 6, p. 148; PANS, MG1, Akins Collection. Family papers, Insurance Journals of Thomas Akins, Vol. 1, 15 February, and 10 May, 22 June 1805; 16 April, 24 and 31 May 1806; 13 July 1807; HCCH, bk. 37, fol. 261, deed of transfer, Robert Lester and Robert Morrogh to Charles R. Prescott and William Lawson, 1806.

7 Mrs. Ann Bell advertisement, NSRG, 20 February 1810; Prescott & Lawson notice, NSRG, 3 January 1809; E. Collins advertisement, The Halifax Journal, 10 June 1811; Prescott, Lawson & Co. notice, NSRG, 6 November 1811, 15 January 1812; HCCH, bk. 39, fols. 345-6, deed of transfer, Prescott to Collins, 1811.

8 Enos Collins and Joseph Allison advertisement of sale of Prize Vessels and their cargoes, captured by the privateers Sir John Sherbrooke and Liverpool Packet, Acadian Recorder, 24 April 1813; J. S. Martell, "Halifax during and after the War of 1812," The Dalhousie Review, Vol. 23 (1943-44), p. 291; Janet E. Mullins, "The Liverpool Packet," The Dalhousie Review, Vol. 14 (1934-35), pp. 193-202; Joseph Schull, "The Black Joke," Weekend Magazine, Vol. 8, Nos. 30 and 31, 1958; PANS vert. file S Ships (2), No. 25; C. H. J. Snider, Under the Red Jack, Privateers of the Maritime Provinces of Canada in the War of 1812 (Toronto, 1928), pp. 7-52.

9 HCCH, bk. 39, fols. 14-16, deed of transfer, Prescott and Lawson to John Clark, 1810; J. Clark advertisements, NSRG, 23 May and 20 June 1809.

10 HCCH, bk. 47, fols. 303-6, legal agreement, John Clark to Enos Collins, 1822; notice, Acadian Recorder, 12 May 1821; Victor Ross, Bank of Commerce, Vol. 1, App. III, p. 430; auction notices, The Free Press, 15 February, 7 March, 4 April 1820; John Clark advertisements, Acadian Recorder, 6 January 1821, 6 April 1822; The Novascotian, 20 December 1827; 14 February, 17 April 1828; 28 October 1829; "Shipping Intelligence," The Novascotian, 1829 and 1830, passim.

11 PANS, MG1, No. 221, Paysant & King papers, Last Will and Testament of John Clark, probated 10 October 1838, copy; Geo. H. Starr advertisements, British Colonist and North American Railway Journal, 27 September, 3 October, 27 November 1851; 27 October 1853; 11 March 1858; Nugent's Directory, 1858-59.

12 PANS, MG1, No. 221, Last Will and Testament of John Clark. For discussion of the transfer of the property in 1859, see "Simon's Building," paragraph 3; HCCH, bk. 127, fols. 248-50, Fraser to William Tarr and William Chisholm, 1859; Halifax Directory, 1863. This portion of the property has not been subsequently divided; HCCH, bk. 139, fols. 235-9, assignment of equity of redemption, William Tarr et al. to Enos Collins, 1862; bk. 148, fols. 151-3, deed of transfer, Enos Collins to George C. Harvey, 1864; City Directory, 1869-70.

13 City Directory, 1869-70 to 1882-83; HCCH, bk. 259, fols. 504-8, mortgage, George C. Harvey "of Kenwood, Huntingdon Valley, Pennsylvania," to John T. Spencer, 1886.

14 City Directory, 1887-88 to 1904-05; HCCH, bk. 364, fols. 724-8, deed of transfer, A. J. M. Harvey to Margaret E. Wood, 1904; City Directory, 1894-95 to 1930, and see Figs. 17, 18.

15 HCCH, bk. 820, fols. 388-91, deed of transfer, G. M. Wood to C. J. Burke, 1941; Insurance Plan 1939-51, block 112, in possession of the Nova Scotia Board of Insurance Underwriters; HCCH, bk. 1806, fols. 544-6, deed of transfer, Mary C. Burke to the City of Halifax, 1962.

16 The "Panoramic View of the City of Halifax Nova Scotia 1879" (Fig. 23) incorrectly shows six apertures on each floor.

17 Architectural Investigation. For construction of the structure adjoining to the west, see "Simon's Building."

Wooden Storehouse

1 For history of the wharf prior to 1859, *see* "Privateer's Warehouse." HCCH, bk. 127, fols. 248-9, deed of transfer, R. W. Fraser to William Tarr and William Chisholm, 1859; bk. 127, fols. 250-5, mortgage, Tarr and Chisholm to Enos Collins, 1860; bk. 139, fols. 235-9, release of equity of redemption, Tarr et al. to Collins, 1862; *Halifax Directory*, 1863.

2 HCCH, bk. 148, fols. 151-3, deed of transfer, Collins to George C. Harvey, 1864.

3 The overlaying of Figs. 10-14 which revealed the presence of this structure by 1830 fails to confirm conjectures that the existing storehouse east of the Privateer's Warehouse may have been the building depicted on the site by the late 1850s.

4 *City Directory*, 1869-70 to 1882-83; 1877-1935; HCCH, bk. 364, fols. 724-8, deed of transfer, Alexander John McRae Harvey, executor of George C. Harvey, to Margaret E. Wood, wife of Joseph Wood, 1904; bk. 820, fols. 388-91, deed of transfer, George Mackenzie Wood to Cyril J. Burke, 1941.

5 HCCH, bk. 820, fols. 388-91, Wood to Burke, 1941.

6 HCCH, bk. 1806, fols. 544-6, deed of transfer, Mary C. Burke to the City of Halifax, 1962.

7 Observation, accompanied by Mr. John Bigelow of Halifax; Wood Analysis Report by Canadian Forestry Association, Eastern Forest Products Laboratory.

8 For discussion of the apertures in this wall, *see* "Privateer's Warehouse."

9 Because of such obvious errors as the omission of the wall of the Ordnance Yard on the north side of the Central Wharf, the "Panoramic View of the City of Halifax Nova Scotia 1879" (Fig. 23) should be used with caution where other evidence does not exist to confirm the information contained in it.

10 A Department of National Defence photograph taken in 1944 shows the dormers still in place: National Air Photo Library, Ottawa (REA 253/5). EDHCH, Building Permit Registers, Vol. 3, 17 October 1945, permit issued to C. J. Burke & Company, No. 30662 and Vol. 4, 14 May 1946, permit issued to C.J. Burke & Company for "repairs to Chimney," No. 31318.

Bibliographic Essay

A report primarily for restoration purposes draws upon a wide variety of published and unpublished sources. While material of a directly or indirectly structural nature becomes of principal interest to the historian, this is not in most cases the emphasis of the papers consulted. Moreover, many materials of a non-structural character are also required by the researcher.

Because of the considerable controversy generated during the struggle to save the Halifax waterfront buildings, both architectural and historical examinations of the complex predate the present departmental study. Photographs and plans presented in October 1960 as part of the Halifax Waterfront Proposal for a Maritime Museum of Canada remain at the Nova Scotia Museum where the Maritime Museum, formerly in the Ordnance Yard adjoining the buildings, is now housed. Some of the buildings also appear in the "Halifax-Darthmouth Survey Report. A Study for the National Inventory of Buildings," prepared in 1964 by C. A. Fowler & Company, an architectural and engineering firm of Halifax, with Marion Moore and John Stevens. The buildings are treated in detail in "The Halifax Waterfront – A Feasibility Study," commissioned from Keith L. Graham & Associates, Architects, of Halifax in October 1968. Harvey Freeman, as a student of the School of Architecture at the Nova Scotia Technical College, submitted a "Report on the Historical Halifax Waterfront with Measured Drawings of Four Mid-nineteenth Century Offices." A number of articles, mainly by Marion Moore, have also appeared in various magazines and newspapers of the maritime region. Some of the buildings are, as well, featured in L. B. Jenson's *Vanishing Halifax* (Halifax: 1968) and in the Heritage Trust of Nova Scotia publication *Founded Upon a Rock; Historic Buildings of Halifax and the Vicinity Standing in 1967* (Halifax: 1967).

The most obvious point of beginning research is with the standard histories of Nova Scotia. Of these, T. B. Akins' "History of Halifax City" (*Collections of the Nova Scotia Historical Society*, Vol. VIII, 1892) is unquestionably the most helpful. Akins provides detailed information on aspects of the physical evolution of the town as well as the activities of the townsmen. T. C. Haliburton's classic, *An Historical and Statistical Account of Nova Scotia* (2 vols., Halifax: 1829), concentrates upon the Acadian presence in the province and its very early British settlement. Beamish Murdoch's *A History of Nova-Scotia, or Acadie* (3 vols., Halifax: 1865-67), on the other hand, is heavily dominated by political events and is based upon documentary sources rather than, like much of the most useful of Akins', upon the author's personal familiarity with individuals and points of interest. Despite its title, Duncan Campbell's *Nova Scotia, in its Historical, Mercan-*

tile and Industrial Relations (Montreal : 1873) emphasized the political rather than the commercial aspects of provincial growth, while A. W. H. Eaton's early 20th-century essays (*Americana*, 1915-19, passim) are fragmented studies which rarely touch upon the economic life of the previous century. Phyllis Blakeley's "Business in Halifax" in *Glimpses of Halifax 1867-1900* (Halifax : 1949) is a concise study of late 19th-century commercial emergence in the city. T. W. Acheson's "The National Policy and the Industrialization of the Maritimes, 1880-1910" (*Acadiensis*, Vol. I, No. 2, spring 1972, pp. 3-28) brings new insights and techniques to the study of the industrial development of the region at the turn of the century.

Various other books and articles have also been found relevant. Among the latter are George Nichols' "Notes on Nova Scotian Privateers" and G. F. Butler's "The Early Organization and Influence of Halifax Merchants" in the *Collections of the Nova Scotia Historical Society* (Vol. XIII, 1908, pp. 111-52, and Vol. XXV, 1942, pp. 1-16) ; Janet Mullins' "The *Liverpool Packet*" and J. S. Martell's "Halifax during and after the War of 1812" in *The Dalhousie Review* (Vol. XIV, 1934-35, pp. 193-202 and Vol. XXIII, 1943-44, pp. 289-304) ; W. R. Copp's "Nova Scotian Trade During the War of 1812" and S. A. Saunders' "The Maritime Provinces and the Reciprocity Treaty" reprinted in G. A. Rawlyk, ed., *Historical Essays on the Atlantic Provinces* (Toronto : 1967, pp. 82-98

and 161-78) ; Bray Hammond's "Banking in Canada before Confederation, 1792-1867," in W. T. Easterbrook and M. H. Watkins, eds., *Approaches to Canadian Economic History* (Toronto : 1967, pp. 127-68), and Joseph Schull's "The *Black Joke*" in *Weekend Magazine* (Vol. 8, Nos. 30 and 31, 1958). C. H. J. Snider's *Under the Red Jack, Privateers of the Maritime Provinces of Canada in the War of 1812* (Toronto : 1928) as well contains a chapter on Collins' famous *Liverpool Packet*.

Because the waterfront buildings to be restored are situated on wharfs which were immediately south of the headquarters of the British army's Ordnance department, a variety of military command records provide information about the structures. First of all, they sometimes appear on early 19th-century plans of the Ordnance Yard and environs before the Commanding Royal Engineers abandoned the practice of showing buildings outside the Ordnance wall on departmental maps. Moreover, the proximity of the site to the yard resulted in an early entrepreneurial offer to sell the property to the army establishment. Later, the convenient location of the buildings made them prime rental space when the Ordnance storekeeper had insufficient stores within the yard to house his supplies. Contracts, correspondence, and plans in War Office 44 and 55 and in PAC Record Group 8, C series, therefore afford evidence as to usage and structure of neighbouring privately owned buildings.

Fire constituted one of the most prevalent and most dreaded urban enemies of the 19th century, and fire damage frequently resulted in significant structural alterations to existing

buildings. *The Bicentennial of the Halifax Fire Department. 200 Years of Fire-fighting. 1768-1968* (Halifax : 1968) contains a brief, illustrated and very general account of the evolution of fire-fighting practices in the town and includes a short discussion of several major 19th-century fires. The Fire Department itself, however, possesses much more useful records in the form of registers of all fires reported in Halifax since 1907. These provide not only the date of the conflagration and the address and ownership of the property concerned, but also information as to the insurance carried, the extent of damage incurred, and the type of building burned. From there, newspaper reports can also be easily traced. Newspapers usually gave extensive coverage to fires in the town, and although their reports concentrate upon the drama of fighting the blaze, they frequently offer incidental information as to the size and type of structure, the situation of apertures and the style of roof. If the circumstances surrounding the fire appeared suspicious, a magisterial investigation was often ordered. The testimony of such a hearing upon a waterfront fire in 1904 is found in the Pickford & Black papers at the Public Archives of Nova Scotia. It describes in detail such features as types of structures, their apertures and connections to adjoining premises, and the contents of the buildings.

The Fire Department is not, however, the only branch of city government whose files contain materials of use to the structural historian. The building inspector's office at City Hall possesses four registers of building permits issued since 1892 (1908-28 missing). The information is scanty and often incomplete, and no permits exist to elucidate what is recorded; nevertheless, from ownership and street reference it is possible to determine when construction or repairs occurred, and sometimes the lists include a brief description of the work undertaken. The Engineering and Works Department, in addition, possesses an extensive collection of manuscript plans of various properties in the city. Dating mainly from the 1870s and later, these reflect the appointment in 1872 of a full-time city engineer. His annual reports regarding streets, sewers and city buildings are found in the published *Report of the Several Departments of the City Government of Halifax, Nova Scotia . . .* (Halifax: various dates) which series also contains reports of the Board of Works, the mayor, a city architect in the 1860s, and committees on streets and city property. The Public Archives of Nova Scotia has a fairly complete run of the annual reports from the early 1860s onward and has also some late 19th-century minute books of the city council.

Further useful records relating to property include assessment rolls, city directories, and registered deeds, leases and mortgages. Few assessment records for Halifax have survived. The Public Archives of Nova Scotia has, nevertheless, one book dated 1817 but probably earlier (1812?), as well as several books of the 1820s and 1830s, 1841 and 1862 (RG 35-A). The institution is shortly to receive from City Hall the similar ward books for ca.

1879-1905. These enumerate owners and occupants by ward and street in an approximately geographic sequence; the assessable value of real and personal property, in addition to the amount of tax due, is indicated. *McAlpine's Halifax City Directory for 1869-70 to 1929*, published annually, also provides detailed information as to occupancy, cross-listed nominally and professionally. *Nugent's Business Directory of the City of Halifax for 1858-9* (Halifax: 1858), *The Halifax, Nova Scotia Business Directory for 1863* compiled by Luke Hutchinson (Halifax: 1863), and *Hutchinson's Nova Scotia Directory for 1866-67* (Halifax: 1866) are similar, earlier compilations. Property deeds for the city are registered in the Halifax County Court House. Primarily, these record the transfer of land ownership, but they may give, as well, details of buildings included in or excluded from the property transfer and the size or type of structures adjoining. The deeds are often accompanied by mortgages which reveal lines of financial connection where the holder of the mortgage is not, as was frequent, the previous owner. Occasional legal agreements between property owners also afford information regarding such arrangements as docks, joint fences, and overhanging roof fixtures.

Not only city records but the files of several federal departments may be helpful in tracing structural history. Many privately owned buildings were used in the 19th century for governmental purposes; of these, some records as to facilities, repairs or alterations, and rent may remain. For instance, in addition to the fully indexed manuscript records of the Department

of Public Works are their annual reports upon government owned or rented buildings which are published in the sessional papers. Moreover, many prominent merchants had on their wharfs at least part of a building used as a bonded warehouse, in which goods were stored awaiting transhipment or local delivery upon the payment of import duties. Owners were required to submit plans of the warehouses to be so designated for prior approval by the local customs officer. The Customs and Excise Department may therefore have records concerning such houses. Those for Halifax, however, are scant, most apparently having been destroyed accidentally in a fire at the customs house or deliberately in the subsequent demolition of the building. Ambitious merchants also frequently obtained appointments as consuls of foreign countries to facilitate trade relations or to handle international shipping matters arising near the Canadian coast. The Department of External Affairs records date only from the establishment of the department in 1909. Application to the several consulates whose representatives in the late 19th and early 20th centuries had offices on Pickford & Black's wharf revealed that surviving records relate mainly to appointments and resignations which can more readily be determined by referral to the city directories or the annual lists submitted by the Department of External Affairs for publication in the sessional papers. The current work of federal departments, such as Energy, Mines and Resources' charting of the water level of Halifax Harbour, may also prove relevant.

Business publications to advertise the commercial interests of the city, like *Halifax and Its Business : containing Historical Sketch, and Description of the City and its Institutions* (Halifax : 1876), *Our Dominion. Mercantile and Manufacturing Interests. Historical and Commercial Sketches of Halifax and Environs* (Toronto : 1887), and *The City of Halifax, The Capital of Nova Scotia, Canada. Its Advantages and Facilities* (Halifax : 1909), contain succinct accounts of the principal local companies. They usually refer to the previous history of the firm and its premises as well as to the main fields of its activity. Published histories of corporations, such as Victor Ross' *A History of the Canadian Bank of Commerce with an Account of the Other Banks which now form Part of its Organization* (3 vols., Toronto : 1920-34), when available, provide more detailed description of all aspects of a company's operation. Manuscript records of business firms are, of course, a rich source of material when their creators have been the owners or occupants of the buildings being studied. The Canadian Imperial Bank of Commerce Archives was unable to provide any information regarding the Halifax Banking Company building, but the Bank of Nova Scotia Archives afforded some comparative notes concerning plans, fixtures and the bank vault. Moreover, although many papers of

both extinct and existing companies have been destroyed, some have been housed in public institutions. The Public Archives of Nova Scotia, for instance, has several fine collections, including Pickford & Black's registers for Lloyd's of all ships entering and leaving the port of Halifax. The Archives of Dalhousie University is rapidly acquiring papers of Nova Scotian firms, among which William Stairs, Son & Morrow, J. E. Morse & Company, and Pickford & Black are represented. These records include items like bills, invoices, cash books and bills of lading which show quickly with whom, where and upon what scale a firm was doing business. The bills of important companies as well frequently bore a sketch of their premises as letterhead. Correspondence and letterbooks afford a fuller picture of the company's activities, including the nature, range and volume of its operations. John Grant's and William Forsyth & Company's letterbooks (PAC, MG23, C8, and PANS, MG3, No. 150), for example, illustrate some late 18th-century activities of lessees and owners of the wharf, while the Seely & Gough letterbook (PANS) describes arrangements regarding building materials ordered by Enos Collins in 1830. Daily journals, apparently kept by many companies, also reveal the particular interests of a firm and sometimes harbour forgotten photographs of significant events in the life of the company. I. H. Mathers & Son's journals and Pickford & Black's similar diaries of the 1920s will shortly be available at Dalhousie. The founding members of a firm are usually named in newspaper advertisements, as are subsequent changes in partnership arrangements. Under the Nova Scotia Companies' Act (R.S.

1900, c. 128), firms were incorporated by duly registering with the provincial registrar of joint stock companies ; that office's files do not, however, include earlier firms nor do they retain information concerning extinct companies. Prior to 1900, incorporation was obtained by individual acts of the provincial legislature, of which record may be found in the statutes and assembly journals with their related papers.

Records not only of the firms themselves but of those with whom they did business may provide material of structural importance. Inquiries in this line regarding the Halifax waterfront buildings have, nevertheless, proved unrewarding. Insurance companies do not normally retain detailed information concerning a building more than three years after the expiry of a policy upon it. Holding and mortgage companies or construction and engineering firms with which the owners of the buildings dealt may, however, still have records of their transactions.

Newspapers can provide a great deal of information regarding the commercial life of a community and the role in it of particular individuals, firms, lines of business or geographic areas. In addition, advertisements reveal occupation and usage of buildings as well as descriptions of property for rent or sale. A wide variety of Halifax papers is available at the Public Archives of Nova Scotia and for the 1850s to 1870s at the National Library, Ottawa. Major alterations to premises of important firms or construction of significant buildings may be noticed by the daily press, but less generalized business journals such as *The Mar-*

itime Merchant and Commercial Review are more likely to comment. *The Commercial News*, the publication of the Halifax Board of Trade, usually notes managerial changes in local firms as well as containing from time to time histories of long-standing Haligonian companies.

Information about prominent figures who may have been associated with the buildings is available from a wide range of sources. The most obvious of these is the published biography or other work focusing upon the individual, such as C. B. Fergusson's *Letters and Papers of Hon. Enos Collins* (Halifax: 1959) and Kay Grant's *Samuel Cunard, Pioneer of Atlantic Steamship* (Toronto: 1967), a rather romanticized view of a close associate of Collins. Personal papers, either in archives or privately held, are of course most helpful, but these exist for comparatively few citizens. City directories, regional business directories, civic lists of aldermen and mayors, and general reference compilations from C. B. Fergusson's *A Directory of the Members of the Legislative Assembly of Nova Scotia 1758–1958* (Halifax: 1958) to John F. Kennedy's *Who's Who and Why in Canada (and Newfoundland), A Biographical Dictionary of Eminent Living Canadians and Notable Men of Newfoundland* (Ottawa: 1912) are among the many tools available to provide basic biographical data. Newspaper articles in the possession of firms or families, obituaries and wills may also be of use.

For restoration purposes, nevertheless, pictorial representations, not written records, are the most valuable documentary source available. The extensive collections of the Nova Scotia Museum and the Public Archives of Nova Scotia both contain photographs of the waterfront buildings to be restored. Sketches and photographs of business premises also occur in advertisements in newspapers (particularly special issues) and city directories. More appear, however, in such advertising pamphlets as *Rogers' Photographic Advertising Album* (Halifax: Joseph S. Rogers, 1871, reprinted for the Heritage Trust of Nova Scotia, 1970) and *The City of Halifax, The Capital of Nova Scotia, Canada. Its Advantages and Facilities* (Halifax: 1909), which were intended specifically to promote the commercial interests of the city. Furthermore, the provincial Legislative Library and the Halifax Regional Library, as well as the Public Archives of Nova Scotia, have good collections of late-19th- and early-20th-century illustrated guide books to the city; although these normally depict public buildings, views of the elegant Granville and Hollis streets, showing privately owned business edifices, are not uncommon. In addition, Archibald MacMechan's prolific writings about Halifax frequently contain both photographs and sketches of the city. A search through files of such periodicals as the *Illustrated London News* and the *Canadian Illustrated News* (Montreal) proved disappointing. While extensively illustrated, their issues picture almost exclusively public buildings with occasional houses, but very rarely include such mundane structures as long-standing offices and warehouses. The photographic collection of the Public Archives of Canada reveals a similar emphasis, while their selection of drawings and paintings was likewise unproductive of specific illustrations of the waterfront buildings. Inquiries of several federal government departments indicate that most of their dormant records, including any old photographs, have already been transferred to the Public Archives. The notable exception to this is the National Air Photo Library (Department of Energy, Mines and Resources) whose well-catalogued files date from the early 1920s. The Notman Collection in the McCord Museum, Montreal, includes a number of excellent late 19th-century views of the Halifax waterfront, but all are too distant to distinguish the particular buildings of the Pickford & Black and Central wharfs. A study of the catalogues of various Canadiana collections (such as those of the J. Ross Robertson and Sigmund Samuel Collections in the Toronto Public Library and of Manoir Richelieu at Murray Bay), as well as applications to archives and museums in the Maritime Provinces and New England, did not discover pictorial representations of the buildings unavailable in Halifax. An advertisement placed in *The Chronicle-Herald* evoked little response and failed to produce any significant material. In fact, the most prolific single source of photographs in this project proved to be the old files still retained by companies which had once occupied the buildings to be restored.

Maps as well as photographs are valuable documentary sources for the structural historian. They often give the first evidence of the existence of a structure whose dimensions are similar to those of the present building, while maps without buildings may show alterations to a site such as the extension of a wharf or the alteration of a street. In addition to plans in the possession of the Engineering and Works Department of the City of Halifax, the Public Archives of Nova Scotia and of Canada have extensive map collections. The latter's Halifax holdings are, however, not large, and a dearth of city maps from 1800 to 1860 prevails in both Halifax and Ottawa. An excellent and detailed plan of the central portion of the town in 1831 is housed in War Office 55/2594, but it is not until Hopkins' *City Atlas of Hal-ifax, Nova Scotia* (Halifax: 1878), nearly a half-century later, that a map of equal precision has been found. Although "A Panoramic View of the City of Halifax Nova Scotia 1879" affords a fine visual representation of the city, numerous inaccuracies, such as the omission of the south wall of the Ordnance Yard, make confirmation of its detail from other sources necessary. The series of urban maps prepared by Charles E. Goad in the late 19th and early 20th centuries are, in contrast, both specific and reliable. Frequently known as insurance plans, they illustrate by symbols not only the size, window patterns, and roof types of existing structures, but also indicate such minute features as cornices, firewalls (including any openings), hoists, partitions, and connections with adjoining buildings. Their completeness varies, nevertheless, from structure to structure, and only four of Halifax, covering the period from 1889 to 1939, have been located. Two of these are in the British Museum, London, one in possession of the city clerk's office, Halifax, and the latest in possession of the Nova Scotia Board of Insurance Underwriters.

Consultation of a wide range of sources and attention particularly to those outside public repositories have been found most useful in completing this report on the Halifax waterfront buildings.

Canadian Historic Sites: Occasional Papers in Archaeology and History

1 Archaeological investigations of the National Historic Sites Service, 1962-1966, John H. Rick; A Classification System for Glass Beads for the Use of Field Archaeologists, K. E. and M. A. Kidd; The Roma Settlement at Brudenell Point, Prince Edward Island, Margaret Coleman. $3.00

2 Contributions from the Fortress of Louisbourg—No. 1 Archaeological Research at the Fortress of Louisbourg, 1961-1965, Edward McM. Larrabee; A "Rescue Excavation" at the Princess Half-bastion, Fortress of Louisbourg, Bruce W. Fry; An Archaeological Study of Clay Pipes from the King's Bastion, Fortress of Louisbourg, Iain C. Walker. $3.00

3 Comparisons of the Faunal Remains from French and British Refuse Pits at Fort Michilimackinac: A Study in Changing Subsistence Patterns, Charles E. Cleland; The French in Gaspé, 1534 to 1760, David Lee;

The Armstrong Mound on Rainy River, Ontario, Walter A. Kenyon. $3.00

4 A Brief History of Lower Fort Garry, Dale Miquelon; The Big House, Lower Fort Garry, George C. Ingram; Industrial and Agricultural Activities at Lower Fort Garry, George C. Ingram; The Sixth Regiment of Foot at Lower Fort Garry, William R. Morrison; The Second Battalion, Quebec Rifles, at Lower Fort Garry, William R. Morrison. $3.00

5 Excavations at Lower Fort Garry, 1965-1967; A General Description of Excavations and Preliminary Discussions, James V. Chism. $3.00

6 A History of Rocky Mountain House, Hugh A. Dempsey; The Excavation and Historical Identification of Rocky Mountain House, William C. Noble. $3.00

7 Archaeological Investigations at Signal Hill, Newfoundland, 1965-1966, Edward B. Jelks. $3.00

8 The Canals of Canada, John P. Heisler. $5.00

9 The Canadian Lighthouse, Edward F. Bush; Table Glass Excavated at Fort Amherst, Prince Edward Island, Paul McNally; Halifax Waterfront Buildings: An Historical Report, Susan Buggey. $6.00

10 The Architectural Heritage of the Rideau Corridor, Barbara A. Humphreys; Glassware Excavated at Fort Gaspereau, New Brunswick, Jane E. Harris; Commissioners of the Yukon, 1897-1918, Edward F. Bush. $5.00

11 The Battle of Queenston Heights, Carol Whitfield; A History of Fort George, Upper Canada, Robert S. Allen; The Battle of Châteauguay, Victor J. H. Suthren. $5.00

Available from Information Canada,
Publications Division, Ottawa, Ontario,
K1A 0S9

Articles appearing in this series are
abstracted and indexed in Historical
Abstracts and/or America : History and
Life.

Canadian Historic Sites : Occasional
Papers in Archaeology and History is
also published in French under the title
Lieux historiques canadiens : Cahiers
d'archéologie et d'histoire. For more
information, write Information Canada,
Publications Division, 171 Slater Street
Ottawa, Ontario K1A 0S9, Canada